INSTITUTE OF SOCIAL AND RELIGIOUS RESEARCH

NEGRO PROBLEMS IN CITIES

NEGRO PROBLEMS
IN CITIES

A Study Made Under the Direction of

T. J. WOOFTER, Jr.

GARDEN CITY   NEW YORK
DOUBLEDAY, DORAN & COMPANY, INC.

CONTENTS

PART I: NEIGHBORHOODS
By T. J. Woofter, Jr.

CHAPTER		PAGE
I	INTRODUCTION	17
	Emphasis on Neighborhoods. The process of urbanization. Signs of neighborhood improvement. Scope of study.	
II	THE RAPID CITY GROWTH	26
	Movement from country to city. Summary 1900 to 1920. Concentration in large cities. Natural increase in city and country.	
III	RACIAL SEPARATION	37
	Different patterns of separation. Character of mixtures. Expansion of Negro areas. Segregation ordinances. Deed restrictions. Social pressure and violence. Race solidarity. Avoiding trouble.	
IV	CONGESTION AND EXPLOITATION	78
	Density. House-crowding and lodgers. Land-crowding. Property values. Density and death. Density and morals.	
V	THE NEIGHBORHOOD SCALE	96
	Northern and southern neighborhoods. Migrant neighborhoods. Central colonies. Middle-class neighborhoods. Home-owning neighborhoods. Municipal improvements.	

PART II: HOUSING
By Madge Headley

VI	EQUIPMENT AND CONDITION OF HOUSES	115
	Classification. Rooms. Equipment. Lots. Repair.	
VII	RENT	121
	Range. Rent and the family budget. Rent and equipment. Negro and white rents. Rent increase. Rents, values, and investment returns.	

CHAPTER   PAGE

VIII HOME BUYING 136
Rapidity. Buying in typical cities. Financing of
home buying. Financing through mortgages.
Building and Loan Associations. Contract buying.
Contractor-builder sales.

IX CONSTRUCTIVE FORCES 152
Need for more building. Municipal control. Volunteer Organizations. Model house and industrial
projects.

PART III: SCHOOLS
By W. A. Daniel

X NORTHERN TRENDS AND POLICIES 173
Migration and adjustment. Distribution and segre-
gation. Negro opinion on segregation. Handling
Negro pupils in mixed schools. Overage pupils.
Curricula and extra-curricular activities. Use of
intelligence tests.

XI NORTHERN ENVIRONMENTAL FACTORS . . . 191
Moving and transfer. Working mothers. Employment of pupils. Poverty and crowding. The
gang. Closer coöperation between parents and
schools. Visiting teachers. Outside organizations.

XII SOUTHERN ADMINISTRATION AND ORGANIZATION . 201
Finances. Standards. Teachers' pay and certifica-
tion. High schools. Industrial training. Differentiation of instruction. Attendance laws. Volunteer aid.

XIII SOUTHERN BUILDINGS AND EQUIPMENT . . . 219
Need of long-range program. Sanitation. Educa-
tional equipment. Crowding. Location of site.
Bond issues.

PART IV: RECREATION
By Henry J. McGuinn

XIV RECREATIONAL NEEDS 227
Neighborhood environment and recreation. Recreation and juvenile delinquency.

CONTENTS

CHAPTER   PAGE

XV   MUNICIPAL FACILITIES 231
       Parks. Playgrounds. Libraries.

XVI ORGANIZATIONS 240
       Y.M.C.A. Y.W.C.A. Boy Scouts and Girl
       Scouts. Boys' clubs. Institutional churches.

XVII COMMERCIAL RECREATION 258
       Theaters—mixed, galleries, neighborhood show-
       houses. Dance halls—equipment, order. Pool
       rooms.

      APPENDIX 283

LIST OF TABLES

TABLE		PAGE
I	URBAN AND RURAL POPULATION, BY RACE	27
II	PER CENT. OF URBAN AND RURAL POPULATION, BY RACE	28
III	NEGRO URBAN POPULATION	30
IV	NUMBER OF NEGROES IN CITIES HAVING NEGRO POPULATIONS OF 25,000 OR MORE IN 1920	32
V	NATURAL INCREASE PER THOUSAND IN THE UNITED STATES, 1923	34
VI	NEGRO NATURAL INCREASE PER THOUSAND IN CITIES, 1923	35
VII	DENSITY OF POPULATION, 1925	79
VIII	DENSITIES OF SELECTED CITIES BY SECTIONS, 1925	80
IX	PERCENTAGE OF NEGRO DWELLINGS CONTAINING TWO OR MORE PERSONS PER ROOM	84
X	LODGERS IN NEGRO FAMILIES	87
XI	NEGRO DENSITY AND DEATH-RATES, BY WARDS, PHILADELPHIA, 1924	91
XII	DEATHS IN OLD AND NEW LAW APARTMENTS, MANHATTAN	92
XIII	NEGRO DENSITY AND ILLEGITIMATE BIRTHS, PHILADELPHIA, 1924	93
XIV	NEGRO DWELLINGS BY CLASSES, FIFTEEN CITIES	115
XV	ROOMS IN NEGRO DWELLINGS, FIFTEEN CITIES	116
XVI	USE OF ROOMS, FIFTEEN CITIES	117
XVII	EQUIPMENT OF NEGRO DWELLINGS, FOURTEEN CITIES	117
XVIII	TOILET FACILITIES IN NEGRO DWELLINGS, FOURTEEN CITIES	118

TABLE   PAGE

XIX   WALKS IN YARDS OF NEGRO HOUSES, FOURTEEN CITIES   119

XX   REPAIR OF NEGRO DWELLINGS, FOURTEEN CITIES   120

XXI   RENTS OF ROOMS AND DWELLINGS FOR SELECTED CITIES   122

XXII   DISTRIBUTION OF FAMILIES ACCORDING TO WEEKLY RENT PER DWELLING . . .   123

XXIII   RENTS PER WEEK FOR DWELLINGS OF A, B, C, AND D CLASSES   125

XXIV   RENTAL FIGURES FOR NEW YORK CITY . .   129

XXV   WEEKLY RENTALS IN PHIPPS TENEMENTS NO. 2   131

XXVI   PROPERTIES OFFERED FOR SALE IN CHICAGO, JANUARY, 1926   132

XXVII   RENTS AND ASSESSED VALUES, HARLEM AND COLUMBUS HILL   134

XXVIII   HOME OWNERSHIP IN FIFTEEN CITIES . .   137

XXIX   NEGRO HOME BUYING IN MEMPHIS . . .   139

XXX   NEGRO HOMES IN OUTLYING WARDS OF MEMPHIS   140

XXXI   NEGRO HOME OWNERSHIP IN FIVE BOROUGHS, NEW YORK CITY, 1920   141

XXXII   NEGRO HOME OWNERSHIP IN SEVEN WARDS, CHICAGO, 1920   142

XXXIII   NEGRO HOMES IN PHILADELPHIA OPERATED BY OCTAVIA HILL ASSOCIATION   166

XXXIV   NEGRO AND WHITE ENROLLMENT IN INDIANAPOLIS HIGH SCHOOLS BY SEMESTERS (JANUARY, 1919, TO JUNE, 1924)   174

XXXV   RETARDATION IN CHICAGO SOUTH-SIDE SCHOOLS .   175

XXXVI   PERCENTAGE OF NEGROES IN PHILADELPHIA SCHOOLS   178

XXXVII   PERCENTAGE OF NEGROES IN INDIANAPOLIS SCHOOLS   179

TABLE   PAGE

XXXVIII   OVERAGE AND SLOW-PROGRESS PUPILS IN ONE
SCHOOL 184

XXXIX   NEGRO PROMOTIONS IN ONE SEMESTER IN FOUR
OVERAGE CLASSES 185

XL   OCCUPATION OF MOTHERS OF 317 PUPILS,
GRADES 5–8 193

XLI   PER CAPITA CURRENT EXPENSES (BASED ON
AVERAGE ATTENDANCE) 203

XLII   TEACHERS' SALARIES IN FOUR CITIES . . . 206

XLIII   PERCENTAGE OF TEACHERS BY CLASS OF CER-
TIFICATE 207

XLIV   ENROLLMENT BY SUBJECTS IN INDIANAPOLIS
HIGH SCHOOLS 214

XLV   KINDERGARTENS IN EIGHT SOUTHERN CITIES . 215

XLVI   STATUS OF PUPILS IN FOUR SOUTHERN CITIES . 216

XLVII   PERCENTAGE OF THE ENROLLMENT BY GRADE IN
FOUR SOUTHERN CITIES 216

XLVIII   JUVENILE DELINQUENCY IN SEVEN CITIES . 227

XLIX   NUMBER OF PLAYGROUNDS IN TEN CITIES . 233

L   LIBRARIES FOR NEGROES 238

LIST OF MAPS

NORTHERN CITIES

NUMBER			PAGE
I A			
I B	Buffalo, New York	. 40-41
II A			
II B	Chicago, Illinois	. 42-43
III A			
III B	Dayton, Ohio	. 44
IV A			
IV B	Gary, Indiana	. 45
V A			
V B	Indianapolis, Indiana	. 46-47
VI A			
VI B	New York City	. 48-49
VII A			
VII B	Philadelphia, Pennsylvania . . .	. 50-51

SOUTHERN CITIES

VIII A			
VIII B	Charleston, South Carolina . . .	. 52-53
IX A			
IX B	Knoxville, Tennessee	. 54-55
X A			
X B	Lexington, Kentucky	. 56-57
XI A			
XI B	Louisville, Kentucky	. 58
XII A			
XII B	Lynchburg, Virginia	. 59
XIII A			
XIII B	Memphis, Tennessee	. 60-61
XIV A			
XIV B	New Orleans, Louisiana . . .	. 62-63
XV A			
XV B	Richmond, Virginia	. 64-65
XVI A			
XVI B	Winston-Salem, North Carolina . .	. 66-67

xiii

LIST OF DIAGRAMS

DIAGRAM   PAGE

I   IDEAL ARRANGEMENT, TWO-ACRE BLOCK (U. S. HOUS-
ING CORPORATION)   81

II   PHILADELPHIA BLOCK   82

III MEMPHIS BLOCK   83

IV   HARLEM BLOCK, NEW YORK CITY   83

PART I: NEIGHBORHOODS
By T. J. Woofter, Jr.

Chapter I

INTRODUCTION

The great concentration of Negroes in cities is a new phenomenon. In 1870, only 750,000 lived in cities, and most of these were in the small cities of the South. As late as 1900, only 2,000,000 Negroes dwelt in cities; but from 1900 to 1925 this city population doubled. There was, moreover, a pronounced trend towards the larger cities—a concentration in metropolitan areas.

Such a wholesale displacement of population necessitates fundamental readjustments in the communities from which Negroes move, in the communities to which they move, and in the pattern of Negro life. It has produced a new set of contacts between the races, and it involves a very significant change in the relation of the Negro to American life and the assimilation of a new type of culture. The effects of this new phenomenon are not yet fully known, and therefore need to be carefully appraised.

But to ascertain and to appraise all these effects would require a very comprehensive study indeed. In this survey, made by the Institute of Social and Religious Research, it was therefore decided to limit the inquiry to aspects of city Negro neighborhoods that relate to general neighborhood characteristics, to housing, to recreation, and to schools; and it is believed that these are among the most interesting and significant factors in Negro adaptation to city life.

During such rapid expansion of city population, it was inevitable that old neighborhoods should grow and that entirely new neighborhoods should be colonized. These changes have not been accomplished without heavy strains on racial goodwill. The expansion of Negro residence areas has frequently occasioned intense friction similar to that which resulted in the Chicago riots. It has caused a housing shortage with attendant evils in the restricted areas from which

Negroes can choose residence sites. It has thrown unexpected burdens and problems upon the public school system and has created new problems in the recreational and social life of city neighborhoods.

Among the essential features of a healthy and happy neighborhood life are: the neighborhood contacts with adjoining neighborhoods; the municipal services such as paving, sewerage, lighting and police protection, through which the city exerts its influence to create progressive communities, the housing conditions, the school facilities, and the recreational opportunities. The effort of this study has been to ascertain the extent to which these neighborhood essentials are available to Negroes who move into the city, and the manner in which the newcomers adapt themselves to the neighborhood institutions.

Other important contacts of the Negro with city life are omitted. The industrial adjustments of the migrants and the growth of their religious and social organizations are important phases of the urbanization process; but these are special phases which are not subject to direction by the municipal government to such an extent as are the housing facilities, the public schools, and the recreational activities. Also they are not such direct determinants of neighborhood life.

The objective of this study has therefore been to interpret the new city Negro in terms of certain new factors in his city environment. It is essential that these environmental influences be emphasized, since they prove to be important factors in disease, crime and morality. Many people attribute excessive Negro death-rates from tuberculosis, pneumonia and the diseases of infants to inborn racial traits, others attribute crimes of violence and irregularities in family life to peculiar emotional equipment of people of African descent. Regardless of whether these traits are influenced to some extent by heredity or not, this analysis of the city environment indicates that they are also profoundly influenced by the conditions of life in cities. In fact, future knowledge concerning Negroes in cities will depend largely upon more thorough analyses of the effects of this environment. This study is merely a beginning—a summation of some of the most obvious interactions between the city and the incoming colored citizens.

PROCESS OF URBANIZATION

The adjustment of these rural people to city life is found to be a definite process, a sequence of experiences by which they become urbanized. The first experience is the migration itself, which sorts out the population leaving certain classes on the farm and shifting the more ambitious into the industrial and business establishments of the city. Segregation is the next experience. The newcomers enter a variety of occupations and are stratified into a variety of economic and social classes. These classes, however, tend to be separate from the same class of old-established residents. Laborers separate within the factory by processes. Professional and business men of each group serve their own clients and have limited contact with their confreres in the other group. More powerful still is the residential segregation which occurs when the newcomers settle into more or less solid colonies. These colonies are perpetuated by the growth of neighborhood organizations, institutions and businesses. As a corollary of this segregation, there is a concentration of population as new waves of migration settle in the same area. This opens the way for the neglect of the interest of the minority group and an exploitation of their position. Equality of opportunity is often theoretically advocated; but as soon as there is a well-defined separation of one group from another, discriminations creep in to the disadvantage of the minority. As a result of this neglect, an intense community consciousness develops within the segregated neighborhood and activity for self-improvement intensifies. Finally, the whole community becomes aware of the situation and the effort to ameliorate conditions may become general.

Foreign-speaking groups, as they have moved to American cities, have gone through a process with strikingly similar phases. In fact, in most northern cities, Negroes have moved into the neighborhoods formerly occupied by incoming foreigners and are subjected to the same housing exploitation as their predecessors. In a few cities it was noted that Mexicans, as the latest comers, are beginning to occupy the worst sections formerly held by Negroes; and they are probably beginning the same cycle.

Since the Negro city population is relatively new, it is now possible to see this process of migration, segregation, concentration, neglect, self-improvement, and amelioration at work. The following chapters trace this process. By observing conditions in a number of cities, some in the North and some in the South, it was possible to see different phases of the process in different places and to secure first-hand knowledge of its effects. Such a study shows that the urbanization of Negro population signifies far more than the mere transference of two million people. It involves a profound cultural change and demands multiple readjustments.

During this whole process a determining factor is the nature of the contact between the members of the white and the colored groups. Since the tendency toward segregation both by occupations and by neighborhoods is so pronounced, the contacts in the city are impersonal and corporate, totally different from the personal contacts involved in farming and in small-town life. On the plantation, the colored farmer was long in contact with the culture of the rural South; but the culture of metropolitan centers is vastly different. In the city, the Negro newcomers from the rural South have been dependent upon their contacts with other groups and with city institutions to adjust themselves to the bewilderingly new conditions. Their contacts have conditioned their chance to enjoy city civilization and to profit by it. On the other hand, the city must depend upon these contacts to adjust these rural-minded people to its life, or let them remain a separate, alien mass within its gates.

The problems of the new environment have proved grave for the Negroes and for the cities into which they have moved. In a number of cities they represent a very vexing series of social maladjustments. The difficulties of adapting these country people to city houses, city schools and city neighborhood organizations are real. The exploitation of their ignorance of city conditions and of their position when segregation restricts their choice of residence or activity is discouraging, even though this exploitation is often similar to that of white groups of similar economic status. But the person who is interested, either because of sympathy for colored people or because of a desire for civic progress, can find genuine encouragement in the tendency toward improvement in newer neighborhoods, in the increased interest of cities in these sections, and in the movement of Negroes from the poorer to the better sections within each city.

SIGNS OF NEIGHBORHOOD IMPROVEMENT

There is a home-making ladder that ambitious migrants climb. From country cabins, they step to the shacks or tenements of the city, thence to a somewhat better type of rental house, and finally, in increasing numbers, they are purchasing neat, comfortable and homelike houses. This latter tendency toward home ownership, so pronounced during the past ten years, is one of the remarkably encouraging signs of genuine advancement which this study reveals. No one can observe the persistent struggles of some Negro families dependent upon humble occupations for a livelihood and yet steadfast in their purpose to build and own real homes, without feeling that here are people who are determined to progress.

The chief obstacles to progress up the home-making ladder are the tardiness in protecting Negro neighborhoods from exploitation and insanitary surroundings, and the financial burdens imposed upon the small home buyer by real estate speculation.

Another great difficulty in the way of Negroes in their struggle for better homes has been a persistence of the attitudes of slavery. The Emancipation Proclamation did not, with a stroke of the pen, strike off the fetters of thought which had been worn for two centuries. During slavery, Negroes lived in cabins in the back yard. It was but a step from these to cabins in some back alley or backwash of the city—down in the hollow, or between the railroad tracks, where land was almost valueless. At first, white people with the slave-holding attitude felt that such places were the natural habitat of the Negro; and colored people with slave attitudes were not accustomed to anything better. In the early days of freedom no one dreamed of putting municipal improvements into these neighborhoods. School facilities were designed to supply merely the sort of education deemed suitable for ex-slaves, and recreation was largely the result of individual inclination. But it did not require much time for the ambition of Negroes to begin to stir in the direction of better homes. A few bought cheap home sites early, and have gradually improved them. Often in the growth and shift of cities these small holdings became valuable and the owner was able to sell, to purchase in a better residence locality, and to erect a neat house with his profits. Municipal authorities also began to see that there are taxable values even in Negro rental property; and beginnings have been made in extending municipal improvements into these places.

The migration northward has been a great stimulant to municipal improvements in southern Negro neighborhoods. Wishing to keep the Negroes who were moving to better their conditions, southern municipalities became more willing to improve their colored communities. When Negroes moved to the larger industrial centers, they learned that they could find better houses there, better neighborhoods, better recreation, and better schools. As a rule, these first-comers to northern cities occupied quarters where immigrants formerly lived; and these neighborhoods had not been neglected as wantonly as had Negro neighborhoods in southern cities.

In turn, those Negroes who stayed in the South began to inquire why they could not have better living conditions in southern cities. Along with this awakening of the public conscience there came, in southern cities, the quickening of civic pride which accompanies vigorous growth. The South has been rural, but with the beginnings of its industrial development scores of urban centers have begun to experience vigorous and healthy expansion. This has caused a greater interest in civic improvement. The cities have become more conscious of themselves and have begun to exert greater effort to serve all neighborhoods. The movement to the

North, and the consequent entry of the Negro into industry, have gone far towards unshackling the bonds of slave psychology.

On the whole, then, the situation is encouraging; but much remains to be done in legislation for better housing, in building stronger institutions, and in educating the masses of colored people to higher standards of living, for there is bad housekeeping as well as bad housing.

SCOPE OF STUDY

In approaching the task of observing the significant contacts between the races, it was decided that the most profitable information would come from a study of them in several places, rather than from a very detailed analysis of urbanization processes in any one city. The study therefore brought together data regarding outstanding general conditions.

The plan involved first-hand observation in sixteen cities in the United States, seven in the North and nine in the South. These included four of the six cities with a Negro population of more than 100,000, and six of the sixteen with a Negro population of between 25,000 and 100,000. In addition, a few smaller places were taken merely for the sake of contrast and comparison. The study therefore is concerned primarily with the most intense form of urbanization—that of large cities.

In addition to data gathered in the sixteen cities visited by the staff, material was available from six other places. In Cincinnati, the Better Housing League has recently made a neighborhood survey, and in Baltimore the Urban League has gathered much data on housing. In Dallas, the Interracial Committee was making a very useful neighborhood survey at the time this study was projected. The same house-card which was used in this study was used in Charlottesville, by C. L. Knight, of the University of Virginia; by L. M. Bristol, in Gainesville, and by Maude Carmichael in Conway. Thus the housing-data are drawn to some extent from twenty-two cities and towns.[1]

1 In addition school and recreational data were gathered in Atlanta, Ga.

The staff consisted of four people, two white and two colored, each primarily interested in some one phase of the study, but all coöperating in the interest of unity. They were T. J. Woofter, Jr., Director; W. A. Daniel, Associate Director, specializing on schools; Madge Headley, specializing on housing; and H. J. McGuinn, specializing on recreation. This staff was occupied from September, 1925, to June, 1926, in gathering data in the cities for this report.

The study has been greatly facilitated by the interest of local people who possess an intimate knowledge of the situation in each city. Without their valuable coöperation in getting information, it would have been impossible to secure details as to the local situations in the time at the disposal of the staff. Acknowledgment of a real debt to these local helpers is due:

Philadelphia—Bernard J. Newman, Philadelphia Housing Association; Forrester B. Washington, Armstrong Association.

New York—Mabel Bickford, St. Phillip's Parish House, and the staff of the Tenement House Department for courtesy in allowing use of their records.

Buffalo—The Buffalo Foundation and W. M. Jackson, Secretary, Michigan Avenue Branch Y.M.C.A.

Indianapolis—Alva Taylor, Chairman Interracial Committee, and especially the colored members of that committee, F. E. De Frantz and L. F. Artis of the staff of the Y.M.C.A.

Chicago—Mary E. McDowell, of the Chicago Department of Public Welfare, and the Sociology Department of the University of Chicago.

Gary—C. O. Holmes, Secretary of the Interracial Committee, and Thyra J. Edwards, Probation Officer.

Dayton—C. H. Wehrly, Dayton Community Chest, and J. O. Greene, Secretary, Fifth Street Y.M.C.A., and members of his staff.

Louisville—James Bond, Interracial Secretary.

Lexington—J. H. Fouse, Principal, Dunbar High School.

Knoxville—J. H. Davies, Librarian, Free Colored Library; W. L. Porter, East Tennessee News.

New Orleans—Bradley Buell, New Orleans Community
Chest, and Leonie Bauduit, Principal, McDonough
Public School.

Memphis—Dr. T. O. Fuller, Secretary of the Interracial
Committee.

Charleston—Mrs. C. P. McGowan, Mrs. F. H. Horl-
beck, Chairman of the Interracial Committee, and
Edna P. Morrison, Chairman, Colored Women's
Section.

Winston-Salem—S. G. Atkins, President, Slater Normal
School.

Lynchburg—Mrs. L. P. Stephens, Secretary, Colored
Y.W.C.A.

Richmond—R. W. Miles, Interracial Secretary; Mrs.
W. H. Harris, Jr., Community Recreational Association.

In addition, the city officials, especially the health officers and their sanitary inspectors, were uniformly cour-
teous and interested. In practically every city, Miss
Headley was invited to make regular rounds of inspection in the Negro neighborhood with a sanitary inspector.

The detailed information on housing was secured in each
city by filling in a number of house-cards to constitute a sample of housing conditions. The actual canvass of the neighborhood to fill in the cards was done by a group of volunteers in each city. These workers showed a real interest in
the housing situation and contributed materially to the in-
timacy of detail about the way the families are housed.

The report of this study therefore is the result of an effort
to put together data about Negro neighborhoods [2] obtained
by the work of many persons. The very fact that so many
have been at work on some one phase or another of this
question indicates that a very healthy community interest is
developing—an interest that can be used to stimulate constructive movements.

[2] A more detailed statement as to the method used in arriving at the
facts presented in different phases of this study will be found in the
Appendix.

Chapter II

THE RAPID CITY GROWTH

The migration of Negroes is ordinarily spoken of as a movement from South to North; but to state it in these terms is to state only a half-truth. Fundamentally it is a movement from country to city. In proportion to their size, the southern cities have received as substantial increases in their Negro population as have the northern cities; but the increases of northern cities have been more spectacular by reason of the fact that before the movement began the Negro population of these cities was negligible, and because the trend has been toward the industrial cities, a majority of which are found in the North.

In other words, the movement of Negroes to cities is only a part of the general American movement from rural to urban centers. While the white population in cities was increasing faster than the Negro population from 1900 to 1910, the Negro increase was much more rapid from 1910 to 1920, when the stoppage of immigration slackened the white increase. In the past, several factors operated to prevent any such movement of colored population on a large scale. At first Negroes were traditionally bound to southern agriculture, and there was a current fiction that they were ill-adapted to machine industry. As long as the demands of industry were satisfied by the rapid influx of immigrants, no one put this theory to a test. The war removed the barriers. It restricted the supply of foreign labor, increased the demands of industry, and led many manufacturers to experiment with Negro labor. The success of these experiments exploded the myth of inadaptability to machine industry and justified exceptional efforts to secure Negro workers. The old order was upset. Labor agents canvassed the South for men and, coming on the heels of the disorganization of cotton farming caused by the boll weevil, they secured large

TABLE I—URBAN AND RURAL POPULATION, BY RACE

	POPULATION			INCREASE*	
	1900	1910	1920	1900-1910	1910-1920
Total United States					
Negro Urban........	2,002,008	2,684,797	3,559,473	682,789	874,676
Negro Rural........	6,831,986	7,142,966	6,903,658	310,980	−239,308
White Urban........	28,305,409	39,379,294	50,620,084	11,073,885	11,240,790
White Rural........	38,503,787	42,352,663	44,200,831	3,848,876	1,848,168
Southern States					
Negro Urban........	1,364,796	1,854,455	2,250,969	489,659	396,514
Negro Rural........	6,558,173	6,894,972	6,661,262	336,799	−233,710
White Urban........	3,051,916	4,761,463	7,043,262	1,709,547	2,281,799
White Rural........	13,470,054	15,785,957	17,088,952	2,315,903	1,302,995
Northern and Western States					
Negro Urban........	637,212	830,342	1,308,504	193,130	478,162
Negro Rural........	273,813	247,994	242,396	−25,819	−5,598
White Urban........	25,253,493	34,617,831	43,576,822	9,364,338	8,958,991
White Rural........	25,033,733	26,566,706	27,111,879	1,532,973	545,173

* Italics denote decrease.

numbers. When these migrants began to write home, others followed without solicitation. This was the great pulling force that drew Negroes to the cities.

Added to this pull was a push from the southern rural districts. The boll weevil ravaged hundreds of thousands of acres of fertile cotton fields, and southern farmers passed through a discouraging trough of depression. Many of them reached the point where they told their laborers to leave, as it would be impossible for them to advance money for food as had been the custom. Negroes began to discern the poverty of educational facilities and the insecurity of life in certain rural communities. As a result of this push, and the removal of the obstacles to movement, the cities gained rapidly in Negro population.

Table I (page 27) indicates the volume of this movement for a twenty-year period as shown by the United States Census.

Table II puts this distribution of the population into percentage.

TABLE II—PER CENT. OF URBAN AND RURAL POPULATION, BY RACE

	POPULATION			INCREASE *	
	1900	1910	1920	1900-1910	1910-1920
Total United States					
Negro Urban....	22.7	27.3	34.0	34.1	32.6
Negro Rural	77.3	72.7	66.0	4.6	−3.4
White Urban....	42.4	48.2	53.4	39.1	28.5
White Rural	57.6	51.8	46.6	10.0	4.4
Southern States					
Negro Urban....	17.2	21.2	25.3	35.9	21.4
Negro Rural	82.8	78.8	74.7	5.1	−3.4
White Urban....	18.5	23.2	29.2	56.0	47.9
White Rural	81.5	76.8	70.8	17.2	8.3
Northern and Western States					
Negro Urban....	69.9	77.0	84.4	30.3	57.6
Negro Rural	30.1	23.0	15.6	−9.4	−2.3
White Urban....	50.2	56.6	61.6	37.1	23.0
White Rural	49.8	43.4	38.4	6.1	2.1

* Italics denote decrease.

Summary, 1900 to 1920

Tables I and II show:

1. That from 1900 to 1920 Negro city population increased more than a million and a half, while the Negro population of rural areas increased less than 72,000, or about 1 per cent. The white drift to the cities was also striking, especially in the South; but despite this drain the white rural population managed to increase slightly.

2. That the greater part of this movement occurred from 1910 to 1920, during which decade the Negro city population increased 875,000 and the rural population actually decreased 240,000. The 1925 estimates of the Census Bureau indicate a further increase of some 600,000 in the Negro city population, making a total increase of more than 2,100,000 for the twenty-five-year period, a growth of over 100 per cent. The fundamental importance of the shift of so great a number of people within the space of one generation can hardly be estimated.

3. Contrary to the general impression that the movement has been entirely northward, these tables show that from 1900 to 1920 the southern cities increased by 886,173 Negroes, while the northern and western cities increased by 671,292. On a percentage basis, however, the gain in the North[1] was 105 per cent., as against 65 per cent. in the South. During the latter half of the twenty-year period the gain in the North was considerably more rapid than between 1900 and 1910. This only serves to emphasize the fact that both in the South and in the North the trend of the Negro population is definitely cityward, and that both the North and the South are concerned with the problems of the city Negro.

Since emancipation, nothing more astounding than this shift of Negroes to cities has occurred to affect the contact between the races.

---

[1] North here refers to areas outside the census divisions South Atlantic, East South Central and West South Central. The majority of Negroes in the "North" are in New England, Middle Atlantic, East North Central and West North Central states.

CONCENTRATION IN LARGE CITIES

It is interesting to analyze further the type of city into which this movement has shifted. Table III shows the increase in Negro population according to size of cities.

TABLE III—NEGRO URBAN POPULATION

	In All Cities	In Cities of 2,500 to 10,000	In Cities of 10,000 to 100,000	In Cities of 100,000 and Over
Total United States				
1900	2,002,008	540,199	793,555	668,254
1910	2,684,797	652,186	1,009,050	1,023,561
1920	3,559,473	667,848	1,207,049	1,684,576
Incr. 1900-10.........	682,789	111,987	215,495	355,307
Incr. 1910-20.........	874,676	15,662	197,999	661,015
Per cent. incr. 1900-10	34.1	20.7	27.2	53.2
Per cent. incr. 1910-20	32.6	2.4	19.6	64.6
Southern States				
1900	1,364,796	424,033	608,040	332,723
1910	1,854,455	539,516	766,056	548,883
1920	2,250,969	554,544	910,881	785,544
Incr. 1900-10.........	489,659	115,483	158,016	216,160
Incr. 1910-20.........	396,514	15,028	144,825	236,661
Per cent. incr. 1900-10	35.9	27.2	26.0	65.0
Per cent. incr. 1910-20	21.4	2.8	18.9	43.1
Northern and Western States				
1900	637,212	116,166	185,515	335,531
1910	830,342	112,670	242,994	474,678
1920	1,308,504	113,304	296,168	899,032
Incr. 1900-10 *	193,130	—3,496	57,479	139,147
Incr. 1910-20	478,162	634	53,174	424,354
Per cent. incr.* 1900-10	30.3	—3.0	31.0	41.5
Per cent. incr. 1910-20	57.6	.6	21.9	89.4

* Italics denote decrease.

It is apparent that the greater portion of the growth has been in cities of 100,000 and over, and that this trend to large cities was especially notable during the decade 1910 to 1920, during which the southern cities of 100,000 and over in-

ployment more rapidly than those in the smaller communities, which are unaccustomed to Negro workmen.

This abnormal concentration in large cities and neglect of the smaller cities is more emphasized in the North than in the South; because each city in the South is immediately surrounded by a rural Negro population which can be drawn in as trade and industry expand. The migration to northern cities, however, is from long range. In most cases, the destination is selected by the migrant on the basis of knowledge that others who have moved to that city have made a success. This tends to draw newcomers to places where migrants have already gone in large numbers.

Thus we may sum up the situation in 1920. More than three and a half million, or over a third of the Negro population, lived in cities. Of these, 1,685,000 were in cities of 100,000 and over, and 1,875,000 in cities of less than 100,000. The 1,685,000 in cities of 100,000 and over were equally divided between the North and the South, and the 1,875,000 in cities of less than 100,000 were for the most part in the South. The bulk of the increase between 1900 and 1920 was in these cities of 100,000 and over, North and South. In addition, a very considerable number of Negroes in the South—probably 800,000, or 10 per cent. of the southern Negro population—were in incorporated villages of fewer than 2,500 inhabitants.

Natural Increase

The sources of this movement to cities are in the open country of the South. In fact, it is evident from the examination of Negro birth-rates and death-rates that the large city populations barely maintain themselves by excess of births over deaths. When the population was badly upset by migration, deaths actually exceeded births in many places. In New York City, for ten years preceding 1916, there were 400 more deaths than births.

This comes about both through decrease in the birth-rate and through increase in deaths. The movement of the two sexes in different directions, the men in larger numbers to some cities and the women in larger numbers to others, upsets the ratio of the sexes and postpones marriage. The higher standard of living in the city also tends to postpone marriage, and probably reduces the number of children through conscious birth control. The result has been that the rapidly growing city populations have been recruited from the rural districts of the South where there is a substantial excess of births over deaths.

Table V shows the birth-rates and death-rates for the registration area in 1923.

TABLE V—NATURAL INCREASE PER THOUSAND IN THE UNITED STATES, 1923

	Birth-rate	Death-rate	Natural Increase
Total Registration Area			
White	22.1	12.0	10.1
Negro	26.3	17.7	8.6
Cities (over 10,000) in Registration Area			
White	22.2	12.4	9.8
Negro	25.2	22.0	3.2
Balance of Registration Area			
White	22.0	11.5	10.5
Negro	26.9	15.2	11.7

Table V indicates that in the whole area included by the Census for the registration of births and deaths the rate of Negro natural increase is less than the rate of white natural increase. There is also a marked slowing down of the rate of natural increase of both races in the city; but this is especially true of the Negro population, which shows a natural increase of only 3.2 per thousand in cities of over 10,000 population and of 11.7 per thousand in cities under 10,000 and in rural districts.

In interpreting these figures it is necessary to bear two things in mind, first that in adopting a population of 10,000 as the dividing line between urban and rural in the registration area, the Census classes many villages and towns as rural. Shifting these places to the urban category, however,

would serve only to raise the natural increase in urban territory slightly, and also to raise the rate of natural increase in
the rural territory, thereby leaving the difference between
the two about the same. The second consideration is that
only a small proportion of the southern Negro population is
in the registration area for births. This gives a fairly accurate analysis of city conditions both North and South, but
an incomplete one of rural increase, since the states omitted
are those that have the greatest rural Negro population and
that seem to have the greatest excess of births over deaths
when judged by the number of migrants they have furnished to other sections of the country. Another inaccuracy
results from the incomplete registration of births. Probably
there are more unregistered Negro births than unregistered
white births, and this would account in part for the lower
rate of natural increase; but the failure to register births in
the country is more frequent than in the city. Consequently,
perfect registration would probably tend to emphasize this
discrepancy of the natural increase in country and in city.

When the contrast is drawn between northern and southern cities, as in Table VI, it is seen that the Negro natural
increase in southern cities is slightly greater than in northern
cities.

TABLE VI—NEGRO NATURAL INCREASE PER THOU-
SAND IN CITIES, 1923

	Birth-rate	Death-rate	Natural Increase
Southern cities................	23.5	18.7	4.8
Northern cities................	25.7	21.4	4.3

This is owing to the more disturbing effects of migration
in northern cities than in southern cities. If the registration
of births were more accurate in the southern states, this discrepancy would be emphasized.[2]

[2] States included in above figures are, Northern: California, Connecticut,
Illinois, Kansas, Massachusetts, Michigan, Minnesota, Nebraska, New
Jersey, New York, Ohio, Pennsylvania; Southern: Delaware, Maryland,
Mississippi, North Carolina, South Carolina, Virginia, Kentucky. The
northern states in the registration area have a Negro urban population of
1,289,932 and the southern states a Negro urban population of 667,967.

This means that the increase in cities comes largely from the rural-minded people who move from the simplest American agricultural communities. On the plantation, the laborer and tenant are looked after in many respects by their landlord. House and fuel are furnished, credit is arranged for, labor is simple and closely supervised, and in many ways habits are formed that are ill-adapted to city conditions. The movement from the one extreme of plantation conditions to the other of metropolitan life in the largest cities renders the task of adjusting the migrant to conditions of city living all the more difficult.

There is some evidence that the low rate of natural increase in cities is not permanent. As the migration settles down to a more normal flow, the ratio between the sexes is adjusted and the birth-rate increased. As larger and larger proportions of the migrants become accustomed to the strains of city life, and as cities adjust their public health programs to the new conditions, the death-rate is lowered. If this trend continues, the future will witness an increase of Negro city populations, both by excess of births over deaths and by migration.

Tables I and II indicate that up to 1920 the rapid increase of Negroes in cities had not slackened to any degree. During the present study the 1925 population was estimated as carefully as possible from census material, school censuses, and house-counts, and it is apparent that the city movement continues. As industry develops in the South, southern city populations will draw more and more from the surrounding rural districts, and nothing short of a revolution in the present agricultural system will hold the Negroes on the farm.

The expanding Negro neighborhoods will be an increasingly important part of the industrial and civic life of the municipalities. The problems involved in their expansion should be weighed, therefore, and preparation should be made to solve them on some basis that will allow Negroes to develop a desirable home life and wholesome neighborhood surroundings.

Chapter III

RACIAL SEPARATION

A number of forces have been at work to segregate Negro from white residence neighborhoods, but the separation is seldom entirely complete. Social pressures have been used, laws have been passed, and the economic and social cohesion of Negro groups have tended to solidify them. Each city visited has examples of all degrees of separation. Some servants live under the same roof as their employers, and occasionally white and Negro families occupy the same apartment-houses or duplex dwellings. There are many cases, both in the South and in the North, where white and colored people are mixed in the same block, and in other instances the dividing line can be more or less definitely traced along streets.

DIFFERENT PATTERNS OF SEPARATION

Each city has a pattern of its own determined by the percentage of Negroes in the total, the distribution of Negro employment, the distribution of the areas where property is within the means of colored families, the attitude of the people toward segregation, and the rate of expansion of business and manufacturing sections. While there is wide variation from city to city, several general patterns may be described.

In order to classify cities according to the pattern of racial separation, it is convenient to consider any area with a population more than 90 per cent. Negro as a concentrated Negro area, and any area with a population more than 90 per cent. white as a concentrated white area.[1]

[1] For the purpose of determining population scatter, the area used was the United States Census enumeration district. These districts range

The first group is typified by New York and Chicago, where the concentration of Negroes is great and yet where it affects only a small part of the whole city area. In Chicago this pattern seems to be changing as the Negroes spread more southward. In New York, 96 per cent. of the white people are in concentrated white areas and 28 per cent. of the colored people are in concentrated colored areas.

The second group is typified by Richmond, and includes most of the large southern cities where Negroes are highly concentrated in several rather large parts of the city and lightly scattered in others, thus leaving a large proportion of the white people in areas from 10 to 90 per cent. Negro. In Richmond 53 per cent. of the white people are in concentrated white areas and 25 per cent. of the Negroes in concentrated Negro areas.

The third group is typified by Charleston, and is limited to the older southern cities and towns which have a heavy percentage of Negroes in their total population, and consequently a heavy scattering of Negroes throughout the city. In Charleston there are no enumeration districts that have a population less than 10 per cent. colored, and none that have a population less than 10 per cent. white, placing all members of both races in districts from 10 to 90 per cent. colored.

Group four is composed of cities with light colored infusion, where the diffusion of Negroes affects only a very small area of the city and is somewhat scattered within this area. In Gary, 89 per cent. of the white people are in concentrated white areas and no Negro districts are more than 90 per cent. Negro.

Two series of maps are presented to show the distribution of Negro population in the cities studied. Series 1-a to xvi-a indicates the areas in which Negroes constitute the majority of the population. Series 1-b to xvi-b shows the dispersion of the population by means of dots representing a fixed number of Negroes per dot.

from 500 to 3,500 in population. A special tabulation of the population by race by enumeration districts was secured from the bureau. In New York the tabulations of the N. Y. Census Committee by sanitary districts were used.

From the enumeration district figures and from the maps it is obvious that it is impossible to generalize as to the extent and character of segregation, except to state that, while separation is practically never complete, all cities have some areas where the large majority of the population is Negro. It is in these areas that the masses of the Negroes live.

When the spread of population is looked at as a process it would seem that Negro settlements start scatteringly in a small area. As the proportion of Negroes in the city increases, the newcomers settle with the older population and tend to fill up the area, thus creating a solid district, or rather a district from 50 to 90 per cent. Negro. When this district begins to fill up, or when some of its residents begin to desire homes in better neighborhoods, new scattering groups are thrown off and later population increments tend again to solidify and expand them.

The advance is somewhat like that of an army. A small outpost is thrown out ahead, and, if the terrain is favorable for occupancy by larger numbers, the mass advances. The only marked difference between the North and the South in this process of spread is that in northern cities the advance is made into areas already built up. It is a process of occupying houses previously filled by white families. In the South, however, the cities are smaller and there is more vacant space. These cities therefore usually expand into vacant territory. In the largest cities of the South, however, there is an occasional instance of depreciation of values in a white neighborhood adjoining a colored neighborhood followed by a change from white to colored occupancy.

CHARACTER OF MIXTURE

Almost without exception the groups which are most heavily mixed with Negroes in the North are Jewish and Italian. This is owing in part to the fact that Negroes have moved into neighborhoods formerly occupied by these foreign groups, and some of the original occupants remain. Those least mixed are the Irish and native white people. In the South the mixture arises from occupancy of servants'

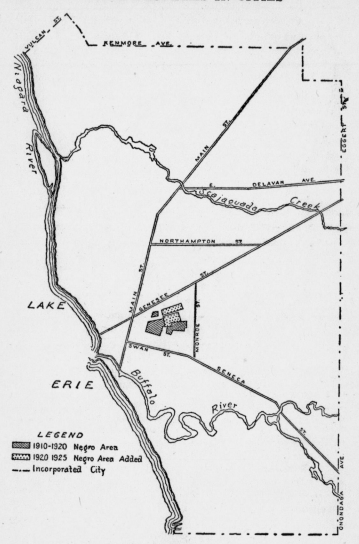

MAP I-A. BUFFALO, NEW YORK.

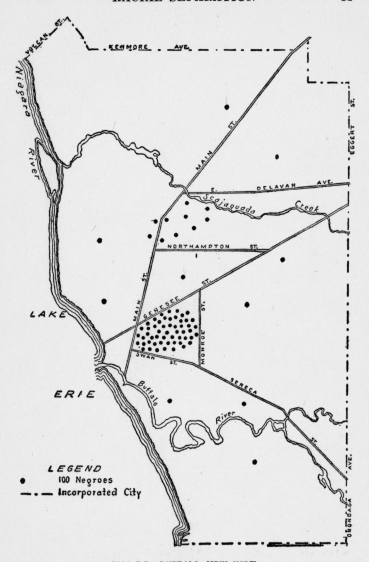

MAP I-B. BUFFALO, NEW YORK.

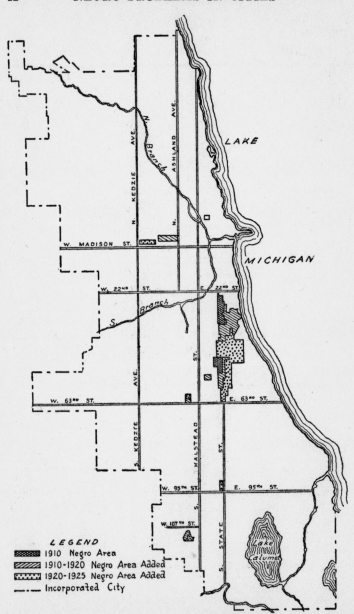

LEGEND
▓▓▓ 1910 Negro Area
░░░ 1910-1920 Negro Area Added
▒▒▒ 1920-1925 Negro Area Added
—··— Incorporated City

MAP II-A. CHICAGO, ILLINOIS.

MAP II-B. CHICAGO, ILLINOIS.

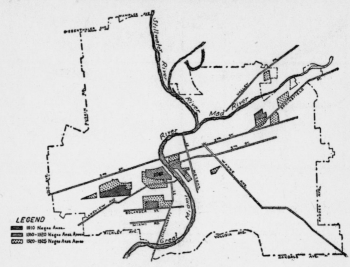

MAP III-A. DAYTON, OHIO.

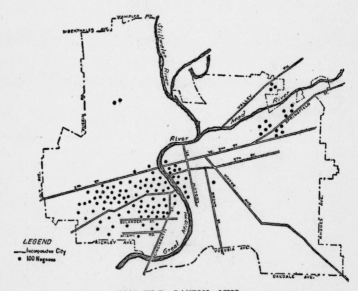

MAP III-B. DAYTON, OHIO.

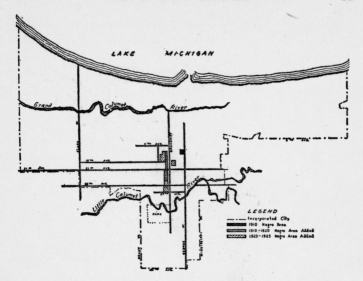

MAP IV-A. GARY, INDIANA.

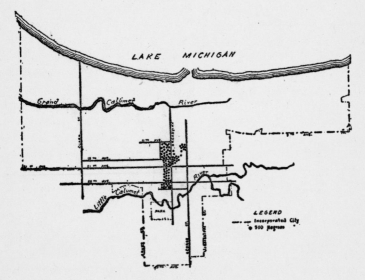

MAP IV-B. GARY, INDIANA.

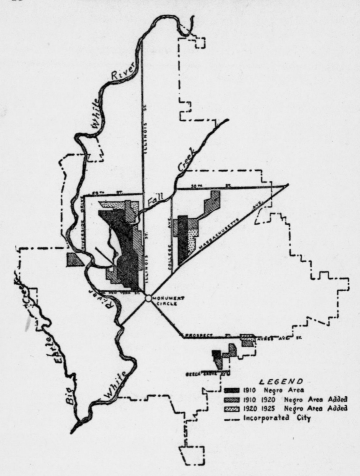

MAP V-A. INDIANAPOLIS, INDIANA.

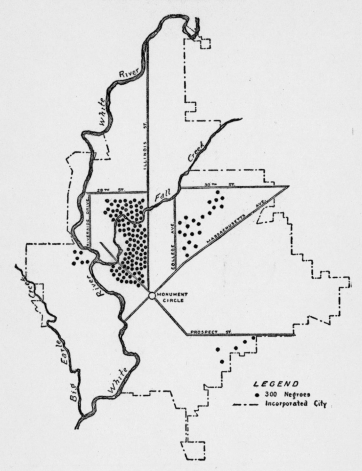

MAP V-B. INDIANAPOLIS, INDIANA.

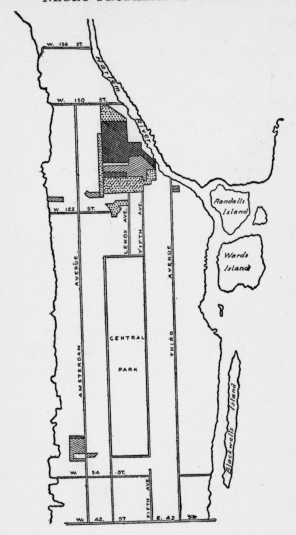

LEGEND
- 1910 Negro Area
- 1910-1920 Negro Area Added
- 1920-1925 Negro Area Added

MAP VI-A. NEW YORK CITY (UPPER MANHATTAN).

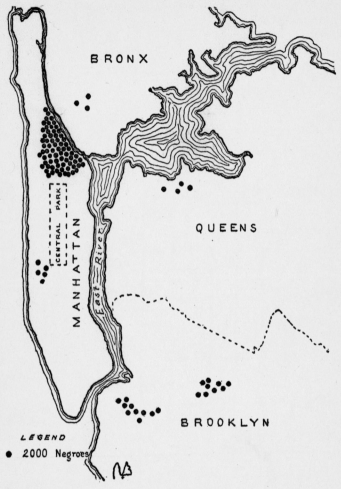

MAP VI-B. NEW YORK CITY.

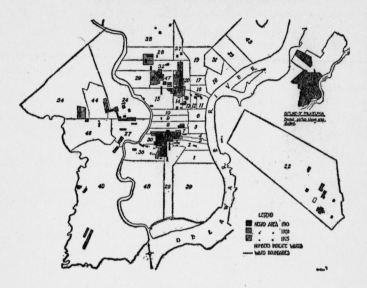

MAP VII-A. PHILADELPHIA, PENNSYLVANIA.

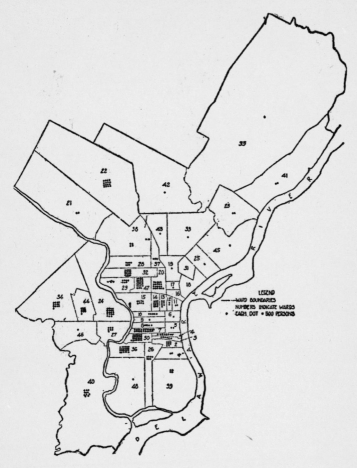

MAP VII-B. PHILADELPHIA, PENNSYLVANIA.

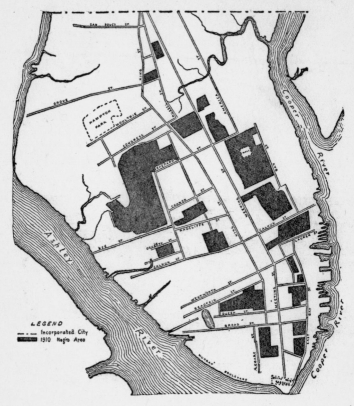

MAP VIII-A. CHARLESTON, SOUTH CAROLINA.

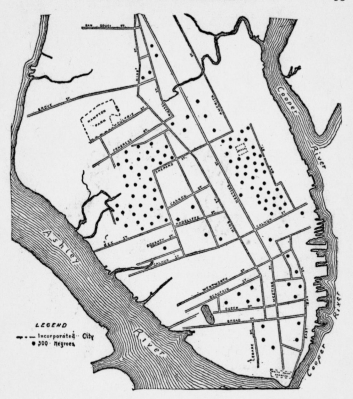

MAP VIII-B. CHARLESTON, SOUTH CAROLINA.

MAP IX-A.   KNOXVILLE, TENNESSEE.

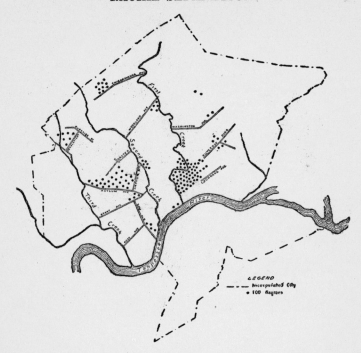

MAP IX-B. KNOXVILLE, TENNESSEE.

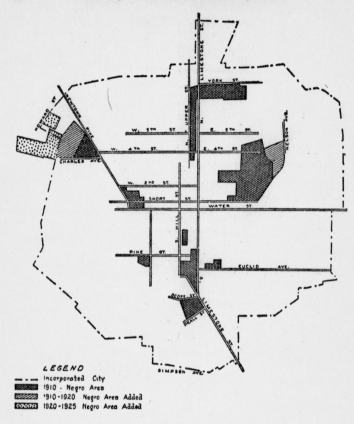

MAP X-A. LEXINGTON, KENTUCKY.

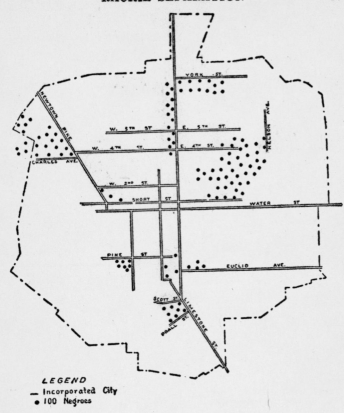

MAP X-B. LEXINGTON, KENTUCKY.

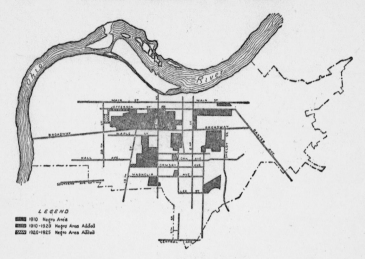

MAP XI-A. LOUISVILLE, KENTUCKY.

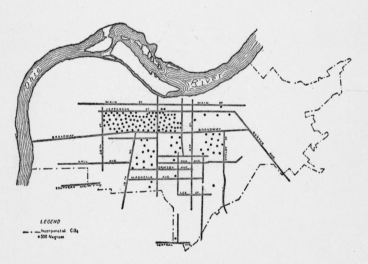

MAP XI-B. LOUISVILLE, KENTUCKY.

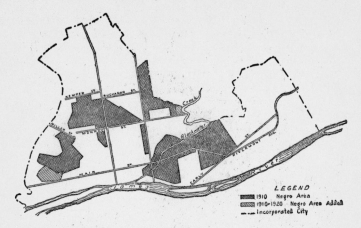

MAP XII-A. LYNCHBURG, VIRGINIA.

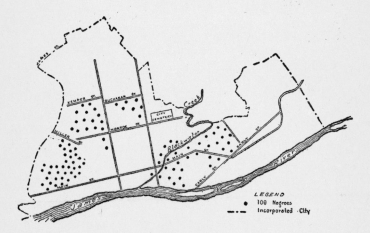

MAP XII-B. LYNCHBURG, VIRGINIA.

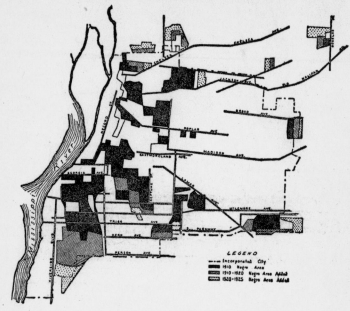

MAP XIII-A. MEMPHIS, TENNESSEE.

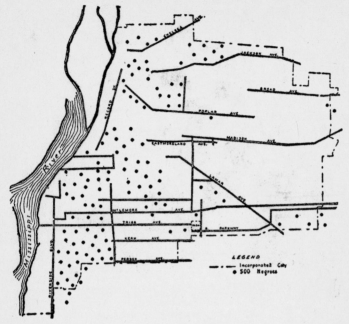

MAP XIII-B. MEMPHIS, TENNESSEE.

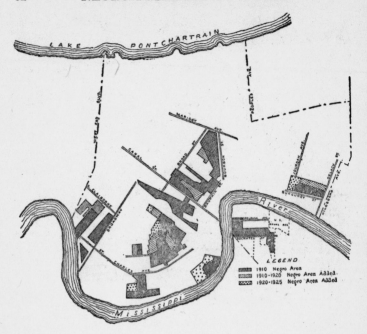

MAP XIV-A.   NEW ORLEANS, LOUISIANA.

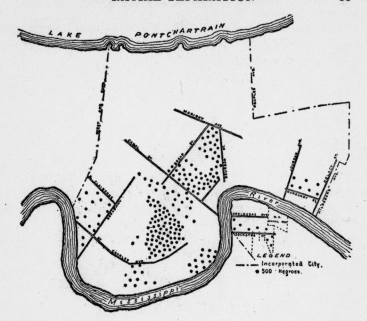

MAP XIV-B. NEW ORLEANS, LOUISIANA.

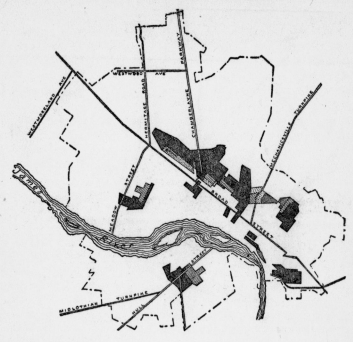

LEGEND
- · — Incorporated City
- 1910 Negro Area
- 1910-1920 Negro Area Added
- 1920-1925 Negro Area Added

MAP XV-A. RICHMOND, VIRGINIA.

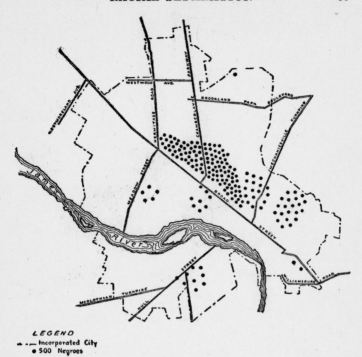

LEGEND
— . .— Incorporated City
● 500 Negroes

MAP XV-B. RICHMOND, VIRGINIA.

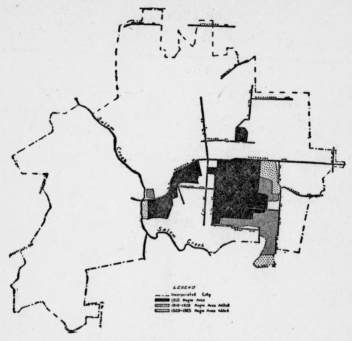

MAP XVI-A. WINSTON-SALEM, NORTH CAROLINA.

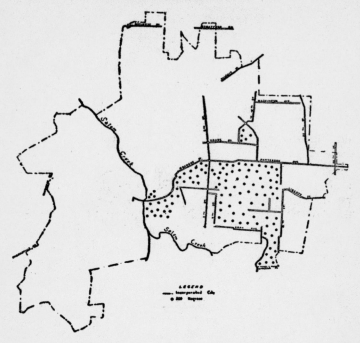

MAP XVI-B. WINSTON-SALEM, NORTH CAROLINA.

quarters on white premises, from the proximity of alleys in
the rear of white residence streets, and from the contiguity
of Negro residence areas to those of native white people.

EXPANSION OF NEGRO AREAS.

Maps i-a to xvi-a show the extent to which areas containing a majority of Negroes have expanded. It is difficult to
determine just what was the extent of the Negro area in
these cities in 1910, but from all available facts in the cities
studied it seems that the addition in area has been at a
slightly faster rate than the addition to the population. This
rapid expansion of Negro areas seems to have involved friction in every city studied and in many others known through
the press. During the transfer from white to Negro occupancy, race prejudice often flares up and this agitation takes
the form of: (1) passage of segregation laws, (2) deed restrictions, (3) social pressures, (4) violence.

Fortunately, however, these outbreaks seldom recur—
each city has one attack and afterwards seems to be immune.
After much discussion some degree of understanding is arrived at. This is apparently the reason for the recent greater
frequency of outbreaks in northern cities than in southern
cities. The former have only recently entered on their period
of rapid expansion of Negro areas and are going through a
corresponding period of acute prejudice. The southern cities
passed through this period some time ago, but there are still
flare-ups as new cities begin to expand vigorously.

In Chicago the first rapid expansion of the old south-
side area led to such intense friction that more than sixty
bombings of Negro residences occurred, and these incidents
culminated in the bloody riots of 1919. Since that time,
however, there has been further rapid expansion of Negro
residence areas with very little friction. The riot seemed to
clear the atmosphere and bring about the realization that the
rapid expansion of Negro population makes the expansion of
residence areas inevitable.

SEGREGATION ORDINANCES.

The passage of segregation laws has always taken the form of an effort to designate certain blocks as white and others as Negro, and to prevent any further movement of white people into colored blocks and colored people into white blocks. The first group of these ordinances was passed by Louisville, Baltimore, Richmond, and Atlanta in 1912 and 1913. The most famous of these, the Louisville ordinance, was passed first and served as a model for the others. It provided that any block containing a majority of white people should be designated a white residence block, and any block containing a majority of Negroes should be designated a Negro residence block, and that no colored people could move into white residence blocks and vice versa.

These ordinances were promptly declared unconstitutional. At the time the Louisville and Richmond ordinances were declared unconstitutional by the U. S. Supreme Court, the Atlanta ordinance was in review before the Georgia State Supreme Court, which body declared it unconstitutional.

In rendering the decision against the Louisville ordinance, the syllabus of the Supreme Court decision states:

A City Ordinance which forbids colored persons to occupy houses in blocks where the greater number of houses are occupied by white persons, in practical effect prevents the sale of such lots in such blocks to colored persons, and is unconstitutional.

A City Ordinance forbidding colored persons from occupying houses as residences, places of abode, or public assembly on blocks where the majority of the houses are occupied by white persons for those purposes, and in like manner forbidding white persons, when conditions of occupancy are reversed, and which bases the interdiction on color and nothing more, passes the legitimate bonds of police power, and invades the civil right to acquire, enjoy and use property which is guaranteed in equal measure to all citizens, white or colored, by the Fourteenth Amendment.

Such prohibition cannot be sustained upon the grounds that, through race segregation it serves to diminish miscegenation and promote the public peace by averting race hostility and conflict, or that it prevents deterioration in the value of property owned and occupied by white people; nor does the fact that upon its face it applies impartially to both races relieve it from the vice of discrimination or obviate the objection that it deprives of property without due process of law.   165 Kentucky, 559, Reversed.

In stating the opinion of the court, Mr. Justice Day said:

> The authority of the state to pass laws in the exercise of police power, having for their object the promotion of public health, safety and welfare, is very broad, and has been affirmed in numerous recent decisions. . . .
> The concrete question here is, may the occupancy of the property be invaded by the state, or by one of its municipalities, solely *because of the color* of the proposed occupant of the premises.[2]

Even though residential segregation by law is thoroughly discredited by these early court decisions, city lawmakers in at least two cities have enacted such legislation recently. These cities were New Orleans and Indianapolis. Although attempts have been made in these recent ordinances to change the wording in such a way that the objections to the Louisville ordinance would be avoided, the principle of block segregation remains the same.

In New Orleans the ordinance was in force at the time the staff of this study was there and its effects were apparent.[3]

The first thing observed was the impossibility of accomplishing the separation of the races by an edict of this kind. It was pointed out in the beginning of this chapter that in most cities there are large numbers of colored people in districts less than 10 per cent. Negro and considerable numbers of white people in districts less than 10 per cent. white.   In New Orleans in 1920 there were 272 census enumeration districts, only six of which were solidly white, while none was solidly colored.   With 10 per cent. as the dividing line we find that 6,328 Negroes are scattered in ninety-six enumeration districts that are less than 10 per cent. Negro. Using the 50 per cent. prescribed in the ordinance as the dividing line, the census enumeration district figures show that 54,000, or about half of the city's Negro population, live

---

[2] For decisions of Georgia and Maryland Supreme Courts on Baltimore and Atlanta ordinances, see: *Jackson* v. *State,* 132 Maryland, 311; *Cary* v. *City of Atlanta,* 143 Georgia, 192.

[3] After this report was written the New Orleans ordinance was declared unconstitutional by the United States Supreme Court.

in districts less than 50 per cent. Negro, and that 24,500 white people live in districts less than 50 per cent. white. Not all in the mixed enumeration districts live in mixed blocks, but a very considerable proportion do. Conservatively estimating the number of persons involved, it appears that some 8,000 white persons and 18,000 Negroes would have to be moved to accomplish segregation by blocks in New Orleans. The result of such a social change, even if gradually effected, is seemingly beyond the comprehension of those who enacted the ordinance.

Even if this chimerical objective could be attained, the results would be insignificant, as the pattern remaining would be that of a checker-board of white and colored blocks, with virtually as much contact along the bounding streets as there now is within the mixed blocks, and the increase in separation would be negligible.

The second result, which stands out sharply, is the financial loss involved for holders of colored property in mixed sections. A large number of cases were noted in New Orleans involving double houses and flats in mixed neighborhoods. If a tenant moves out of such a dwelling, the landlord cannot replace him; for if the block has a majority of white people, no new colored families can establish a residence in the quarters of the outgoing tenant. Under these circumstances the owner has to let his dwelling stand idle. This has seriously embarrassed quite a number of white landlords, as well as colored purchasers who were depending upon rents to help them meet their payments on property in mixed blocks. As a result, many building and loan associations and real estate firms in New Orleans expressed their dissatisfaction with the segregation ordinance.

The third objection is that although theoretically the law is supposed to apply to white and colored alike, in practice it never does. The colored people do not protest against white invasion, while the white people in mixed blocks do not hesitate to protest. Altogether about fifty cases have been made against Negroes under the New Orleans ordinance, and there has not been a single case against a white person.

The unconstitutionality of segregation by ordinance, the

physical impossibility of moving as many people as would have to move if such an ordinance were enforced, the loss imposed upon owners of property in mixed blocks, and the inequitable enforcement of the law all emphasize the error of ordinances of this kind. It might seem useless to give so much space to this matter if it were not for the fact that twelve years after the Louisville ordinance had been declared void by the Supreme Court, the city fathers of two municipalities attempted segregation by ordinance.

But legislation has not been the only method employed to force separation. Restrictive clauses in deeds of sale often provide that the deed is void in case the property is subsequently sold to a colored person. Cases involving various forms of deed restriction are frequent.

There are many court decisions upholding other types of deed restriction. Stipulation as to the type of house, time in which a residence is to be established, amount of the area of the lot that can be covered, and various limitations on the usage of property are common in deeds. Recently in the Michigan Supreme Court and in the District of Columbia Court, restrictive clauses against sale to colored persons were upheld; but the validity of restrictions on the ground of color has yet to be fully tested.[4] Such restrictions, however, are largely individual matters and the prohibition involved applies to a single lot and not to a whole neighborhood.

SOCIAL PRESSURE AND VIOLENCE

Social pressure toward segregation often results in the formation of neighborhood protective associations, particularly when Negroes first begin to invade a white neighborhood. The property holders organize to prevent the threatened change of the neighborhood, hold meetings, and often, under the leadership of some prejudiced person, become very excited. In fact, the segregation ordinance in Indianapolis resulted almost directly from the organization of one of these

---

[4] A fairly comprehensive digest of the opinions on the validity of deed restrictions may be found in 151 Ga. 667 to 680. This brief cites some fifteen cases in various states.

associations, the purpose of which was to prevent the north-ward spread of the Negro area.

The riots of Chicago were preceded by the organization of a number of these associations; and an excellent report on their workings is to be found in *The Negro in Chicago*, the report of the Chicago Race Commission. The endeavor of such organizations is to pledge the property holders of the neighborhood not to sell or rent to Negroes, and to use all the possible pressures of boycott and ostracism in the en-deavor to hold the status of the area. They often endeavor to bring pressure from banks against loans on Negro prop-erty in the neighborhood, and are sometimes successful in this.

The danger in such associations lies in the tendency of unruly members to become inflamed and to resort to acts of violence. Although they are a usual phenomenon when neighborhoods are changing from white to Negro in north-ern cities, no record was found in this study where such an association had been successful in stopping the spread of a Negro neighborhood. The net results seem to have been a slight retardation in the rate of spread and the creation of a considerable amount of bitterness in the community.

Social pressure also often takes the form of violent action against colored persons who have moved into mixed neigh-borhoods. The Report of the Chicago Race Commission contains a mass of illuminating descriptive material relating to these outbreaks. Many similar cases came to the atten-tion of the staff during this study and the testimony of well-informed local social workers and real estate men in other cities indicated that the possibility of violence lurks every-where when Negro neighborhoods spread.

In many of these violent outbursts, it can be observed that the Negroes involved are the victims of circumstances. They are constantly in search of better homes. They buy houses in good faith and cannot get out of their bargains without serious loss when they discover that they are not welcome in the neighborhood. For every Negro purchaser there must be a seller who is usually white. These sellers often make a good profit.

PROPERTY VALUES

One thing that stirs the white people in these neighbor-hoods to opposition is the depreciation of property values when Negroes come in. It was observed during the Chicago study and during this study, however, that the areas that are usually penetrated by Negroes in their expansion are in neighborhoods that are already depreciating in value. There are numerous signs of such depreciation which often escape the observation of neighborhood residents who are not keen observers. Single family residences begin to give way to boarding-houses and apartments. Flats are built, and some-times business or manufacturing establishments come into the neighborhood. Thus an exclusive residence section is cheapened. If one of these depreciating sections lies close to a Negro neighborhood, or if it has good transit service to places where Negroes work, the time finally comes when Negroes are willing to pay more for property there than the white occupants are, and the transition begins. It is a per-fectly normal operation of real estate supply and demand which cannot readily be accelerated by promotion or re-tarded by agitation.

There is considerable controversy as to whether the in-filtration of Negroes further depreciates the value of the property, or whether the new demand for Negro residences sends the price up again. Nothing short of a technical and detailed study of changing values in sections of this kind could determine this point. From the limited observations made in this study it seems probable that prices sometimes rise and sometimes fall under different circumstances of supply and demand. Since Negroes usually pay higher rents than white people for the same type of property, as is shown in Chapter VII, it is also probable that rents and sale prices may take slightly different trends in the same neigh-borhood.

There is undoubtedly a period, just after Negroes begin to move into an area, when the white owners begin to be fully aware of the depreciation, and when their eagerness to sell often approximates a panic. During such a period the shrewd real estate operator can pick up good bargains. In fact Negroes have occasionally been introduced into a neighborhood by these operators for the purpose of creating bargains. On the other hand, if the owners remain calm and hold on to their property, it may even appreciate if the section develops a brisk demand for colored residences. Some sections of Harlem, in New York City, have appreciated in this way. The chief obstacle to rapid appreciation in a section of this kind is the limited income of Negroes of the middle class, who cannot pay high prices for residences. Values often tend to stabilize at the highest prices this class can pay, as happened in the Clay, Leigh, and Marshall Street section of Richmond, which has recently changed from white to colored occupancy.

A study of Olcott's land value maps of Chicago indicates a gradual depreciation during the past five years in the South-side sections that are changing from white to Negro. It is almost impossible to determine whether this is the result of Negro infiltration or merely of the normal depreciation caused by a shift of fashionable residence northward and by industrial invasion. A more detailed study of changes in rents and values in these changing neighborhoods would be interesting.

RACE SOLIDARITY

The forces that tend to separate the races do not all come from without. Within the Negro group there is a considerable economic and social cohesion which accentuates the tendencies toward solidarity.

The economic factors arise in the main from the low incomes of Negroes, which limit the amount they can put into houses, and force them into districts in which values and rents are low. Another tendency toward concentration results from the arrangement of transportation systems. The large settlements of colored people are always either centrally located or are served with convenient transportation facilities. Lack of transportation retards the development of the suburban subdivisions for Negroes. The average colored family has no automobile and is not able to buy in a suburban area even if it is not restricted; therefore, it was found in this study that the movement of Negro population to distant suburbs was limited almost entirely to persons actually employed there.

The social cohesion of the population which fosters concentration derives its power from the social life and institutions in the community. Schools are especially powerful factors in attracting residents. Colored people have a strong ambition for good school facilities, and it was noted in city after city in this study that a neighborhood with a good school showed rapid growth, while settlements not adequately supplied with schools, churches, and recreational facilities were retarded.

This process of separation strikes deep into the social life of the group. It develops neighborhood business and institutions. Before the solidification of the large settlements in Chicago, Philadelphia and New York, there was little Negro neighborhood business, the stores being in the hands of small white merchants. As these settlements grew and became self-conscious Negro business developed and self-improvement organizations took root.

But unfortunately separation also paves the way for neglect and exploitation, as Chapters IV and V indicate. The neighborhood improvements in sewerage, lighting and paving, especially in southern cities, are too often slighted. The intense demand for space is exploited, and the separate schools and recreational facilities that serve the segregated areas are too often neglected.

AVOIDING TROUBLE

The concentration, spread, and reconcentration of Negro population within the city needs to be recognized as an inevitable result of the coming of a large new group of laborers. These are processes that follow normal laws of supply and demand, and that do not yield to community excitement and agitation, although on occasion they do create much excitement. Consequently a Negro seeking to better his home conditions is frequently in danger of violence, in spite of the fact that he is acting under his legal rights as a citizen.

Many white persons resent Negro intrusion into a neighborhood on the ground that the move is made merely because of the desire of the Negroes to live among white people. The strength of economic and social cohesion among the colored people, however, indicates that this is not true. The preference is given to home sites near the centers of their social, economic and religious life; but except in cases of occasional individuals they are driven from these centers by neglect and exploitation of such neighborhoods, by lack of sanitation, and by poor police protection. The man with ambition naturally tries to find a better place for his home.

It is most important that these matters should be generally understood. The experience of two cities that have dealt constructively with this problem of the spread of Negro population should be of general value in working out a solution. Convinced of the futility of segregation laws and of the demoralizing effects of violence, the cities of Winston-Salem and Dallas have approached their neighborhood problems successfully on the basis of coöperation.

In both of these places the rapid spread of Negro population began to cause friction, and trouble threatened. In both, a systematic canvass of the situation revealed the trend of Negro population and the probable rate of expansion. The facts were discussed in a series of neighborhood meetings attended by both white and colored persons; and an understanding was reached as to the direction to be taken in the spread of the white population on the one hand, and in the spread of the Negro population on the other, though naturally Negroes did not relinquish their right to hold property anywhere in the city. The Negroes at these meetings made clear their right to have better neighborhoods and better facilities for the making of good homes. As a result, the white and colored neighbors together attacked the problem of getting the municipality to improve colored districts. Already there has been, in response to this joint effort, a great stimulation of the school-building, paving, sewerage, and recreational programs of the two cities; and friction seems to be at a minimum.

Chapter IV

CONGESTION AND EXPLOITATION

If there are barriers that block the natural expansion of a neighborhood, an increase in population will result in an increase in density. The forces that tend to separate the Negro community from other communities and to restrict the area occupied by Negroes, therefore tend to concentrate the population; and there is concentration to an alarming degree in Negro communities where migrants have been limited in their selection of home sites to certain parts of the city.

Density

The density of Negro areas in most cities is much greater than the density of white areas. In some cities it is four times as great. Table VII gives the average net residence densities for cities studied.[1]

The density varies widely from city to city. It ranges from 336 per acre in New York City to twenty per acre in Winston-Salem. On account of their size and intensive growth, the large cities have much greater density of population than the small cities.

In fact, the smaller cities, which are now just approaching the metropolitan proportions, have an opportunity to

[1] Net residence area used in Table VII excludes parks, playgrounds, schools, water and manufacturing sites. Business section is excluded from both white and Negro area. Street spaces are, however, included.

The areas are calculated by two methods: (1) Measurement of Negro area delineated on large maps drawn to scale, and (2) check on this method by use of the densities calculated by small sections of the city by the telephone companies in their house counts. The population for 1920 was obtained by census enumeration districts which divide the city into small areas. Increases in these areas from 1920 to 1925 were estimated closely by noting the new building, the number of blocks changing from white to Negro, the increases in school census figures and, in some cities, from recent telephone company family counts. These estimates were checked by comparison of the total population of the city with census estimates for 1925 and by calculation of birth-rates and death-rates.

78

avoid the mistakes that marred the growth of older centers. The last generation drifted into the error of allowing a dense, unplanned, exploitative growth in the central parts of large cities. With the examples of these mistakes before them, the smaller cities can give attention to city plans, zoning ordinances, and building codes, which, if wisely made

TABLE VII—DENSITY OF POPULATION, 1925

City	White			Negro		
	Population	Net Residence Area (Acres)	Density Per Acre	Population	Net Residence Area (Acres)	Density Per Acre
New York (Manhattan)	1,926,983	8,644	223	148,081	441	336
Philadelphia	1,815,460	64,387	28	163,250	1,468	111
Chicago	2,966,200	94,464	31	154,800	2,320	67
Charleston	34,700	1,851	19	31,056	544	57
Richmond	131,254	11,840	11	57,770	1,247	46
Buffalo	529,216	34,596	15	9,800	245	40
Lexington	33,111	*	*	13,400	335	40
Louisville	218,781	9,486	23	40,505	1,362	30
New Orleans	304,700	22,038	14	109,380	3,671	30
Indianapolis	316,702	21,256	15	42,980	2,100	21
Knoxville	83,523	14,460	6	13,842	5,737	24
Gary	68,739	14,760	5	9,700	472	21
Memphis	114,703	8,737	13	69,394	3,340	21
Winston-Salem	39,200	2,075	19	34,400	1,746	20
Dayton	161,502	9,415	17	11,440	582	20

* Not available.

and administered, will distribute city growth more normally and stabilize land uses and values.

Density also varies within the city from one section to another. Table VIII, which gives the densities by sections for selected cities, shows that the average density is lowered by a few outlying sections with sparse population and a considerable amount of vacant space, and that the populous central sections are much denser than the average. In fact, in many cities the majority of the Negroes live in sections whose density is greater than the average for the city. (See

TABLE VIII—DENSITIES OF SELECTED CITIES*
BY SECTIONS, 1925

City and Section	Population	Net Residence Area in Acres	Density, People per Acre
Philadelphia			
South Side.....................	51,000	368	139
Lower North Side	23,978	198	121
Upper North Side	26,539	244	109
West Philadelphia.............	30,489	347	88
Germantown	7,885	100	79
Chicago			
South Side	126,000	1,629	77
Halstead Street (near Hull House)	1,600	20	80
Lower North Side.............	2,600	45	58
West Side....................	8,600	152	57
Ogden Park...................	2,900	58	50
Oakwood	4,300	110	39
Morgan Park.................	2,800	160	18
Memphis			
Central (Looney Ave.).........	3,647	110	33
Central (Overton St.)..........	2,244	60	37
Central (Monroe-Calhoun).....	5,942	164	36
Central (Poplar-Forest)	4,171	170	25
South (Calhoun-City limit)	33,344	1,688	20
South (Calvary-Cemetery).....	2,870	273	11
Extreme N. West..............	1,817	102	18
Klondike (North)	4,009	320	13
Orange Mound	2,340	287	8
New Orleans			
Wards 1, 2, 10, 11, 12..........	38,700	845	46
Lower 1 and 10................	6,800	180	38
Ward 7	11,500	298	39
Wards 4, 5, and 6.............	18,500	576	32
Wards Upper 14 and 16........	3,230	115	28
Wards Lower 16...............	1,750	72	24
Ward 3	9,800	427	23
Wards Lower 12 and 13........	5,400	255	21
Algiers	4,700	355	13
Ward 17......................	3,800	317	12
Industrial Canal	3,300	327	10

* Includes only areas with a majority of Negro population.

Tables VII and VIII.) The average density for New Orleans is thirty; but 75,500 of the 109,380 Negroes live in sections where the density is thirty-two or more.

It will also be noted from the sectional densities in Table VIII that although the average for the smaller cities is not high, there are, within these cities, very dense spots in Negro neighborhoods. It is evident also that if there are whole sections, embracing many blocks, that have a high average density, there are some blocks within these sections in which the population is even more dense. Diagrams I-IV show the arrangement of some of these dense blocks, alongside an ideal arrangement set up by the United States Housing Corporation. Area covered by houses is shaded.

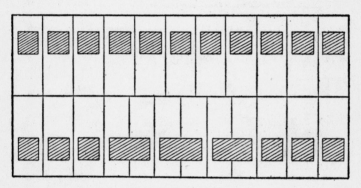

DIAGRAM I. IDEAL ARRANGEMENT TWO-ACRE BLOCK
(U. S. HOUSING CORPORATION).

Housing authorities set the ideal division of an acre of land at ten or eleven lots of about forty by one hundred feet, exclusive of streets. In outlying sections with single family houses, this would accommodate ten families, or slightly more than thirty-five persons. In central sections with double houses it would accommodate twenty families, or somewhat more than seventy persons; and in areas containing flats the density would be higher. It is apparent that many Negro blocks pass this ideal of thirty-five to the acre, and that quite a number have more than seventy persons to the acre. This exploitation of the separate communities produces an indelible impression on the character of the residents and upon the life of the city. It is directly reflected in the health and morals of the people.

Density can be caused by two kinds of crowding. It can result from packing too many people into each dwelling, or

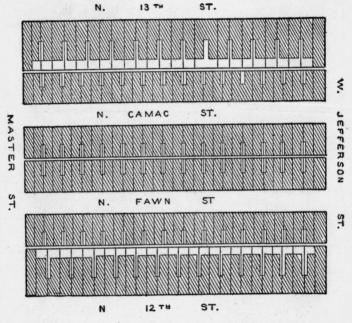

DIAGRAM II. PHILADELPHIA BLOCK.

from packing too many houses into an area. While there is some house-crowding in the lower-class Negro neighborhoods, especially in segregated, high-rent sections, the most serious aspects of density arise from land-crowding.

HOUSE-CROWDING

Sanitary officials often complain of the tendency of Negroes, especially those moving from country to city, to over-

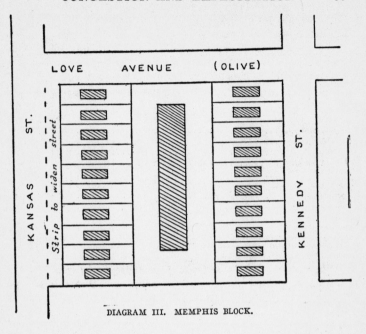

DIAGRAM III. MEMPHIS BLOCK.

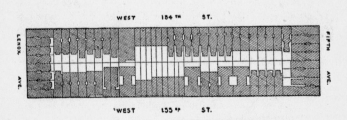

DIAGRAM IV. HARLEM BLOCK, NEW YORK CITY.

crowd houses. Country families are usually large and tenant houses are small. The usual provision for the family of a farm hand is a cabin of two or three rooms. Under these circumstances standards are low. The indications are, however, that standards in the city are higher.

When all the rooms in the house are counted, including

kitchens and small rooms, two persons to a room is excessive crowding. The percentage of dwellings containing two
or more persons for every room is given in Table IX.

TABLE IX—PERCENTAGE OF NEGRO DWELLINGS CON-
TAINING TWO OR MORE PERSONS PER ROOM

City	Percentage *
Charleston	21.5
Philadelphia	16.9
Gary	16.6
New Orleans	16.5
Memphis	12.4
Dayton	10.0
Richmond	9.7
Louisville	9.0
Lexington	8.8
Indianapolis	6.7

* From house-cards, see appendix for method.

While these figures indicate that there is overcrowding
among Negro families, they do not indicate that this is as
bad as it is generally supposed to be.

Crowding is more prevalent in high-rent cities than in cities in which the rent per room is more reasonable. Charleston, where, as is shown in Table XXI, rents are low, is a
notable exception. The reason why Charleston shows the
highest congestion in spite of low rents is that it contains
many two-room cabins of the kind used on near-by farms,
and that these are occupied by families that have come in
from the country.

Room-crowding therefore results from the low economic
level of many Negro families and from the type of house
that is built for them. Houses of several different kinds
contribute to congestion. The worst phase of overcrowding
is found where one room serves as living-room, bedroom
and kitchen and is furnished with table, bed, and cookstove.
Even when it has only one or two occupants it is overcrowded and highly insanitary. A five-room house may
have five families using a common sink and toilet. Old
tenements have as high as twenty-five to thirty families,

each family occupying one furnished room. In New York and Chicago, tenements are more commonly rented out in sleeping rooms with the privilege of cooking in a common kitchen. One-room dwellings are not found outside the tenement cities, except in a few places where, as in Charleston, the country-cabin type of building has been transplanted to the city.

Shacks of two and three rooms and shot-gun houses are sufficient for not more than two adults with one child, or possibly with two small children. They are often occupied by unskilled wage-earning families with more than two children, water supply and toilet facilities being shared by two or more families.

A cottage of four or five rooms is sufficient for a family of four or five persons if there are no lodgers. If one of the rooms is sub-rented to two adults, overcrowding results.

Large single-family houses are often subdivided for multiple occupancy. Richmond has a few of these, Philadelphia, New York and Buffalo have many in proportion to the total number of Negro dwellings. Much of this subdivision is done when a neighborhood changes from white to Negro and when the demand for Negro dwellings is brisk. When the city requires putting in a separate water supply and toilet for each family, this subdividing can, without harm, be carried to the point of providing two or three rooms for a couple with one or two small children. But when an old house is filled up with two or more persons in a room, and sanitary conveniences are the same as they were for the original single family, the situation is serious.

Since 1920 there seems to have been a tendency in all cities to decrease sanitary inspections and to rely upon complaints to bring bad conditions to light. This is manifestly unfair to a group made up of persons unfamiliar with city conditions. Tenants do not know where to make complaints; and many landlords dispossess tenants who complain. In neighborhoods in which the people have difficulty in finding vacant dwellings, reliance upon complaints from occupants of tenement-houses is inadequate.

Usually Negro families must fit themselves into cramped quarters in old houses in which rooms are let at high rentals.

The following examples indicate that the situation of Negroes tends to produce slightly more crowding than is found among white persons in similar areas.

In New York City in 1910 the area containing a majority of Negroes had a total population of 118,032. From 1910 to 1920, when there was little building, the population in the same houses increased by 14,522, largely by a substitution of Negroes for white people in a considerable part of the area. Thus sixteen people to the acre were added with virtually no new building. This was done by slightly greater room-crowding in the apartment buildings and by the sub-division of single-family houses for multiple occupancy.[2]

In Richmond the area comprised in Census Enumeration District 141 and part of 142 in 1910 contained 2,737 white and 227 colored people, or a total of 2,964. By 1920 this total had increased to 3,689, of which 2,376 were white and 1,313 colored. There had been a little flat-building in the area, but the greater part of this increase of 727 people in the area was owing to the subdivision of old houses which in 1910 were occupied by single white families but which were rented between 1910 and 1920 to several colored families.

Lodgers are an important element in room-crowding. Many families that rent have to struggle to pay the high rent with low wages, and lodgers are an economic necessity. Many families that are buying houses have an equally hard struggle to meet the monthly payments and take in lodgers to help out. In fact, as Table X indicates, there are more lodgers among the home-owning families studied than among the families that rent.

The large number of lodgers in the cities that have many Negro migrants is in striking contrast with their comparative absence in the static southern cities, such as Lynch-

2 Computation of New York Census Committee.

burg, Lexington, Charleston and Louisville. This is owing
to the prevalence in a migrant population of unattached persons who must find shelter among families. Part of the
family often remains in the South while one or two mem-

TABLE X—LODGERS * IN NEGRO FAMILIES

City	Total Families Canvassed	Families with Lodgers	Total Number of Lodgers	Percentage of Families with Lodgers
Philadelphia	2,531	948	2,438	37
New York †	1,627	513	874	32
Indianapolis	207	51	131	25
Dayton	231	64	178	28
Buffalo	53	26	62	49
Gary	111	27	64	24
Total North	4,760	1,629	3,747	34
Memphis	193	55	123	28
Louisville	485	51	292	11
Richmond	410	53	108	13
New Orleans	194	11	22	6
Charleston	452	36	76	8
Lexington	190	7	12	4
Knoxville †	3,151	612	1,624	19
Lynchburg	188	15	27	8
Charlottesville	125	14	25	11
Total South	5,388	854	2,309	15.9
Grand Total	10,148	2,483	6,056	24.5
Owners ‡	1,653	500	1,313	30.2
Renters	5,244	1,371	3,143	26.1

* Data from house-cards, see appendix.
† From special study made by local agency.
‡ Knoxville not tabulated as to owners and renters.

bers go in advance and remain alone until they get settled
in the new community.

High rents and high prices for homes in these cities also
contribute to the desire to take in lodgers. There are not
only many unattached persons in need of lodgings, but there
are also many families eager to supplement their income by
renting rooms.

It would seem that the cost of the home has much to do with the taking in of lodgers. In the northern cities, where costs are high, there is a high proportion of home-owning families with lodgers. In the southern cities, where cheaper houses are bought, the proportion of lodgers is not nearly so great.

In a family of adults, lodgers present no serious problems unless the renting family crowds itself too much to release the spare room. With adolescent and young adult children in the family, however, lodgers give rise to serious social problems. Fortunately, in migrant communities where the proportion of lodgers is highest, the proportion of children is lowest. The Chicago Race Commission investigated the lodger problem intensively and discovered a number of neighborhoods where the proportion of lodgers to the total population was about the same as the proportion of children. While this indicates that lodgers are found in greatest numbers in the neighborhoods in which there are few children, it indicates also a serious situation for those few children.

It is only fair, however, to repeat that the landlord is largely responsible for this crowding. The pattern of the city is already made and the newcomers must fit themselves into it.

LAND-CROWDING

Land plats shown in the fire insurance maps of various cities indicate that land-exploitation is at the bottom of much of the congestion of the most depressing slum areas. (See Diagrams I-IV.) Spaces that should have been occupied by single-family houses have been built up thickly with flats. In other places single-family houses have been built with a common wall, the effect of which is to eliminate side yards and to reduce the amount of light and of air-space to less than is necessary for health. Front yards have been eliminated by building flush on the sidewalk, and the rear yards have then been cut in two by alleys and secondary streets on which rows of houses have been built.

Thus in the scramble for profits the land in the central sections of cities has been greatly exploited.

Diagram I shows the ideal arrangement of lots on a block of 2.07 acres, excluding streets. This arrangement houses twenty-three families, or eleven families to the acre. Alongside this block are diagrams showing actual arrangements as disclosed by fire insurance maps in certain of the Negro sections studied. These and the ideal arrangement show striking differences in respect to light and air-space.

Eagerness to squeeze profits from the land is responsible for most of the overcrowding. Congestion in cities has made some intensive use of land necessary; but in many instances the actual crowding caused by a desire for more than a fair return on the value of the land has increased until it has produced deplorable conditions. (See Chapter VII.) In these cases profits pyramid by the following process:

> In a given district, the land values increase with the number of families normally housed on a lot. The speculative builder sees a large opportunity for gain in crowding more families on a lot than has been customary in a neighborhood. He buys a vacant lot at a value based on its net return from use for a one- or two-family house and builds a four-family house, and is usually able to pocket the difference between the cost of a single lot and the cost of two lots. After a considerable number of such small tenements have been erected, and land values have thereby been practically doubled, the same process is repeated. The speculative builder discovers a profit in building six- or eight-family tenements on lots of the size originally used for one- or two-family houses. This process of more and more intensive use of the land and a corresponding increase in land values continues until at length slum conditions are produced.[3]

Many overcrowded areas are on the edge of growing business or manufacturing districts. Strictly speaking, the property is no longer residence property, but is being held until it can be sold for commercial use. Meanwhile the old residences are allowed to stand for the rental they bring in.

The Memphis area in Diagram III, however, is taken from a recently subdivided area. It shows that speculative builders, left to operate without restrictions, will create unsightly,

[3] Robert Whitten, "Housing Density Regulation," *Proceedings*, February, 1925, *American Society of Civil Engineers*.

unhealthy communities in almost any part of a city if they scent a chance for profit. This plat is in open violation of the Memphis zoning law which requires 1,000 square feet per family. In the block shown, the total allotment is about 1,000 feet, but the tenement in the center of the block provides only about 700 feet per family.

This fondness of the Babbitts for speculative profits in land has created cesspools in the midst of American cities. Migrants coming into such a place are powerless to change the situation but must fit themselves into it as best they may. This is especially true of cities in which the Negro neighborhoods are more or less segregated. The newcomers must go there and nowhere else. Here is a situation that affords the exploiter an opportunity to extract as much profit as the community will stand for.

DENSITY AND DEATH

Extreme congestion has a direct bearing on the high city death-rate of Negroes. Two of the most common causes of death among them—tuberculosis and pneumonia—and the death of infants under one year of age, were found to be very closely allied with it. To ascertain this relationship, comparisons between the death-rates and densities were made by wards in Philadelphia. Inasmuch as the comparison was by wards within one city, the variations in public health effort were eliminated; and as only Negroes were included, the racial factor was held constant. Table XI shows by wards the density of Negro population and the infant and tuberculosis death-rates in Philadelphia.

In this table the eye can readily follow the rise of the tuberculosis death-rate as the density rises. The rise of the infant death-rate is not so marked, but there is a positive correlation. The Pearsonian correlation coefficients are: density and tuberculosis death-rate, $+.809$; infant mortality and density, $+.323$.

In New York City the sanitary-district figures are not kept by color, but the total deaths in districts containing a large Negro population vary with the density of the district.

In this connection it is interesting to note that in Louisville the Woman's City Club investigated the incidence of tuberculosis by houses, and listed some 300 dwellings in each of which there had been two or more deaths. A thorough

TABLE XI—NEGRO DENSITY AND DEATH-RATES, BY WARDS, PHILADELPHIA, 1924 *

Ward	Density Per Acre	Deaths per 100,000 Tuberculosis	Deaths Under 1 Year per 1,000 Births
14	63.6	230	8.9
22	78.8	127	10.6
34	80.0	241	6.7
29	89.6	195	8.1
28	96.3	116	10.3
26	106.7	188	9.8
36	109.0	198	11.0
40	110.5	215	14.2
24	111.3	203	8.9
32	114.6	203	9.1
47	116.6	206	12.2
13	118.9	253	15.2
20	120.3	272	10.7
15	121.4	308	11.2
14	123.0	290	13.7
30	140.9	299	10.7
7	164.3	463	12.5
2	169.2	408	15.7
3	170.2	341	8.3
4	170.4	400	13.2

* Hospital deaths in 27th ward omitted. Deaths from *Report of Philadelphia Board of Health.* Densities, see Table VII.

examination of these houses revealed in every one some serious defect in lighting or ventilation.

There are other evidences of the relation of density to death. In New York City the tenement-house department has kept check upon the deaths in tenements and has compared the "old-law tenements" with those erected under the new laws. The "old-law" houses do not allow as much light and air as the "new-law" buildings. The comparative death-rates are shown in Table XII on page 92.

The number of individuals per dwelling doubtless averages slightly higher in the old-law dwellings than in the
new, but not sufficiently to make up for this startling discrepancy in the death-rates. Truly the saying that "one can
kill a baby with a house as easily as with a hatchet" holds
good of the houses in dense Negro neighborhoods.

These relationships between density and death are not
cited to show that density is a primary cause of tuberculosis,
pneumonia, or the diseases of infants. Dense living is some-

TABLE XII—DEATHS IN OLD AND NEW LAW APARTMENTS, MANHATTAN *

Year	Total Deaths per 1,000 Apts.		Tuberculosis Cases per 1,000 Apts.	
	Old Law	New Law	Old Law	New Law
1919	47	34	13.1	7.7
1920	46	30	12.2	7.5
1921	40	26	10.2	6.2
1922	44	30	10.1	6.4
1923	43	28	8.1	5.6
1924	42	28	8.0	5.5
Average	44	29	10.3	6.5

* Data from Bureau of Records, Tenement House Department, New York City.

times undoubtedly the direct cause of pulmonary complaints;
but it is a greater factor in spreading infection than in causing it. What these figures tend to prove, therefore, is that
contagious and infectious diseases in a densely populated
area will cause proportionately more deaths than in one more
sparsely settled.

The effects of bad housing conditions on the death-rate
need to be emphasized, because they are environmental and
subject to improvement. Negro death-rates from pulmonary
complaints and from the diseases of infants have been so
high that some commentators have ascribed the excessive
mortality to inborn racial traits. But in this relationship of
density of population to the death-rate we have a direct
variation with environmental conditions. This but serves to
emphasize the responsibility of cities for the protection of

migrant Negro neighborhoods from ravages traceable to the environment and caused by exploitation and neglect.

DENSITY AND MORALS

Density, especially that arising from room-crowding, also has a relationship to immorality. Family privacy is seri-

TABLE XIII—NEGRO DENSITY AND ILLEGITIMATE
BIRTHS, PHILADELPHIA, 1924*

Ward	Negro Density per Acre	Illegitimate Births per 1,000 Births
44	63.6	127
22	78.8	137
34	80.0	119
29	89.6	100
28	96.3	103
26	106.7	159
36	109.0	96
40	110.5	169
24	111.3	125
32	114.6	79
47	116.6	116
13	118.9	116
20	120.3	128
15	121.4	143
14	123.0	144
30	140.9	165
7	164.3	200
2	169.2	139
3	170.2	119
4	170.4	186

* Data from *Report of Philadelphia Board of Health.*

ously violated in crowded flat-houses where the conveniences are often used in common. It is further invaded when lodgers are included in the same households with young people.

Family case-workers and juvenile-court judges complain constantly of the moral disorders coming to their attention in densely populated neighborhoods where these conditions of crowding prevail.

By noting the fluctuations of density and of the illegitimate birth-rate in the wards of Philadelphia, it is possible to see the connection between them.

The Pearsonian correlation coefficient between density and illegitimacy is $+ .243$. While the correlation is not very high in this case, the great increase in illegitimacy in the very dense wards is significant. Here again density is a contributing factor rather than a primary cause.

The social cost of this concentration, especially when it involves families low in the social scale, is illustrated in the intensive study of a congested block in Philadelphia made by the Housing Association. This block, of slightly more than one acre, houses on the average 110 families and about 330 people, in addition to several business establishments. The Report of the Philadelphia Housing Association for 1924 says:

> During the last three years there were 179 families living in this block reported to the Social Service Exchange. There were 402 case records of these families, handled by 52 agencies functioning in the field of family relief, health and children's work. Generally there was work done by the agency for the family for quite a length of time after the registration, the case often being reopened, which fact did not occasion a re-registration at the exchange. These records revealed 261 social defects against these families, among which were 71 cases of delinquency, 95 of sickness, 6 still-born babies and 56 cases of family relief.
>
> Further the police records were not accessible, thus limiting the cases of delinquency to those recorded by the social agencies, a small percentage of the actual number. But even the police do not know the amount of crime committed in this section, which is hushed up by mutual agreement of the inhabitants.
>
> To prove that this is not merely surmise, special permission to glance over the accident book of a hospital in this district revealed in a period of nine months there were 39 severe lacerations of residents of this block, treated by this hospital alone, and exclusive of those treated at home or in other places.
>
> The following are typical: "Laceration of hand, cut by razor of husband." "Laceration of chest, side and jaw; fight." "Stab wound in the back." "Wound on scapula, hit by hatchet." "Laceration of scalp, piece of ice." "Laceration of forehead, hit by brick." "Shot in right leg." "Fractured clavicle, thrown downstairs." "Human bite on finger."

In this way a tremendous part of the social cost of such dense slums is borne by the community at large which supports courts, hospitals, and social agencies to repair the damage caused in large measure by the land exploiter.

It was noted in the introductory statement that congestion is a phase of the urban cycle, following migration and segregation. The most recently arrived migrants are now in the midst of this phase in large cities. It is encouraging to note, however, that this density is lessening somewhat. The movement of population is outward from the overcrowded central sections, as is shown in the following chapter. It is difficult to estimate just the amount of area occupied by Negroes in 1910; but from all indications the trend from 1910 to 1925 was toward a slightly greater increase in area than in population, slightly lessening the density in most cities.

Several points are worthy of reëmphasis.

1. Congestion comes about largely from conditions over which the Negroes have little control. They are crowded into segregated neighborhoods, are obliged to go there and nowhere else, and are subjected to vicious exploitation. This exploitation is often very loosely supervised by the municipality, so that both the land and the houses become dangerously overcrowded.

2. Overcrowding is increased by the necessity for many families to take in lodgers either to pay high rentals or to meet substantial payments on homes under purchase.

3. Overcrowding saps the vitality and the moral vigor of those in the dense neighborhoods. The environment then, rather than hereditary traits, is a strong factor in increasing death-rates and moral disorders. Since the cost of sickness, death, immorality and crime is in part borne by municipal appropriations to hospitals, jails and courts, and in part by employers' losses through absence of employees, the entire community pays for conditions from which the exploiters of real estate profit.

Chapter V

THE NEIGHBORHOOD SCALE

Each city has its bad and its good neighborhoods, with middle-class neighborhoods predominating, and with many different stages and conditions of home life to be found between the worst and the best. Averages for the whole city tend to give an impression that all the citizens are of one "average" mold, whereas the variations from this average are interesting and significant.

NORTHERN AND SOUTHERN

Negro neighborhoods in the North and in the South are not alike, because they have developed in different ways, and because the cities in which they are located are not alike. Northern migration took Negroes from neighborhoods in which a family had a house with a yard and placed them in densely built-up metropolitan areas that for the most part had been occupied by foreigners. In most of the southern cities, within convenient transportation distance of places of Negro employment, there is vacant space in which Negro neighborhoods can develop; while in the large northern cities, which are already built up, new groups can get into a neighborhood only by crowding other people out.

The attitude of Negroes who go North is different from that of Negro migrants to southern cities. In the South they move in from near-by country districts, largely to improve their economic condition. Many of them take scanty furnishings. They rent any kind of house and get what work they can. Having been badly housed and without conveniences in the country, they do not expect much more in the city. Those who move to the North, however, usually go with the definite feeling that they will improve their standard of living as well as increase the amount they earn. They expect more in the way of houses, conveniences, and institutions. This accounts for much of their moving from section to section in northern cities.

The physical facts of life are much the same in a two-room cabin on a farm, a two-room shack in town, or a two-room tenement in a city. The difference is in contacts, in wider experiences, and in the opportunities that lessen hardships. Migration to the North has been impelled in part by the desire for these contacts, experiences and opportunities, especially for the children of the family. The opportunity to enter northern industry came as the culmination of Negro progress during sixty-five years; and many families were willing to pioneer to grasp the opportunity. They sold whatever they had in the South to go North and take any shelter for which they could afford the rent until they could earn enough to satisfy their ambitions. Some were not adaptable to changed conditions; but most of the first migrants were strong, ambitious young people, ready to take chances. In later migrations, Negro families went North, established homes, and learned, after ten years of experience, that they could live in a variety of districts, in any kind of house they could afford. There is among them as wide a range of culture, of income, of ambition, of shiftlessness and thrift, as in any racial group.

MIGRANT NEIGHBORHOODS

Even though the Negroes that go to cities in the North expect more than migrants to southern cities, their standards, when they arrive, do not measure up to those of the Negroes who were born in the North or who have lived there for some time. This creates a difference between migrant neighborhoods and well-settled neighborhoods within northern cities. The incoming migrants to southern cities are not so definitely separated, but concentrations of newcomers in depressed districts can be found.

Migrants who have friends and who take some money with them soon settle. Unskilled workers, unfamiliar with housing, work, and conditions in cities, have great difficulties. They drift into rooms of lowest rents, staying until they find work, sometimes a long process, and until they learn the city. The process of urbanization places them first in houses that have held many waves of foreign-speech peoples.

In Philadelphia, typical migrant settlements can be found in the second, third, fourth, eleventh and fourteenth wards. Here they find three types of shelter at the lowest available rentals. They are the old court-bandbox houses, tenements, and scattered lodgings.

Court-bandbox houses in the district along the lower river fronts, which have been occupied by wage-earners for seventy-five or a hundred years, consist of three rooms, one set on top of another and with a stairway through a lower room giving access to the room above. These houses are built in long rows the depth of a deep lot, or behind houses facing the street. Entrance is from a narrow side-yard, paved and with a gutter for surface drainage of wash-water and slops; though most of the houses are now underdrained. Walls and chimneys are cracked, plaster is loose, and floors are worn. Many rooms need artificial light all day. Each room houses a family, or lodgers, with entire lack of privacy.

The Philadelphia Housing Association found eleven nationalities in one block. These families, white or colored, rarely go away from the near neighborhood, except as the men go to work, because of the expense of carfare and lack of knowledge of the city.

The old tenement-houses in South Street are better only in that they allow more contacts. A typical house, three and a half stories high, with poorly lighted rooms that had windows only on narrow side-yards, was rented to Negroes in twenty-three apartments, twenty of one room, two of two, and one of three. Long, narrow, dim halls, with dark and dangerous stairways, are in the middle of the house. Seven toilets in the public halls, filthy and odorous, are used in common by twenty-three families. Six apartments have sinks, but seventeen families use in common twelve sinks located in the halls.

Many of the one-room apartments are let "furnished" with an old iron bed, a cheap mattress and two pillows, black and greasy with the dirt of tenants who have slept in their clothing without washing, and who have had neither sheets nor covers. A table and a two-holed stove are filthy, and food is eaten from the papers in which it is wrapped when purchased. Oil lamps for lighting are generally used in the daytime. Temporary tenants do not clean; and floors, walls, ceiling, and windows are thick with dirt.

Rents vary with the amount the tenants can pay and the janitor can extract. Some houses have mixed white and colored occupancy, a few are carefully policed by a janitor who throws families out if there is any rough-house, others are shared by idle girls, waiting for night.

In eleven of these tenement-houses, selected as typical by the Division of Housing of the Health Department, 175 families were living in 354 rooms, an average of two rooms per family. Forty-one families lived in one room, 75 in two, 45 in three, and 7 in four. One hundred and sixteen families shared 48 public toilets.

In New York, Chicago, Buffalo, Louisville, Memphis, and New Orleans, similar conditions were found in tenements, arks, rookeries and rows in old changing areas where multiple dwellings are crowded with migrant families.

Most tenants in these neighborhoods do not stay long, however, before they seek better quarters. Their place is filled by new arrivals. The population of these neighborhoods shifts rapidly but does not increase. Columbus Hill in New York, the Lower South side in Chicago, the South side in Philadelphia (seventh, twenty-sixth, thirtieth, and thirty-sixth wards), Central Memphis, Central Atlanta—all show slight decreases or negligible increases in population, while the better outlying neighborhoods are increasing in population. In Memphis during the past fifteen years there has been a movement of some 5,000 colored people from the congested central districts into the outlying areas. New migrants crowd the old inhabitants of these neighborhoods into newer and better sections of the town and are in turn pushed out by subsequent arrivals. It is genuinely encouraging to note the population increases in outlying neighborhoods that indicate how ambitious families are climbing out of these congested central neighborhoods.

LARGE CENTRAL COLONIES

All the cities have these large central sections which have certain traits in common. They are large, the largest Negro neighborhood usually being centrally located. The South side, in Chicago, probably the largest Negro community in the world, numbers 126,000 people; Harlem in New York, though not a typical central section, numbers 124,000; the South side in Philadelphia, 51,000; Central Memphis, 22,000; and Central Atlanta, 18,000. These are such great aggregations of population that each has a community life all its own. They contain the large churches, schools, theaters, centers of commercial recreation and business houses. The main arteries, Lenox Avenue in Harlem, State Street in Chicago, South Street in Philadelphia, Beale Street in Memphis, Second Street in Richmond, and Auburn Avenue in Atlanta are business streets of bustle and activity, and are the main thoroughfares for thousands of people. The central position of these sections also subjects them all to invasion by business and manufacturing establishments, and to the subsequent depreciation of property for residence purposes. Large areas are so directly in the line of the business and manufacturing expansion of the cities that property is intrinsically worth high prices for commercial purposes though very much depreciated for residence uses. Under these circumstances, landlords, who are holding for profits from sale for commercial purposes, look upon the rental houses on their land merely as a source of temporary income. They make as few repairs and improvements as possible. Neighborhoods of this kind therefore become dilapidated and insanitary, and are eyesores to the city. On other streets where business has actually come in, it is usual to find buildings designed so that the first floor is given over to commercial purposes and from one to seven floors above to tenements. Often these residence quarters are entirely secondary to the business uses of the building and are poorly arranged, poorly equipped, and insanitary.

Because they are central, relatively low in rentals, and not desirable for high-class residences, vice often invades these areas. On the other hand, they are favorably situated for municipal improvements, sewers are usually laid, streets and sidewalks are paved, lights are provided, and police protection is much better than in outlying sections.

In these central sections there are often neighborhoods in which the dregs of the population, of all races and colors, settle. The shiftless, vicious, ignorant, ne'er-do-wells move in and out, dodging rent days, spending irregular earnings on sensuous pleasures. Houses are old and worn, owners or agents are neglectful, city officials are indifferent, social workers have no means of making changes, and police activities are largely confined to raids or searches for criminals. The districts are notorious for indolence, vice, crime, disease and poverty. They are out of sight of the average citizen and are visited only by installment and rent collectors, insurance agents, truant officers, an occasional sanitary inspector and social workers.

In Richmond, the worst district lies in a deep valley and on the steep hillsides of Shockoe Creek and along the railroad. Very old brick and frame houses face on unimproved streets that have no sewers or water mains, so that sanitary conditions are bad.

In Lynchburg, Salem Street has had for years an unsavory reputation for drinking and vice. Factories lie along the tops of the hills, and the street which winds down a valley is rarely used except by occupants of the old houses. Furniture is sketchy, the housekeeping is casual, the families in general have low standards and there is much shiftlessness.

In Philadelphia, the old small streets among which South Street is the main highway are lined with small row-houses, overcrowded and lacking repairs, and with water and toilets in the yards. Many of the ambitious families have moved away.

In New York, Columbus Hill formerly was the desirable district, with amusements, tenements in fair condition for their day, and intense racial community spirit similar to that of to-day in Harlem. Only a few good families are left. Tenements show thirty to forty years of hard wear, have dark rooms and are in an insanitary condition. Stoops are filled day and evening with gossiping women, loafing men and dirty children. Paving is noisy granite block, sidewalks are broken, buildings are defaced, and fire escapes are hung with bright colored garments, badly washed. On the avenue along the river are filthy stores, pool-rooms filled with boys and men from morning to late night, with drunks and frowsy street-women, white and colored. Families are shiftless and content with poor housing so long as they need do little work.

In Buffalo, the large Negro colony overlaps the vice district, with families living in alley and rear houses, sometimes three deep on a lot. On Exchange Place near the railroad stations are lodging and furnished-room houses, sprinkled with cabarets and pool-rooms, filled with casual laborers, floaters, shiftless families and vicious men and women. No worse housing conditions can be found than exist in every large city in these lodging-houses, rooming-houses, light housekeeping apartments, and similar places where homeless men and women live. They are full or empty as work is plentiful or slack. Furniture is old and battered, walls, floors and ceilings are uncleaned, plumbing is abused and out of order, and landlords are indifferent after they receive an advance payment of rent. Within even a week after a thorough cleaning, conditions are as bad as ever.

In Chicago, there are many well-known districts of outworn houses occupied at high rents, and whole blocks are given over to gambling houses, and black and tan cabarets. Their keepers, occupants and supporters are occasionally raided, but are generally politically protected by the weight of the Negro minority vote in city elections.

In speaking of Federal and South Dearborn Streets, a recent survey says:

A dozen years ago, a study of these streets showed that the neighborhood was so run down that the passerby was impressed with the dilapidation of the buildings, only 26 per cent. of which could be considered in good repair. The median rental was $16.00. In the last months of 1924, with twelve years more of neglect and decay, the median rental for some of the same old houses was $30.00 to $35.00.[1]

[1] *Living Conditions of Small Wage Earners in Chicago*, p. 35.

In Gary, "bungaloos" were built twenty years ago to house unskilled workers in the steel mills, and are still rented. A bungaloo is a barrack, two rooms deep, and six to ten rooms long, of the lightest construction that can be expected to stand up, and set on posts. A narrow walk runs between each pair of bungaloos, and each door and window faces a door or window across the passage, making any privacy impossible. A hydrant and a water closet at the end of each two rows represents the sanitary equipment, and the ground in the rear is kept sour and ill-smelling by slops thrown from back doors and garbage.

Rents are not low, but the old bungaloos furnish shelter for the shiftless, ignorant, and vicious, and are kept filled; and an occasional new one, called a tenement, is erected.

In Indianapolis, "Wild Cat Chute" lies in a section of unpaved, deeply rutted streets that often have no sidewalks, and are deep in mud in wet weather. Some of the streets have sewers, but there are still many privy-vaults in the yards. Row-houses, tenements, and old shacks offer poor housing. "The Bottoms" is a near neighbor, both districts being well known to the police and to the charitable.

Louisville has a large down-town area, with fair conditions in houses facing the streets, and extremely insanitary and unhealthful conditions in alley houses. Satisfied or ignorant families live in houses not fit for work animals; children are familiar with vice before they start to school; and unattached men and women who work in tobacco factories lodge with families in overcrowded rooms.

Even the smaller towns do not escape these bad, poorly housed colonies. Salem Street in Lynchburg is matched by Davis Bottom in Lexington, and Willow Street in Knoxville. Houses are in a hollow, with side-hill drainage to a creek that occasionally overflows, and that keeps ground, walls and floors damp at all times. Drainage is poor; the creek is often an open sewer and becomes very offensive when the water is low. Streets are deeply rutted and boards are laid down over puddles. These back-waters beside the active current of city life are places where much that is vicious and criminal occurs or is fostered. No child who lives in such an

environment has any decent chance, and the adults are beyond redemption.

To keep these civic ulcers from poisoning the whole city,
much more stringent municipal control is needed than in
overcrowded, unhealthful areas where migrants get their first
start.

MIDDLE-CLASS NEIGHBORHOODS

According to census figures for 1920, 35,000 of the 61,000
colored population of Memphis live in the large southeastern
area of the city. They were scattered in large colonies, in
smaller settlements, and in units as small as a block over an
area four miles long and two to three miles wide. A large
part of the district was originally built up for wage-earners,
and it is cut by railroads and spotted by factories. All kinds
of homes from cottages to shacks were mixed together. Occasional blocks of cottages of four and five rooms were still
occupied by owners who bought the houses years ago and
are unwilling to move.

The pride of the colony is in the good houses, formerly
built for well-to-do white families along Mississippi Boule-
vard, McLemore Avenue, and neighboring streets. These
houses have been purchased in the past two to eight years by
teachers, postal employees, skilled workmen, and salaried
men who must live near their work. Two physicians have
built homes, costing $12,000 and $15,000. Old houses sold
for from $4,500 to $6,000. A woman undertaker bought a
handsome old residence in large grounds and completely re-
modeled it. Thus a few high-class residence streets may be
found in these middle sections. Many of the families own
one, and some two, automobiles, the children go away to
college, and a high standard of social and community life is
maintained.

The speculative builder and contractor is much in evidence
in these middle-class areas. Long rows of houses exactly
alike, occasional tenements and arks, a sprinkling of shacks,
all built for rental returns and of cheap construction, can be
counted by thousands, and house the largest number of fam-

ilies. Water supply and toilets are in the yard and are often shared by two or more families. There is a general air of unthrift, and a lack of any attempt to make the houses attractive, rather than any positive bad construction or sanitary conditions.

Unless curbed by strict city ordinances and enforcement, these rental neighborhoods fill up with houses that are not weatherproof, and that have too few rooms and inadequate sanitary conveniences.

In Dayton, Negro families are gradually taking over a large area on the near West side containing substantial houses originally built for white wage-earners. Fifth Street is developing with colored business places, offices, and amusements, together with rooming-houses. The cross streets are developed with good one-story and two-story frame houses built twenty to thirty years ago. Streets are paved and have sewers and water. Houses of various sizes and prices meet the needs of various kinds of families. A street of handsome old residences is gradually changing character, and some of the houses have been offered for sale to Negroes. A few houses on side streets have already been sold to them.

Many of the blocks in this district are deep and irregular, with alleys cutting through or making dead-ends. There are already indications of exploitation of the land in the interior of these large blocks. An owner of a double house facing a street has constructed two tenement-houses on the rear of the lot, gaining rentals from ten families. Each family has 780 square feet, the land overcrowding is comparable to that of any large city, and all standards of decent housing are ignored.

Housing conditions south of Fifth Street are still less satisfactory. Houses are of less desirable types, and are among factories and railroads. Some areas are built up with cheap, two-story, four-room houses, greatly in need of paint and repairs. The spaces between houses are narrow, and yards are shallow.

Two prominent colored churches close to some of the worst alley housing have no apparent interest in improving conditions. Sheds and shacks made over into houses, addi-

tions built to existing houses so that virtually all the lot is
covered, dim or dark rooms, and one-room dwellings in tenements, create a slum condition.

HOME-OWNING NEIGHBORHOODS

High rentals, room overcrowding, and scarcity of dwellings have tended to foster one desirable improvement in
housing conditions. In every city, small outlying settlements
are growing up where land is cheaper, and where Negroes
can afford small houses and use street cars or automobiles
to reach their working places. Houses are small, and sold
on terms within the means of unskilled wage-earners, but
community life is active and ambitious.

Whenever a good school building is erected near or in
these settlements, buying increases rapidly, and families
move out to make permanent homes. Too often, however,
the board of education delays the erection of good schools
until the settlement is rather large.

The new colony of Lonsdale, just on the edge of Knoxville, has grown so rapidly without direct city influence that
an analysis is interesting. The men make day wages of
$2.50 or $3.00. About half the women go out to work as
domestic servants, but tend to stay at home as soon as the
husband's income permits. It takes twenty-five minutes to
go down-town by street car, and there the young people go
for recreation; but the fathers and mothers seldom leave the
neighborhood except to work, and spend what they make on
their homes, their church, and their friendly life. Census
figures showed 43 rented houses in 1920, and 41 owned by
the occupants. In 1925, a house-to-house card study made
by a teacher showed 223 families, an increase of 139 in five
years. There were 139 houses owned by the occupants, 78
rented and 6 regarding which the status was not given.
Most of the houses are small, of frame construction, and set
in good-sized yards.

Of these, 31 per cent. have three rooms, 46 per cent. have
have four or five rooms, and the remainder are very small or

very large. There were 452 adults, including 22 lodgers, and 429 children. Only 54 family groups had no children.

											Total Families
Children per family.. None	1	2	3	4	5	6	7	8	9	10	
Number of families .. 54	61	48	23	14	8	6	5	1	2	1	223

In the larger family groups there is considerable over-crowding of rooms. In 27 families there was excessive over-crowding, considering the total number of persons; but because most of the children were small, its effects were not so bad. Eight persons in two rooms was the worst case found; but in this case the family owned its home and planned to add rooms.

Rents differ widely for the same kinds of houses, depending on various conditions.

No. of Rooms	$2	$5	$6	$8	$9	$10	$11	$12	$13	$15	$16	$35
1	1	..	..	1	..	..	..	..	..	..	..	..
2	..	6	2	3	..	..	..	1	..	..	..	..
3	..	2	2	8	2	11	..	7	..	..	..	..
4	..	..	..	3	2	6	1	6	4	2	2	..
5	..	..	..	..	..	1	..	1	..	..	..	..
6	..	..	..	..	..	..	..	1	..	..	..	1
8	..	..	..	..	..	..	..	1	..	..	..	..

The vitality of a community in which 60 per cent. of the families are buying homes cannot be questioned. Any city could afford to help a community of this kind by putting in public improvements as rapidly as possible.

At Morgan Park, near Chicago, is another rapidly grow-ing suburban colony. It was an old, small settlement until about 1915, with houses built on cheap, low land, badly in need of drainage. Some colored city employees, familiar with methods of getting improvements, moved in and secured drainage, a little paving, and some sewers. Further exten-sion of sewerage and paving and improvement of schools is contemplated.

In housing, this colony presents a very ragged appearance. It has grown rapidly since 1920. Many of the older houses, and some of the new ones, are of the typical small, suburban type, well kept and attractive. Several hundred have been built by sections, starting with one, two, or three rooms. Often the owners themselves build them or hire carpenters by the day to do the work. Houses are enlarged by adding rooms, as the family can afford this. Porches and improvements are put in slowly. The effect is that of a boom-town, with temporary shelters run up in a hurry. This type of sectional shack building is found in many new home-owning sections. It is owing, in part, to the difficulty of financing.

However, 25 per cent. of the houses are fully paid for and 50 per cent. are more than half paid for. Many of the good homes started with one or two rooms, and were improved as the money was earned, the owners keeping out of debt. A believer in the future of the settlement said, "Our houses seem poor to eyes accustomed to rows of bungalows and cottages, all exactly alike. Our houses are not so neatly finished, but they are comfortable, full of hope, and not loaded with debts. There are home-loving families in all of them."

A large part of the change in Negro neighborhoods in both the North and the South comes through home-buying. Always since freedom, Negroes have had the desire to own homes. Even in slavery an occasional Negro earned the money to buy himself, his wife and his children, and to own his home. The buying of homes has been as large a factor in the establishing of neighborhoods in the North as in the South. A fuller discussion of home-buying may be found in Chapter VIII.

MUNICIPAL IMPROVEMENTS

In the large central Negro districts which Negroes have inherited from former residents, sewers are sometimes inadequate for the increased density, water mains put in for single family houses are made to supply large tenements, and paving of old types is worn into rough surfaces. The city is usually busy developing new territories and pays no attention to these old districts, in which it would be difficult to get the property owners to stand the expense of improvements.

In these old districts, also, there is apparent neglect from city departments charged with plumbing installation and repairs, with sanitation and garbage and rubbish removal. Local improvement associations must be very active to have laws and ordinances enforced.

Families who break away from the large old central colonies, and move into newer districts, sometimes gain the advantage of more recent improvements on the main streets. These families are on about the same economic level, are intelligent, and know how to obtain service from the city. It was found, however, that the people in nearly all these colonies were reluctant about standing the cost of improvements, particularly of paving for new streets, partly because owners were already making heavy payments on houses purchased, and in part because landlords were unwilling to stand for improvements in rental property.

The disadvantage of outlying colonies is that they must usually wait many years for sewers, water mains, street lights, sidewalks, and especially for paving. For inexpensive housing developments, land is often chosen that is undesirable because of topographical features or neighboring uses.

In some cities the areas occupied by Negroes are those in which engineering obstacles make improvements difficult and land cheap. Until colored families learn that such properties are undesirable investments and bad from a health standpoint, these unimproved spots will continue to exist.

In several cities it was noted that health departments had to be patient with small property holders in the matter of connecting their homes with sewers and water mains, because the expense would be a serious drain on their limited income. Negroes, like the wage-earning groups of white people, are handicapped by lack of facilities for securing loans. In Lexington this situation has been met by the adoption of a plan whereby sanitary improvements can be paid for in installments, like paving.

The most rapid outlying development has taken place in Memphis; and while the suburban colonies there are generally supplied with sewer and water, the pavements, sidewalks and lights are very poor. In Louisville, Richmond,

Knoxville, Lexington and Charleston, the outlying Negro sections are quite poorly supplied with municipal improvements.

The side streets of southern Negro neighborhoods are especially unattractive. The mud and ruts are often so deep that ambulances and fire engines cannot penetrate them. Street lights are far apart, leaving dangerous dark blocks.

In a study of Negro neighborhood conditions of Dallas, which furnish a fairly good sample of conditions in the average southern city, an endeavor was made to ascertain the number of families whose travel to and from their homes in going to church, to school, or to street-car lines, was impeded by poor condition of streets. The results of the canvass follow:

Number of families unimpeded.............. 162 or 13 per cent.
Number of families somewhat impeded........ 239 or 19 per cent.
Number of families almost entirely impeded
  (especially in wet weather)................ 839 or 68 per cent.

"The serious hindrance and at times complete inhibition from attendance at school, church, etc., not to speak of its becoming quite a factor in preventing the fulfillment of work engagements," are illustrated by these figures.

Cities such as Louisville are fairly well paved except in outlying districts; and cities such as Atlanta, Memphis and Richmond have made commendable progress in paving the main arteries through Negro sections, but the side streets are still in deplorable condition. Cities of the type of New Orleans and Charleston, where municipal improvements are very expensive by reason of the necessity for filling and draining, have neglected their Negro sections. In the smaller cities, neglect is the rule rather than the exception; yet improvements could be made even in these places, as is evidenced by the progressive city of Winston-Salem, which is 100 per cent. paved, and by Lynchburg, which is 100 per cent. sewered in spite of engineering difficulties.

It is because of the exploitation by land owners and of disregard by the cities that ambitious families wish to leave these neglected spots. Their moving from the back alleys and congested blocks into better sections of town is a healthy sign of progress. Yet if the districts to which they go abut on white districts, the moving families are accused of trying to inconvenience their white neighbors by moving among them, and are humiliated and often subjected to violence.

The lesson for the cities is plain. Each city needs neighborhoods supplied with municipal improvements into which the better-class Negroes can move without opposition. These neighborhoods should be protected from exploitation by zoning and tenement laws, and should be made attractive by the installation of paving, lighting, sewerage, schools, and playgrounds. Only when neighborhoods of the kind are developed will the movement of Negro population within the city be stabilized.

PART II: HOUSING

By Madge Headley

Chapter VI

EQUIPMENT AND CONDITION OF HOUSES

In the study of Negro housing conditions, 12,123 cards, each giving detailed information about a particular house, were examined. The houses described were in eighteen cities; and in every case were well scattered, so that although they may perhaps have been slightly better than the average, they nevertheless were fairly representative of Negro housing conditions in each city.[1]

CLASSIFICATION

A rough method of summarizing housing conditions is to classify dwellings according to the number of defects found. This was done, and the result is shown in Table XIV. In this classification, *A* does not mean a fine house, but merely a good small dwelling, large enough for the family occupying it and not lacking in any of the items carried on the house-card. Class *B* consists of dwellings inadequate in one major item or in two minor ones; Class *C* of dwellings lacking in two or more major respects or in three minor items; and Class *D* houses were lacking in at least five respects, in many cases even approaching the uninhabitable state.

TABLE XIV—NEGRO DWELLINGS BY CLASSES, FIFTEEN CITIES

	A	*B*	*C*	*D*	Total Classified
Number					
Owners	434	1,150	370	44	1,998
Renters	171	1,247	2,019	801	4,238
Total	605	2,397	2,389	845	6,236
Per Cent.					
Owners	21.7	57.6	18.5	2.2	100
Renters	4.0	29.4	47.7	18.9	100
Total	9.7	38.4	38.3	13.6	100

[1] See appendix for method of taking these cards. They were tabulated by machinery by the Underwriters Statistical Bureau.

It will be noted that the great majority of dwellings are in B and C class, with only 9.7 per cent. in A class and 13.6 per cent. in D class. Dwellings owned by occupants show up much better in this respect, of course, than do rented dwellings. This is true in all the tables in this chapter.

ROOMS

The dwellings are small, averaging slightly more than four rooms each. About 30 per cent. are in the one-, two-, and three-room class.

TABLE XV—ROOMS IN NEGRO DWELLINGS, FIFTEEN CITIES

	1-3 Rooms	4-6 Rooms	Over 6 Rooms	Total Reporting
Number Occupying				
Owners	141	745	784	1,670
Renters	1,221	1,752	772	3,745
Total *	2,469	4,025	1,809	8,303
Per Cent. Occupying				
Owners	8.4	44.6	47.0	100
Renters	32.6	46.8	20.6	100
Total	29.7	48.5	21.8	100

* Totals include Knoxville not separated as to owners and renters.

In these smaller houses living is very cramped. Eighty-eight per cent. of the families occupying them reported having bedrooms separate from cooking and living quarters. Separate living-rooms were reported by 63 per cent., and separate kitchens by 85 per cent. of the families.

The first step in climbing the housing-ladder is taken when the family leaves the dwelling composed entirely of bedrooms and secures a separate kitchen. Most Negro families have taken this step. A smaller number have also taken the second step and secured a separate bedroom, while a still smaller number have a separate living-room.

Partial data were gathered which indicated that a number of city tenements were so planned that the inside rooms were dark, and some of them were without an opening to the outer air.

TABLE XVI—USE OF ROOMS, FIFTEEN CITIES

	Total Reporting	Having Separate Room Number	Per Cent.
Separate Bedroom			
Owners	1,028	913	88.8
Renters	1,725	1,504	87.2
Total	2,753	2,417	87.8
Separate Living-room			
Owners	1,122	931	83.0
Renters	1,849	940	50.8
Total	2,971	1,871	63.0
Separate Kitchen			
Owners	1,132	1,064	94.0
Renters	1,905	1,514	79.5
Total	3,037	2,578	84.9

EQUIPMENT

The equipment of most rental homes is the minimum required to induce the tenant to enter. Migrants from country districts do not expect much equipment, as they have been accustomed to have living-quarters in poorly equipped farm tenement-houses.

The majority of dwellings, especially in southern cities, are unheated except by grates or small stoves. In large northern cities, electric lights and gas are common; but in many houses in the southern cities lamps are used.

TABLE XVII—EQUIPMENT OF NEGRO DWELLINGS, FOURTEEN CITIES

	Total Reporting	Having Specified Equipment Number	Per Cent.
Bath Tub			
Owners	1,565	1,008	64.4
Renters	2,357	1,082	45.9
Total	3,922	2,090	53.3
City Water			
Owners	1,658	1,548	93.4
Renters	3,680	3,565	96.9
Total	5,338	5,113	95.8

Table XVII indicates that about 53 per cent. of the houses have bathtubs and that 96 per cent. are supplied with city water. Often, however, the hydrant supplying the water is inconveniently placed. The investigators who filled out these cards frequently reported such conditions as "one hydrant in yard for four houses," or "water is obtained from hydrant four doors away." In flat buildings, it is usual to place the hydrant in the hall for common use.

TABLE XVIII—TOILET FACILITIES IN NEGRO DWELL-
INGS, FOURTEEN CITIES

	Total Reporting	Water Closet Inside	Water Closet Outside	Privy
Number				
Owners	1,673	1,012	485	176
Renters	3,684	1,236	1,968	480
Total	5,357	2,248	2,453	656
Per Cent.				
Owners	100	60.5	29.0	10.5
Renters	100	33.6	53.4	13.0
Total	100	42.0	45.8	12.2

Table XVIII indicates that outside toilets and privies are more common than inside facilities. Here again the sharing of facilities among several houses in the same block, or several dwellings in the same tenement, is common practice. Sanitary officers are beginning to bring pressure to bear on landlords to compel them to make sewer connection with each dwelling; but in southern Negro neighborhoods one outside toilet for two or four adjoining houses is often considered satisfactory. Because the making of sewer connections is expensive, it would doubtless be facilitated if other cities were to adopt the plan in force in Lexington, whereby the city pays, and the owner refunds in installments, as is often done with paving costs.

Lots

The discussion of congestion in an earlier chapter gives an idea of the extent to which the land in Negro sections is crowded, and Diagrams II-IV indicate some of the worst examples of the crowding of lots with houses.

In addition, many sections of Negro neighborhoods, especially in southern cities, are low and badly drained. Over

22 per cent. of the lots reported in this canvass were only fairly well drained, and 12 per cent. were badly drained. This, taken in conjunction with the fact that about 60 per cent. of the houses were unscreened or incompletely screened, produces a marked malaria hazard.

Furthermore, houses that are provided with a front yard often do not have walks connecting with the street. Table XIX shows the condition of walks, the houses reporting being mostly in smaller cities where they are commonly set back from the street.

TABLE XIX—WALKS IN YARDS OF NEGRO HOUSES, FOURTEEN CITIES

	Total Reporting	Good	Poor	None
Number				
Owners	1,045	715	134	196
Renting	1,380	577	283	520
Total	2,425	1,292	417	716
Per Cent.				
Owners	100	68.4	12.8	18.8
Renting	100	41.8	20.5	37.7
Total	100	53.3	17.2	29.5

REPAIR

An effort was made to evaluate the general repair of Negro houses; but, of course, only the most glaring defects were reported, as volunteer canvassers were used. Table XX gives the result of this canvass.

Members of the staff visited a large number of these houses and found that the amount of poor repair is even greater than that tabulated in Table XX from the house-cards. There are three factors in this situation. First is the age of Negro houses. In the North Negroes have moved into old neighborhoods where houses have served several generations of tenement dwellers. In the South the flimsily constructed frame dwellings age rapidly.

The second factor is the unwillingness of landlords to make repairs in houses of this class; and the third factor is

TABLE XX—REPAIR OF NEGRO DWELLINGS, FOURTEEN CITIES

Item	Total Reporting	Number			Per Cent.		
		Good	Fair	Bad	Good	Fair	Bad
Inside Repair							
Owners	1,126	841	235	50	74.7	20.9	4.4
Renters	2,090	644	903	543	30.8	43.2	26.0
Total	3,216	1,485	1,138	593	46.2	35.4	18.4
Outside Walls							
Owners	1,117	813	246	58	72.8	22.0	5.2
Renters	1,868	685	718	465	36.7	38.4	24.9
Total	2,985	1,498	964	523	50.2	32.3	17.5
Steps							
Owners	1,099	877	176	46	79.8	16.0	4.2
Renters	1,586	810	517	259	51.1	32.6	16.3
Total	2,685	1,687	693	305	62.8	25.8	11.4
Roof *							
Owners	1,124	999	...	125	88.9	...	11.1
Renters	2,199	1,556	...	643	70.8	...	29.2
Total	3,323	2,555	...	768	76.9	...	23.1

* Roofs reported as sound or leaking.

the carelessness of tenants themselves. There is much complaint from landlords of abuse of property and equipment by tenants, especially if there are children in the family. Migrants are lax in this respect. The experience of the model-house experiments indicates, however, that with a reasonable amount of supervision Negro tenants are not more destructive than others at the same economic level.

It was pointed out in connection with land-crowding that renters have little chance to improve their environmental conditions except as better houses are built for them at reasonable rentals. The pattern of the house, as well as of the neighborhood, is laid out for the homeseeker by the builders of rental property and the family must fit itself into the best available quarters.

Chapter VII

RENT

The rent of Negro dwellings is a plain indication of the exploitation of Negro neighborhoods. These rents are excessive whether they are measured by the kind of house and equipment, by the relation of rents paid by Negroes and those paid by white people for similar quarters, by the steady increase in rents, by the relation of rent to the value of the property, or by the proportion which rent forms of the family budget.

The amount of money paid per dwelling (see Table XXI) seems small; but when it is considered in relation to the income of the families and the meager quarters obtained for the money, it is evident that rent assumes a central place in the budget of the lower-class and the middle-class colored people.

The preceding chapter showed in detail the poverty of colored rental houses in the items of equipment necessary to convert a shelter into a real home; and this, in the last analysis, is the true measure of rent.

The low wages of unskilled colored workers, and the pressure of segregation, must be kept in mind as constant factors that can be changed only very slowly by Negroes. Even without the migration to cities, the housing shortage was serious from 1918 to 1922. It was still acute in 1926 for those who earned low wages, because relatively few dwellings have been built for them, and they must continue to live in well-worn houses, doubling up to use all available space.

Rent Range

In southern cities, an established form of investment is based upon the high return from small, cheap dwellings, and the demand for them from those who earn low wages. Large districts are developed, generally in locations undesirable as homes for white persons, but near enough for colored tenants to walk to their work. With rising wages and diversified employment, newer sections with better houses are being developed to meet the needs of a school-trained generation.

In southern cities rents do not vary greatly because of the large numbers of small dwellings of a uniform type. The rentals are based on the wages of domestic servants and day laborers and tend to be about the same in amount no matter what kind of a house is furnished.

In northern cities houses vary widely in types and the rents have been subject to inflation because of the great demand there has been from both white and colored families moving into cities. Prospective tenants have bid against one another, thus increasing rentals, and have been willing to subdivide apartments and share sanitary conveniences in order to get shelter.

Table XXI shows the average weekly rent for rooms and dwellings in the cities studied.

TABLE XXI—RENTS OF ROOMS AND DWELLINGS FOR SELECTED CITIES *

City	Dwellings Reported	Rent per Room per Week	Rent per Dwelling per Week
Buffalo, N. Y.	49	$1.36	$9.02
Philadelphia, Pa.	1,932	1.57	7.95
Gary, Ind.	50	1.78	7.20
New York, N. Y.			
Columbus Hill............	880	1.21	4.50
Harlem	747	1.66	7.19
Chicago, Ill.			
Lower North Side.........	500	1.25	†
Dayton, O.	84	1.19	6.00
Indianapolis, Ind.	96	1.13	5.68
Louisville, Ky.	203	1.00	4.54
New Orleans, La.	103	1.18	4.52
Richmond, Va.	147	.88	4.46
Memphis, Tenn.	110	1.16	3.73
Lexington, Ky.	110	1.06	3.55
Knoxville, Tenn.	1,637	.80	3.37
Charleston, S. C.	295	.91	3.11
Charlottesville, Va.	40	.72	3.06
Lynchburg, Va.	33	.60	2.27

* Data from house-cards, see appendix for method.
† Not tabulated.

The average for the northern cities is $7.19 per dwelling per week, and for southern cities $3.74 per dwelling per week. Rents run from a minimum of sixty cents per room per week in Lynchburg to a maximum of $1.78 per room per week in Gary. The figures from the housing-cards are borne out by similar studies recently made in Buffalo, Chicago and Gary.

The tendency toward wide fluctuations in the North and toward uniformity in the South is evident from the distribution of rents paid by families in five northern and eight southern cities, shown in Table XXII.

TABLE XXII—DISTRIBUTION OF FAMILIES ACCORDING TO WEEKLY RENT PER DWELLING

Rent Paid (nearest dollar)	Northern City Families	Per Cent. of Total	Southern City Families	Per Cent. of Total
$1.00	4		51	
2.00	40	2	234	27
3.00	150		269	
4.00	217		207	
5.00	297	30	123	58
6.00	252		45	
7.00	158		28	
8.00	200	28	31	10
9.00	192		14	
10.00 and over	706	40	39	5
Total	2,216	100	1,041	100

It will be observed from this table that 58 per cent. of southern Negro families were in the 3-dollar, 4-dollar and 5-dollar rent-groups; and that only 42 per cent. of the families paid rents above or below the average; while in the North this proportion was reversed, and 28 per cent. of the families paid from six to eight dollars, while 72 per cent. paid amounts above or below this average.

RENT AND FAMILY BUDGET

When these rental figures are considered in relation to the low wages earned by Negroes it is evident that rent consumes too large a proportion of the family budget. The investigations of the U. S. Department of Labor indicate that, for wage-earners of this class, rent should not exceed 20 per cent. of the total family expenditure. Yet even with the mass of Negroes paying amounts close to the three-dollar average in the South, it will be seen that the family income would have to be $15.00 to $20.00 a week every week in the year for rent to be in proportion. This amount, however, is considerably above the average wage of the mass of domestics and common laborers. Rent runs for 365 days in the year, and it is the exceptional day laborer who earns his daily stipend for more than 250 days.

Even in New York, where the range of wages is considerably higher and rents in Negro sections not quite so high as in Buffalo, Gary and Philadelphia, it was discovered that rent took 23.4 per cent. of the total family income of 747 Harlem families studied. It was pointed out in Chapter IV that such high rents lead many families to eke out their budgets by crowding in lodgers.

In a study made by the sanitary inspectors of the Board of Health of Buffalo in 1925, the range of rents was obtained for 1,463 colored families out of the total of 1,721 for the entire city; and it was found that 12.5 per cent. were living in dwellings for which they paid up to $20 per month, or 20 per cent. of a monthly income of $100; 65.9 per cent. of 1,463 families paid between $20 and $40, or 20 per cent. of a family income of $100 to $200 a month; and 21.6 per cent. paid from $40 to $95 per month, indicating a considerable number of families with incomes from skilled labor, business or professions, or with two or more wage-earners.[1]

Rent and Equipment

The preceding chapter indicated the meager equipment of Negro rental dwellings. Table XXIII, showing rents by

[1] Number of families in Buffalo paying specified monthly rents

Under $10	$10 -14	$15 -19	$20 -24	$25 -29	$30 -34	$35 -39	$40 -49	$50 -59	$60 -69	$70 -95
6	44	133	222	243	241	258	197	82	27	10

TABLE XXIII—RENTS PER WEEK FOR DWELLINGS OF A, B, C, AND D CLASSES*

	A CLASS DWELLINGS			B CLASS DWELLINGS			C CLASS DWELLINGS			D CLASS DWELLINGS		
	Number	Rent per Dwelling	Rent per Room	Number	Rent per Dwelling	Rent per Room	Number	Rent per Dwelling	Rent per Room	Number	Rent per Dwelling	Rent per Room
Richmond	24	$7.12	$1.21	110	$5.45	$1.12	94	$4.47	$1.04	5	$3.00	$.89
Memphis	9	7.77	1.44	26	4.89	1.14	52	4.31	1.12	33	2.85	.99
Louisville	2	10.00	1.51	31	5.48	1.54	106	4.40	1.23	39	3.77	1.13
New Orleans.....	14	5.79	1.16	29	5.24	1.15	38	3.98	1.14	21	3.43	1.29
Philadelphia	†	†	†	354	11.78	1.90	797	8.15	1.56	316	5.35	1.77
Dayton	5	7.20	1.71	44	7.00	1.24	36	5.84	1.29	2	4.50	1.28
Indianapolis	6	7.50	1.32	39	6.47	1.13	41	5.61	1.17	12	4.00	1.00

* From house-cards.
† None reported.

class of house, indicates that there is not a great spread between the price charged for a wholly satisfactory house of the *A* class and one of the almost uninhabitable houses of the *D* class.

The great mass of Negroes, however, were found in neither the best kind nor the worst, but in houses rated as *B* or *C* class which had from one to four or five notable defects, and the rentals for which are very uniform within a city.

The Dallas study, covering 1,130 rental dwellings, disclosed the same trend for houses classified as (1) average, (2) wholly without conveniences, (3) not fit for habitation. While the general average weekly rental was $1.21 a room, the rental in houses entirely without conveniences was $1.08, and in houses not fit for habitation, $1.07. Thus almost as high a rental is charged for these very poor houses as for those of the average kind.

NEGRO AND WHITE RENTS

There is a preponderance of evidence indicating that Negroes pay more rent for houses than is paid by white tenants for houses of the same kind. The report of the Department of Public Welfare of Chicago, involving 1,224 colored families, states:

> As a group, Negroes are paying much more for shelter than the other classes of the community.
> The median rental in unheated flats was $20 to $25 for native whites; $15 to $20 for foreign born; and $25 to $30 for Negroes. A similar difference was found in the heated apartments, where the median rental for white families was $55 to $60, but for Negro families from $65 to $70.
> It is probable that the difficulty of finding a place in which to live at a rent which they could afford has been instrumental in increasing home-buying . . . especially among Negroes.

The report of the Urban League on the Lower North District of Chicago, including 527 colored families, states:

> The high rents in other sections of the city, especially on the South Side whence about 63 per cent. had come, were compelling them to seek cheaper quarters. As rents increased with the

demand for homes, landlords used any kind of broken-down dwellings in poor physical condition and with low environment.

A scale of $4 to $5 monthly per room is paid by the tenants. Dwellings which were formerly rented for $8 to $20 to white families were now bringing from $12 to $45 per month. There were 197 families paying an average of $7.04 per month per room, 243 paying an average of $4.48, while eighty-seven families were paying an average of $2.68.

In January, 1925, a survey of 341 white families and 594 colored families was made in Gary, a town twenty years old. In rentals, colored families were shown to be at a decided disadvantage, and especially so considering the equipment and condition of the houses in which they live.

	White	*Colored*
Average rent per dwelling..............	$16.00	$22.51
Average rent per room	4.00	5.64
Average rent per family................	15.76	16.53
Renters paying less than $20.00..........	63	154

The equipment of the houses shows the higher sanitary standards and conveniences of a new town.

	PER CENT. WITH EQUIPMENT	
	White	*Colored*
Bathrooms	34	18
Inside toilets	64	64
Outside toilets	4	10

The report of the Board of Health for Buffalo, including 1,463 colored families, states:

> The rents in most cases are too high for the accommodations offered.
> A number of colored families doubled up, or boarded from one to five relatives to meet expenses.

The following comparative rents where white and colored families lived in the same tenement-house were noted:

White	$ 7	$50	$26	$50	$20
Colored	25	45	55	70	28

It is therefore apparent that Negroes forced to compete for homes must pay a higher rental than white tenants of the same class of residences.

Rent Increase

It is also apparent that during the period of rapid rent increase brought on by the housing shortage the Negroes suffered greater increases than white people of similar neighborhoods.

The report of the Philadelphia Housing Association for 1923 [2] states:

> Last year the Negro population was subjected to a more difficult rental situation than the whites. Over 61 per cent. of the Negro tenants were forced to pay higher rents, as compared with 35 per cent. of the white tenantry. For the city, the average increase was 14 per cent., while the average for the white element was 11.5 per cent. and for the Negroes 18 per cent. . . . The greatest contrast was shown in the northeast and northwest where the rate of increase for the Negroes was 26.7 per cent. and 21.5 per cent. respectively, and for the whites, 9.5 per cent. and 8.6 per cent. respectively.

The same Philadelphia report also states: [3]

> Contrary to the records of preceding years, the Negro tenants experienced a higher percentage of rent increase. The rate for whites was 61.5 per cent., and for Negroes 71.86 per cent. The Negro tenants south of Market Street between the rivers were affected in greatest numbers.

According to these reports excessive rental raises occurred in at least two successive years.

In the two large Negro centers in New York City, known as Harlem and Columbus Hill, the demand for dwellings has been so great that landlords have been able to double their rents, a large part of the increase occurring between 1920 and 1924. The New York rent laws are invoked to some extent by Negroes, but as leases are generally not made, it is easy for the landlord to give notice to a tenant who complains, and rent to another one at a higher rate.

In many tenements apartments of five and six rooms have been divided into two or more units, each of which is rented for about as much as was formerly charged for the original apartment.

2 *Housing in Philadelphia*, Philadelphia Housing Association, 1924, pp. 22-25.
3 *Ibid.*

In Table XXIV rents of typical apartments are given, from data collected by inspectors of the Tenement House Department. Average blocks were selected for the making of card schedules, and every tenement-house in the block was covered, a procedure that removed any question of selected buildings.

TABLE XXIV—RENTAL FIGURES FOR NEW YORK CITY *

Type of Building	Monthly Rental Range in Dollars		
	1910	1920	1924
HARLEM †			
5 story buildings (old law)			
5 apartments....................	$30–33	$80–100	$100–125
11 apartments (divided into 21)..	23–26	15–28	15–40
10 apartments...................	17–20	18–25	24–27
10 apartments (divided into 20)..	18–20	15–24	21–38
11 apartments...................	23–26	25–40	40–55
11 apartments...................	21–23	20–27	20–40
9 apartments...................	16–18	12–19	12–36
10 apartments...................	17–20	10–35	10–35
11 apartments...................	20–22	10–40	15–60
6 story buildings (new law)			
28 apartments...................	19–23	16–32	23–45
33 apartments...................	14–21	15–50	19–70
COLUMBUS HILL ‡			
5 story buildings (old law)			
9 apartments	$19–20	$16–30	$ 6–50
20 apartments...................	6–14	10–12	12–26
20 apartments...................	9–12	9–13	11–17
20 apartments...................	10–12	8–18	13–24
18 apartments...................	7–9	8–9	15–30
20 apartments...................	10–14	9–15	13–23
18 apartments...................	10–14	8–20	13–22
22 apartments...................	9–12	9–14	12–26
8 apartments and 2 stores........	18–21	18–24	22–26
8 apartments and 2 stores........	18–21	19–35	24–35
16 apartments and 2 stores.......	10–13	9–16	13–30

* Data from records of Tenement House Department, New York City.
† Data for eleven typical tenement-houses in the block Lenox to Fifth Avenues and 133rd to 134th Streets.
‡ Data for eleven typical tenement-houses in the block Amsterdam to West End Avenues, 61st to 62nd Streets.

The average rent increase in Harlem from 1920 to 1924 was 32.2 per cent. In Columbus Hill it was 35.2 per cent.

The increases on individual apartments varied from 1.6 to 260 per cent.

In restricted Negro districts the demand for rental property has been so intense that tenants have bid for quarters until an exorbitant rental has been placed upon their dwellings. In other words, the price has been placed close to the amount which the tenant would stand regardless of the kind of dwelling and equipment furnished. This condition was indicated by the fact that apartments occupied by old residents were not raised much, while the newcomers stood the stiffest raises.

Such illogical raises have left the rent with little relation to the quarters furnished. These cards showed wide variation in charges for apartments of the same size and location in the same building.

A block of tenement-houses, called Phipps Houses Number 2, were built on Columbus Hill, New York City, in 1907. Through the courtesy of the manager, figures were given showing the necessary increases in rents to take care of higher upkeep, taxes, and other expenses.

These buildings are of high-grade construction, with a minimum of depreciation. Repair and upkeep have always been under the supervision of a competent manager. Records were examined back to 1912 and no change was found in rents until 1919, so that it is probable no increases were made from 1907 to 1919. Rents have always been collected weekly, making a thirteen-month year.

Four increases were made in the years from 1919 to 1923.

Date	Increase per Room per Week
July, 1919	10 cents
Jan., 1920	10 cents
Sept., 1920	15 cents
May, 1923	20 cents

The investment rate had increased approximately 2 per cent. during the term and the rates of increase in rent have been fixed to cover the increase in this rate, as well as in expenditures. It does not include the usual speculative investment rate common in tenement-house property.

The increase in rents works out over a period of ten years according to the following table:

TABLE XXV—WEEKLY RENTALS IN PHIPPS TENE-
MENTS NO. 2

Size of Apt.	Conveniences	Aug. 1912	July 1919	Jan. 1920	Sept. 1920	May 1923
3 rooms	Heat, WC and water	$3.90	$4.20	$4.50	$4.95	$5.55
3 rooms	Heat, bath, WC and water	4.05	4.35	4.65	5.10	5.70
4 rooms	Heat, bath, WC and water	5.80	6.20	6.60	7.20	8.00
2 rooms	Heat, bath, WC and water	2.75	2.95	3.15	3.45	3.85

These increases amount to about 33 per cent. in ten years, but have been put on the rooms in about four years. The increases cover charges on a building with 200-foot frontage, with 82 rooms on each of the five floors. There are ten apartments of two rooms, four of three rooms, with toilet and sink, also fourteen three- or four-room apartments, with sink, toilet and bath. Rooms are larger than the legal requirements and larger than those usually found in tenement-houses in New York City.

A definite plan of repairs is carried out by the management; but many tenants make unreasonable demands. When the last raise was made in rents, eighteen tenants combined, employed a city official as lawyer, and went into court under the New York Rent Laws. The manager was on the stand eight hours and his entire staff and all his books were required to prove that the raise was justified, and to win the case.

RENTS, VALUES AND INVESTMENT RETURNS

In the study of Dallas, appraisals of property were made by a "competent and reliable evaluator." On the basis of this valuation, the financial return on 181 houses in five districts was computed, and the gross percentage returns of 12.6, 14.5, 16.9 and 22.6 per cent. respectively for the districts were revealed. The report states that there was ample evidence of exploitation of Negroes as to both rentals and outright sales of property.

Table XXVI shows property listed for sale by a real estate firm in Chicago.

TABLE XXVI—PROPERTIES OFFERED FOR SALE IN CHICAGO, JANUARY, 1926

Type of Building	No. of Apts.	No. of Rooms	Conveniences	Sale Price	Rentals Year	Gross Return %	Net Return %
Apartment	3	3-3-4	stove heat elec. light	$7,750	$1,260	16.3	9.3
Dwelling	2	4-4	hot water heat elec. light	8,000	1,260	15.7	8.7
Apartment	3	7-8-8	2 car garage	20,000	3,420	17.1	10.1
House and store		9		8,500	1,524	17.9	10.9
Dwelling	2	4-6	detached	8,500	1,140	13.4	8.4
Apartment	3	6-7-7	hot water heat elec. light	17,500	3,120	17.8	10.8
House		12	furnace elec. light	7,500	1,080	14.4	9.4
Dwelling and store	2	2-3-7		8,500	1,200	14.1	7.1
Dwelling	2	6-7	2 furnaces elec. light 3 garages	10,000	1,680	16.8	9.8
House (3 story frame)		10	hot water heat	9,500	960	10.1	5.1

To get the net return a liberal allowance of 2 per cent. for depreciation, 2 per cent. for taxes and assessments and 3 per cent. for maintenance and repairs has been made. Five per cent. is allowed on small houses which cost less for upkeep. It must be borne in mind that these prices are the "asked" amounts, and that the actual sale price is often less.

These prices are typical of those quoted in the down-town area, in Woodlawn, and in some other sections, and represent the general types of buildings now being purchased by Negroes. Families that bought during the peak of the migration to get a home are now selling and reinvesting in better properties, or in apartments from which there will be an income. The high rate of return is a potent selling argument.

Cases were found of colored landlords whose exploitation was fully as extreme as that of white landlords. With the increase in the purchase of apartments by Negroes as an investment it seems probable that neither lower rents nor improved conditions in Negro neighborhoods will result from Negro ownership of rental properties.

Two blocks occupied by Negroes were chosen by the Tenement House Department for a study of increase in rents. A careful card-record was made by experienced inspectors of every house and family in these blocks, one in Harlem and one on Columbus Hill. In the early years of the century Columbus Hill was the active and vivid center of Negro life, as Harlem is to-day.

From the books of the Board of Assessors, figures were taken for appraisements in 1915 and 1925, showing a small increase when spread over a period of increasing rents and land values. Assessments in New York City are made on full valuation of real property, and it is therefore possible to combine rents and assessments and get a fair idea of the returns.

The tenement buildings on Columbus Hill are reported as very old, with a large number of rooms without windows to outer air except in small air shafts, and water closets and sinks in halls shared by two to four families. Some buildings are so old and dilapidated that assessments have been decreased while rents have increased.

The tenements of Harlem are usually of the same old-law types as those of Columbus Hill, but in better repair, and usually with sinks in kitchens. Two new-law tenements were included.

In addition to such high returns, which can be gauged by relation to assessed value, there is another type of Negro rental house that has depreciated so far that it is almost valueless. These old houses are usually in changing districts, and landlords merely let them stand until they can sell the lot for business property. The rent collected in the meantime is that much clear profit. Owing to the knowledge that the condition of such houses seldom affects the sale price of the lot, the owners make the minimum amount of repairs and replacements.

It is difficult to estimate the depreciation in buildings resulting from their use by Negroes. In northern cities, foreign-speech people will have followed one another into buildings before the Negroes come, at which time the buildings may be from thirty to fifty or more years old. The migration of the years from 1917 to 1920 went into buildings that were receiving no repairs because of the high cost and because landlords could always find tenants.

TABLE XXVII—RENTS AND ASSESSED VALUES, HARLEM AND COLUMBUS HILL

No. of Bldgs.	No. of Apts.		Annual Rent 1924	Assessment 1925	Gross Return %	Net Return %
		HARLEM				
1	5	....	$6,900	$24,000	29.2	22.2
2	21	....	6,948	26,000	26.7	19.7
3	10	....	2,790	17,500	15.9	8.9
4	10	....	5,400	20,000	27.0	20.0
5	19	....	5,664	22,000	25.7	18.7
6	11	....	4,248	19,000	22.4	15.4
7	10	....	3,540	17,000	20.8	13.8
8	27	....	9,720	57,000	17.1	10.1
9	33	....	10,908	57,000	19.1	12.1
10	11	....	4,680	17,000	27.5	20.5
		COLUMBUS HILL				
11	9	....	3,172	17,000	18.7	11.7
12	20	....	3,804	16,000	23.8	16.8
13	19	....	3,108	17,000	18.3	11.3
14	20	....	4,536	17,000	26.6	19.6
15	18	....	4,548	14,000	32.5	25.5
16	20	....	3,984	15,000	26.6	19.6
17	18	....	4,032	15,000	26.9	19.9

Careful landlords and real estate agents accustomed to handling the lower-price houses agreed that rural migrants, unaccustomed to city dwellings, were hard on halls, stairways, and plumbing, and were not careful in the upkeep of their rooms. Many families took lodgings with the expectation of moving as soon as they could find better rooms and lower rents. Flats rented to one family were sublet to lodgers, often a family to a room, with common use of sanitary conveniences and of the kitchen. Standards of living rose slowly, if at all, among many of the low-wage, uneducated families accustomed to a cabin on a farm. It is possible to find in every city families that have not made adjustments either in industry or in housing, and that float from one part of the city to another, or from city to city, leaving unpaid bills behind them.

There is also a considerable loss from tenants who move their few possessions, after getting into arrears for several months' rent. It is difficult for rural families, accustomed to a settling once a year, to pay rent every week, bi-weekly or monthly, out of irregular wages which do not stretch to cover the more expensive living of a city. Costs of collection are high when an agent must make several calls.

A careful study of depreciation, of rents, and of investment returns, would be necessary to indicate the real net return from properties rented to Negroes. At present it would seem that rents are sufficiently high to cover all possible losses.

With the high returns indicated in the foregoing rent tables, it is evident that landlords could well afford to spend more on the upkeep and equipment of these meager dwellings and still have a fair return from their investment. There are such large numbers of these houses in every city that the rent situation cannot materially improve until better houses are built and equipped for about the same rental so that these tenants can move out. To do this in any one city would require large sums of money. There is indeed a great opportunity for civic-minded investors who are willing to accept 5 or 6 per cent. from rental houses instead of the present high rate of return.

Chapter VIII

HOME BUYING

The number of Negroes who bought houses in cities increased markedly between 1910 and 1920, according to census figures, and still more between 1920 and 1925. It was only in the last period and the two years immediately preceding it, however, that the buying was really speeded up by migration in northern cities. Since 1920 this development has been attended by increased activity among real estate men and by the expansion of financing operations, as well as by the growth of new Negro home-owning subdivisions; increase in home ownership having kept pace with increasing opportunities in industry, higher wages, and a widening knowledge of city living conditions.

Unfortunately a large proportion of the properties purchased by Negroes have been old houses, as only a few men of the professional and business class have been able to build for themselves, and not many speculative builders have been building to sell to colored people.

RAPIDITY

Of eight southern cities for which census figures for 1910 and 1920 were obtained, four showed a large increase in buying, two a steady development, and two a tendency for the total number of homes to decrease and the number of occupant-owned homes to increase. In northern cities figures for 1920 indicate that there had been some buying. Even in Harlem, where tenement-houses involve an investment of at least $15,000, there was some buying. In Dayton, 28.8 per cent. of all colored families owned homes in 1920, and the percentage is now greater.

TABLE XXVIII—HOME OWNERSHIP, FIFTEEN CITIES*

City	Total Number		Colored Homes Number Owned		Per Cent. Owned			All Homes Per Cent. Owned		
	1920	1910	1920	1910	1920	1910	Change	1920	1910	Change
Philadelphia	30,995	18,095	3,778	905	12.2	5.0	7.2	39.5	26.6	12.9
New York	36,412	22,452	1,163	545	3.2	2.5	.7	12.7	11.7	1.0
Chicago	25,684	10,421	1,912	662	7.4	6.3	1.1	27.0	26.2	.8
Gary	1,414	†	135	†	9.5	†	†	34.8	...	...
Indianapolis	8,754	5,818	1,525	853	17.4	14.7	2.7	34.5	33.0	1.5
Dayton	1,959	1,324	504	302	28.8	22.8	6.0	41.9	38.1	3.8
Richmond	13,307	10,507	2,010	1,646	15.1	15.7	−.6	25.9	24.0	1.9
Lynchburg	2,121	2,296	686	615	32.3	26.8	5.5	36.7	33.3	3.4
Louisville	12,456	10,962	1,190	708	9.6	6.5	3.1	29.8	26.6	3.2
Lexington	3,852	3,158	796	644	20.7	20.4	.3	32.2	29.7	2.5
Memphis	19,132	14,878	2,867	1,672	15.0	11.2	3.8	28.9	25.2	3.7
Knoxville	2,698	1,835	722	324	26.8	17.7	9.1	40.4	23.1	17.3
New Orleans	24,942	22,064	2,103	2,438	8.4	11.0	−2.6	23.1	23.1	.0
Charleston	9,858	9,387	1,016	836	10.3	8.9	1.4	20.2	17.6	2.6
Winston-Salem	4,763	†	820	†	17.2	†	†	29.8	...	...

* Data from the Federal Census. Includes less than 1 per cent. other colored than Negro.
† Not shown by color in 1910.

Between 1910 and 1920, 2,517 homes were acquired in the eight southern cities shown in Table XXVIII. This is an increase of 29 per cent. in the number of Negro-owned homes. In every city except Richmond and New Orleans, this increase in owned homes was more rapid than increase in total homes, leaving a substantial favorable change in the per cent. of families occupying their own homes.

It will be observed that in northern cities Negro home ownership had progressed well by 1920, though it had hardly commenced in 1910. There was an increase between 1910-1920 of 5,675 owned homes in the five northern cities included, a percentage increase of 174 in the number of home owners. This was because of the rapid migration and of the special need for Negroes in the cities to buy. In the South, Negro and white ownership seem to fluctuate together. The cities showing a healthy increase in the total number of houses owned by occupants also show a healthy increase in the number of houses owned by Negro occupants, while cities with a sluggish increase in the general total showed small increases in Negro home ownership.

The indications are that since 1920 home ownership among Negroes in northern cities has about doubled. This is evidenced by the brisk buying in Harlem, New York City, where fewer than two hundred dwellings were owned by Negro occupants in 1920; by the wide extension of the Chicago areas containing occupant-owned houses; and by two new large Negro districts of the same kind in Philadelphia, which have grown very rapidly since 1920. In southern cities the increase has been substantial but not so rapid as in northern cities.

A frequently expressed general belief about Negroes is that they live huddled together because they like to. It is true that they like to live near their churches, schools and friends, finding comfort in racial solidarity; but the movement to new areas and to suburbs shows that they are not willing to accept bad housing and living conditions if it is possible to find, and to afford, better. In every city studied, this movement was notable.

Buying in Typical Cities

Memphis, a rapidly growing industrial city, with characteristics of both North and South, furnishes a good example. Between 1910 and 1920 the per cent. of Negro homes owned increased from 11.0 to 15.0. In actual numbers, 1,195 houses were acquired to be used as occupant-owned residences. Comparing total homes with owned homes, the increase is more remarkable.

TABLE XXIX—NEGRO HOME BUYING IN MEMPHIS *

Year	Total Homes	Total Owned	Owned Free	Owned Mortgaged	Owned Unknown
1920	19,132	2,867	1,673	940	254
1910	14,878	1,672	1,039	522	111
Per cent. increase	28.6	71.5	61.0	81.4	...

* Data from the Federal Census.

Homes owned free represent buying over a long period of years. Mortgaged homes represent homes bought within ten or twelve years, and on which payments are being made. The higher per cent. of mortgaged houses in 1920 indicates somewhat the rate of buying.

The increase in home buying is large in new areas and outlying wards. City growth caused old Negro districts to be crowded out by expansion of business areas, and a considerable number of displaced families, together with others ambitious to have better homes, moved from the down-town areas. In the newer areas home owning is popular, business centers are growing, and church and community life is active and wholesome.

In the outlying wards of Memphis for which data are given in Table XXX, there was a rapid increase not only in home buying but also in the number of homes owned free, showing the tendency of Negro families to pay off their obligations. Along with home buying, however, there was some speculative buying, and failure to foresee the difficulty of making payments over a long period resulted in the usual losses.

Providence Park in Richmond, Morgan Park in Chicago, Douglass Park in Indianapolis, Cherry Hill and Columbia Hill in Winston-Salem, the Hill Street District in Louisville, Lonsdale and Park City in Knoxville, are similar growing suburbs, occupied by Negroes who own their homes. In

TABLE XXX—NEGRO HOMES IN OUTLYING WARDS OF MEMPHIS *

Ward and Year	Total Homes	Total Owned	Per Cent. Owned	Increase in Owned Homes
Ward 14				
1920	878	204	23.2	...
1910	601	79	13.1	125
Ward 29				
1920	618	335	54.2	...
1910	55	31	56.4	304
Ward 34				
1920	419	196	46.8	...
1910 †	...	...	...	...
Ward 35				
1920	799	405	50.7	...
1910 †	...	...	...	...

* Data from Federal Census.
† Ward added since 1910.

the smaller cities there are colonies in new areas in which ambitious families that break away from the old colored districts can find houses they are able to buy, and where they can give better living conditions to their children.

One of the largest housing projects undertaken by Negro promoters and capital was the purchase for cash of Truxton, one of the developments of the United States Housing Corporation for colored laborers, near Portsmouth, Va. Competition was in open market, and $141,000 was raised by a Negro syndicate to bid it in.

The property comprises 100 acres, 253 houses, a ten-room brick school, hard-surface streets, sewers, water and lights.

It has the highest elevation of any section of Portsmouth. Most of the houses have five rooms and bath, a few are double houses of ten rooms and bath for two families. Houses are sold on an easy-payment plan of $25 a month. The prices range from $1,700 to $2,200, and virtually all had been contracted for by representative middle-class families. Portsmouth includes the school in the city system and pays for the employment of ten colored teachers. There is street car connection with the center of town and a growing business center in the colony.

In New York home owning is difficult for any average wage-earner because of the general tenement-house development and the speculative prices of land. Only business and professional men, and salaried employees, have incomes stable enough to enable them to buy. Yet a number of houses have been bought in Manhattan since 1920. A start has been made by wage-earners in the coöperative buying of apartment-houses, and in group-buying.

There is movement to areas other than Columbus Hill and Harlem, with a large percentage of home ownership in Queens Borough, on Long Island, and on Staten Island.

TABLE XXXI—NEGRO HOME OWNERSHIP IN FIVE BOROUGHS, NEW YORK CITY, 1920

Borough	Total Homes	Owned Homes	Per Cent. Owned
Brooklyn	7,791	477	6.1
Bronx	975	76	7.8
Manhattan	26,156	184	.7
Queens	1,173	370	31.5
Richmond	317	56	17.9
Total city	36,412	1,163	3.2

Less than 1 per cent. of the Negro families in Manhattan owned their homes in 1920; but it is estimated that Negroes now own more than $2,000,000 worth of property in Harlem. A large number of handsome residences, including some high-grade, artistic ones developed by Stanford White, have been purchased and are maintained as homes. Individual owners have bought from one to fifteen or more tenement-houses each, and are large investors. This has mostly taken place in five years.

There is also some movement to Jersey and Westchester towns, the congestion of Harlem being largely created by the constant influx of migrants and floaters.

In Chicago, where home buying had started several years earlier than in other northern cities, and where it has continued, Negroes are scattering into many parts of the city. Table XXXII shows that 85 per cent. of the dwellings were in seven wards, and 58 per cent. of the dwellings in the second and third wards. Home ownership was largest in the sixth, thirty-first and thirty-second wards, all of which were new or changing areas.

TABLE XXXII—NEGRO HOME OWNERSHIP IN SEVEN
WARDS, CHICAGO, 1920 *

Ward	Total Homes	Owned Homes	Per Cent. Owned
2	10,714	558	5.2
3	4,369	346	7.9
6	1,463	149	10.2
14	1,744	69	4.0
30	1,944	106	5.5
31	1,061	209	19.7
32	399	189	47.4
Total city	25,684	1,912	7.4

* Data from the Federal Census.

Ward 2 is in the oldest part of the down-town colony, which grew south into the third ward, and later into the sixth. Probably 90 per cent. or more of the owned homes in these wards have been purchased since 1918, roughly 1,050 in number. Buying continues, with investment increasing in better houses and apartments. Ward 6 includes the Hyde Park districts, where bombings, intimidations and other violent methods were used previous to 1922 to prevent sales to Negroes.

In Ward 14, which includes the West Side colonies, home buying is not active for either white or colored, because of changing uses. Ward 30 has a number of small scattered colonies, occupying a few blocks each, with an occasional owned home.

Ward 31 has the Ogden Park Colony, one of the first to go to an outlying district. This colony has grown slowly, but is a community of stable, comfortable homes.

Ward 32 includes the colony in Morgan Park, which is made up of families with a keen home-owning desire, progressive ideals and civic pride, and who are actively working to obtain municipal improvements in sewers, paving, and water supply.

FINANCING OF HOME BUYING

Few wage-earning families have the cash to pay for a house, and payments must be financed over a period of years. To borrow money, even with friendly relations, is a test of character. Steady employment, prospects, character, and savings must be considered.

Negroes are standing this test of borrowing for home buying, and are steadily overcoming the prejudice against lending money to them, though this is still one of the greatest obstacles to home owning. Their own financial institutions are commencing to influence loan money, but the difficulties in securing this type of small loans are still great.

Negroes are also standing the test of payments running over a period of ten or twelve years, and have belied their general reputation for hand-to-mouth living. In every city studied, white and colored bankers, brokers, real estate dealers and builders stated that families buying a home rarely default, except because of some disaster, or very poor judgment in buying. One dealer who had sold 700 houses in five years had had only three foreclosures, and another who had sold 900 houses had had none. There is, however, a decided tendency to get behind in payments, which makes it necessary for those who collect to be both patient and persistent in keeping them regular.

The increase in buying in northern cities started at a time when loan-money was in demand and rates high.

Negroes bought old properties, and had great difficulty in getting mortgage money, even at advanced rates, partly because of the depreciated values of the houses they purchased and partly because of prejudice against a new type of clients. Mortgage firms willing to take the paper found difficulty in selling it. This attitude has changed slowly.

In southern cities, colored families, through friendly relations with white families, usually make arrangements for borrowing more easily, though this of course depends on the character of the borrower and the kind of property purchased.

Negroes are learning to use their own financial institutions with greater confidence, both for depositing and for borrowing, as correct banking methods are established and the number of failures decreases. One bank is typical of many started within the past ten years.

This typical bank began business in February, 1921. It now has between 700 and 800 stockholders, 2,840 commercial accounts, 2,558 savings accounts, and school savings of $7,000 to $8,000. The daily ledger sheet of December 31st, 1925, showed real estate loans of $169,993.61, with an estimate of 98 per cent. on homes. In the same city there is another Negro bank, as well as three building and loan associations, all with an increasing number of stockholders and investors.

In Chicago in January, 1926, an old state bank owned and staffed by colored people had $412,775 in real estate loans. A life insurance company of the same city, five years old, had over $100,000 in mortgages; another company three years old had $130,000. In Philadelphia, thirty-six Negro building and loan associations, operating under the State Banking Department, are estimated to have a capital of over five million dollars.

As Negroes gain confidence in their own financial institutions, savings increase and become the basis for varied activities. At the same time, white banks report that the number of Negro depositors and the stability of their accounts steadily increase. It was estimated for the Commission on Race Relations of Chicago in 1921 that Negroes had upwards of fifteen million dollars in down-town white banks. It was estimated for this study that the amount had at least doubled.

These resources, controlled by, or open to, Negroes, materially affect home buying. It is easier to place or renew mortgages, and a family that gets into difficulties about payments can often find help where formerly it stood to lose. There is some buying beyond means, some speculative buying, and the average amount of losses through default in payments; but in each case the amount involved grows less, and fewer home buyers fail to pay out.

Financing of home buying in each city or town usually follows the customs of the place. In general all methods sum up to a cash payment of 10 per cent. or more; and monthly payments, arranged to cover the balance, with interest, taxes, insurance, and other charges, amount to about 1 per cent. of the total per month, running ten to twelve years to complete title. Financing is done through mortgages, building and loan, and different forms of contract sale.

When the terms of sale include payments over a long period of years, with a cash payment smaller than 10 per cent., and a higher cost for the balance due, an equity is gained so slowly that the buyer is really paying rent plus interest, taxes, and insurance, the title to the property remaining with the seller. These charges are a heavy burden. It is probable that a detailed study of buying by Negroes who are unfamiliar with values and financing would show a considerable amount of this form of exploitation. At the worst, however, the home is usually owned eventually and the family life has been given stability and purpose.

In Richmond, Lynchburg, New York, Buffalo, Chicago, Charleston, Winston-Salem, Louisville and Atlanta, houses are usually sold on cash payment and first and second mortgages, with a few financed on the building and loan plan. In Philadelphia, Dayton, Indianapolis, New Orleans, and Lexington, building and loan associations are active. In Memphis, Gary and Indianapolis, the contract-lease form of sale is common. In Knoxville, and to some extent in all cities, there is direct sale from owner to buyer, or from contractor-builder to buyer. In Harlem (New York City) and in Indianapolis, group-buying is starting, in the former place because of the large investment in a ten to twenty-four family tenement-house, and in the latter for a quick turn and profits on small houses.

Whatever the method used for financing, real estate dealers in each city stated that Negroes are satisfactory clients if property is sold to them on correct principles, and if patience is exercised in helping them to keep up to their payments.

FINANCING THROUGH MORTGAGES

Active home buying in northern cities started with the high wages and housing shortage of the war-industry period. Pressure for a place to live induced many families to undertake larger obligations than in normal times. Loan money did not go freely to this new group of buyers, partly because of prejudice making it difficult to sell mortgages on property of Negroes, and partly because of the buying of old homes of doubtful resale values. Negroes in some instances paid as high as 25 per cent. for loan money on second mortgages, adding materially to the cost of buying. Second mortgage money is seldom secured for less than 12 per cent. First mortgages were often reduced in amount on renewal, or appraisals of property placed so low that first mortgage money bore little relation to the selling price.

Gradually, as real estate brokers, money-lenders and financial institutions have learned from experience that money knows no color, first mortgages have been readily renewed, the rates have declined, and loan money has become more plentiful, though it is probable that Negroes still pay a higher rate, distributed in fees, searches of abstracts, renewal commissions and other additions to the legal rates, than do white buyers.

The large amount of loan money seeking investment has also favored Negro buyers, who have learned more about sources for borrowing. To some extent, the financial resources of Negro institutions are affecting loans, though these are not yet sufficient to cover all mortgages.

The placing of first mortgage loans, dependent upon appraisals for the amount loaned, is not difficult, especially in cities that have building and loan associations with strong resources. The placing of second-mortgage money to cover the differences between the cash payment and the first mortgage from the selling price is still difficult, and will continue to be until the tenacity of colored families in paying out for their homes is generally recognized, and until the second mortgage field is more highly developed. A detailed study of this feature of buying would show the difference in rates and methods of handling the loans of white and colored buyers. Reliable firms deal fairly with Negroes; but a considerable proportion of their mortgage money comes from lenders who ask for excessive rates, have no hesitancy in foreclosing, and who make a new profit from every resale of property or renewal of mortgage.

Second mortgage money at the legal rate of from 6 to 8 per cent., plus various types of "fees" that bring the rate up to from 12 to 20 per cent., seems to prevail not so much from color prejudice as from lack of organization of this field of investment. White purchasers of cheap property face the same problem, especially in cities where the building and loan plan is not common. All loan companies naturally prefer large loans to small ones, so the more valuable houses are always provided for first, leaving the small purchasers to the smaller loan companies.

The rates seem entirely too high when the character of the risk is considered. Foreclosures are rare, and the risk is largely a moral one, depending on the character and stability of the family. Greater development of second mortgage facilities would greatly stimulate the tendency to home buying, with the stable home life and better conditions for children that are such fundamental needs for an emerging race.

BUILDING AND LOAN ASSOCIATIONS

Strong, carefully managed building and loan associations provide a favorable method of financing the buying of small homes. White associations are not unfriendly to colored investors or borrowers, and the general feeling among Negroes is that appraisals are better than those secured through banks and loan companies. There is also the advantage of personal help and advice, and generally of weekly payments of definite sums over a stated period of years. In most states laws have been passed controlling or limiting building and loan activities, which make associations sound financially. However, some building and loans, organized as stock companies for profit, charge as high rates as mortgage companies.

In Philadelphia, the thirty-six colored building and loan associations are largely developed and officered by church-members, and they give inexperienced buyers the benefit of friendly advice and help in locating a house, judging its value, and in financing. One colored association is over twenty-five years old, and has financed over a million dollars' worth of homes. In Dayton, Negro financing is done principally through one white association, with scattered borrowers in several others, and one small colored association. Dayton shows a high percentage of home ownership, and the houses bought are substantial, well-located property. In Indianapolis, a white association has over three thousand Negro clients, and others have a considerable number. In New Orleans, where buying is not active, financing is usually done on the building and loan plan.

In Lexington, where growth is steady and fairly normal, a building and loan company has had Negro clients for most of its twenty-one years of service. In the spring of 1925 it had about two hundred colored borrowers, and sixty investors. It pays 6 per cent. and has a record of never having lost a dollar. The usual loan to colored clients is 60 per cent. of the appraisal value, rising to 75 per cent. on especially good property.

CONTRACT BUYING

The contract method of buying is a popular one in Gary, Memphis, Indianapolis, and other cities, and is usual in new subdivisions. Its attractions are the small cash payment, and monthly "payments like rent." Its defect is that it allows exploitation, and that special clauses may be inserted which make it easy to claim a default, whereby the buyer loses all that has been paid in. The printed forms of contract to sell that are used are devised to protect the vendor: there is no record of purchase; and additional mortgages may be put on by the vendor after payments have started.

However, protection is necessary for the vendor, since the cash payment is low and an equity is earned only after thirty to forty monthly payments. Careful supervision is necessary to get in the small monthly payments with additional collections to cover repairs, taxes, assessments, and other fees. Under some state laws, it is usual that if a family defaults, it may go on living in the house for a year or more, paying no rent, nor taking any care of the property.

Selling under contract-lease is highly speculative, and is carried on through active advertising and soliciting campaigns in which glowing promises are made. Buyers are tempted to undertake a burden of payments extending over from ten to fifteen years, with constant danger of loss through violation of clauses in the lease contract, or through default.

The method used in Indianapolis is popular and typical of the better class of sales under contract-leases. A small cash payment, $25 to $50, is made covering a part of the fees, and the cost of the abstract, and to bind the bargain. Monthly notes covering a reduction of principal, interest, taxes, insurance, assessments, are made. When about 40 per cent. has been paid in, the buyer arranges a loan, usually through a building and loan association, and is given 50 per cent. of the appraised value. The buyer must also arrange a second mortgage, usually at the legal rate of interest, plus commission, fees, cost of abstracts and other costs which bring the rate to 18 per cent. or higher, running for one year

and renewable. The buyer makes every effort to pay off
this mortgage to avoid renewal fees, paying at the same time
to the building and loan association on the first mortgage.

Enough definite information was obtained in this study to
indicate the need of a special study of this method of selling, to be followed by instruction of buyers regarding its
pitfalls. Negro papers are used for advertising, agents are
sent out to speak in churches on Sunday, following up with
sales on Monday, and Negro families expecting to move put
down their money, often only to find that they have wasted
it on undesirable lots or houses.

CONTRACTOR-BUILDER SALES

The houses offered under contractor-builder terms are
new, located in desirable neighborhoods, and offer a wide
range of size and equipment. Usually the plan of 10 per
cent. cash payment with a first mortgage is followed. The
drawback to this type of purchase is usually the large margin allowed between cost of erection and selling price, to
cover the second mortgage notes which must be discounted
and give the contractor and the lender each a high rate of
return. That is, a house costing $1,700 to build, is sold
for $2,250 to $2,500, with improvements still to be paid for.
The margin is so high that if the contractor holds his own
notes he will make upwards of 25 per cent., and if he is
compelled to sell, he splits as best he can. If he is pressed,
he can sell again, getting what is the equivalent of third
mortgage money.

Where Negroes have successfully bought homes, it is evident that they have done so in the same way as all other
classes of buyers. Small-house buyers are not educated in
property values, the relation of income to payments, and
the necessary expenses of interest, taxes, assessments and
rates, added to or included in payments. The asked price
of the house may be only 50 per cent. of the amount of
cash invested before a title is clear, when interest payments
extend over from ten to twelve years.

Good buying depends on the care taken by real estate

firms or vendors in advising investments, and in making up the schedule of payments. Negroes are eager to learn, but sometimes get into trouble because they are not frank as to how much money they have for the first payment, or what they can pay monthly. Their lack of frankness goes back to the old days when traders found out how much they had, and took it all. Their native shrewdness often keeps them from telling white men, even those whom they trust, what their resources are, and this often prevents them from making the best bargain.

In 1920 Negro home buyers came through a period of business depression and unemployment, with lessened incomes from wages and from lodgers. Even with this handicap, it was found that foreclosures on Negro-owned property were not above the average for the city; in the experience of many dealers they were considerably less, except where forced.

The higher standard of house owners stands out all through Chapter VI, on equipment of houses, and especially in the comparison between owners and renters shown in tables on the number of *A, B, C* and *D* class houses, the separate living-rooms, bedrooms and kitchens, the repair of houses and the upkeep of yards and premises.

There can be no doubt that home ownership and all that goes with it is one of the greatest strides in the rise of the standard of living of families that have had to put up with the conditions in Negro rental sections. The home-buying movement is therefore one of the most hopeful features of the urbanization process.

Chapter IX

CONSTRUCTIVE AGENCIES

Improvement in the housing conditions of Negroes in cities has been effected here and there through municipal control of buildings and sanitation; through privately organized efforts of several kinds; and by philanthropically inclined persons who have provided a few good houses for Negroes in good locations and have found their investments to be reasonably profitable business ventures.

Individual initiative struggling in the direction of the purchase of good homes, as described in the preceding chapter, must be relied upon for the improvement of the housing of most families; and the success of this initiative is, to a large extent, conditioned by the economic well-being of the families. The increased amounts for home-betterment must come from an increasing surplus of family income over and above the amount necessary for a bare subsistence.

The period from 1921 to 1926 was one of great prosperity for Negroes, as well as for the general rank and file of American labor. Unusual opportunities for employment were offered by trade and industry, and the resulting high and regular wages afforded real opportunity for progress toward better living-quarters. It is indeed noteworthy that so much of this increase in earnings has been devoted to a higher standard of living, as is evidenced by the movement of Negroes to better residence sections.

NEED FOR MORE BUILDING

While the individual initiative furnishes the drive toward better housing, the individual who seeks a home worth from $1,500 to $5,000, either for purchase or for rent, usually has to deal with the real estate speculator, the speculative builder if he is purchasing, or the speculative landlord if he is renting. The profit sought by capital in these businesses is high, and it is from this that the housing-evils result.

Some associations that have succeeded in earning a reasonable return without charging excessive rents are described later in this chapter. While these associations have provided good houses for few families in proportion to the great number of ill-housed families, they have shown that decent houses for Negroes can be made reasonably profitable investments. Until very much larger sums are applied to investments of this kind, other efforts for improvement will be merely palliative and not cures for the evils.

There is always the marginal group of families unable to bargain effectively for homes and open to the worst forms of exploitation; and there is always a considerable amount of ignorance or indifference in the middle classes that leaves them also open to certain kinds of exploitation. Much can be done toward alleviating the bad housing among these groups by municipal departments and by private associations. The results of such efforts are described in this chapter.

MUNICIPAL CONTROL

The function of municipal services for bettering the neighborhood was discussed in Chapter V. The modern city, however, does more than merely concern itself with the installation of sewers, lights and water, and with garbage removal and police protection. Zoning laws and building laws give it control of light- and air-spaces and many other matters relating to the construction and equipment of houses.

The fact that Negroes live in depressed areas, or in areas of changing uses, where city departments crowded with work on newer housing-developments are apt to spend little time and energy, has much to do with their health, morals and general welfare. Since Negroes are thus handicapped, it is especially unfortunate that their citizen rights are often disregarded. In no city studied was there evidence that Negro housing-areas are effectively controlled by the health, building, zoning and public-service departments. The health departments, seeking to reduce their mortality and morbidity rates, are least neglectful.

HEALTH SERVICES

It is evident that health problems of Negroes, both native and migrant, call for special methods of control. Their mortality and morbidity rates are much higher than those of white people. In the seventeen cities included in this study, it was noted that while full-time, trained health officers are aware that housing is a factor of Negro health, some are hampered by politics, and more by the protests of influential owners of low-rent dwellings that the rent-returns are not sufficient to provide for sanitary improvements, a claim not borne out by rental studies.

There is no question that the inferior living conditions of Negroes contribute largely to respiratory, intestinal and venereal diseases, and to the high infant death-rate. It is also evident, wherever control has been undertaken, that improvement immediately results. In Lynchburg, a highly organized and effective health department keeps down its rates through education and supervision. In Richmond, the health officer holds each nurse accountable for the death of any baby from intestinal disease. A spot map shows each case reported, white or colored, with a personal explanation following each death. As virtually all parts of these cities have sewers and good water, cleanliness is possible and easy.

HEALTH ORDINANCES

In several cities it was evident that Negroes suffer from lax enforcement of antiquated health ordinances. A common defect in ordinances is the lack of any power on the part of the health officer to compel sanitary installation for each house. Quite generally one set of fixtures for two families is accepted even by health officers as a fair standard. In some cities, only the "property" need be connected, making possible a large number of houses with one hydrant and one toilet in the yard. In one city, through defective ordinances and divided power in enforcement, one owner had equipped thirty houses, facing two streets, with one hydrant and a two-compartment water-closet, both at some distance from most of the houses. In another southern city, with thousands of Negroes living in alley-houses, the court ruled that an imaginary line could be drawn across a lot and the front house connected to sewers and water-mains, without it being necessary to connect the alley-houses.

It is so generally taken for granted that each house in a city has sewer and water-connections that even those interested in health and sanitary conditions are often unaware of abuses in areas of small-rental houses.

SANITARY INSPECTORS

A corps of sanitary inspectors is a comparatively recent addition to the staff of health officers; and their work is not yet stabilized. The result of inspections honestly done, even by untrained men, using common sense, are so evident, however, that their value is not questioned. During this study a large part of the most valuable information was obtained from the regular sanitary men, with whom field-inspections were made.

A few cities are trying out Negro inspectors, nurses and physicians in public health work. It was noted that a conscientious colored sanitary inspector, familiar with his district, could accomplish more through personal instructions than could even the best written orders backed by good ordinances.

In Dayton, a man who understands his own race psychology and who has behind him a progressive health officer, has taken care of all kinds of sanitary and health violations by the use of persuasion, instruction, and orders where needed. In Louisville, an experiment undertaken by civic societies and the health officer developed carded information of great value, through the work of a colored inspector. In Buffalo, a colored inspector is put on the crowded east-side district; and so far as ordinances permit, has good sanitary conditions.

In seven of the seventeen cities studied, zoning ordinances were in effect; in four, plans were in preparation, allowing observation in eleven cities. These zoning plans can be of service to a residence neighborhood by stabilizing usage of land, by protecting it against encroachment by industry and business, and in some neighborhoods by preventing encroachment by apartments and flats.

Two factors are constant in any discussion of the effect of zoning on settled Negro colonies. First, a considerable proportion of colored population lives in areas of changing uses, where business and factories are mixed with dwellings. Second, Negroes are not yet actively concerned with the effects of zoning, although they are no more indifferent than other racial groups. The first zoning ordinance to go into effect was that of New York City in 1916; and the average small property owner is not yet aware of the purpose and effect of city control through zoning.

A study of zoning maps shows that areas occupied by Negroes lie commonly along railroads or waterways, or near business districts. These areas are usually zoned for commerce and industry, and dwellings are given incidental consideration. Negro homes are treated neither better nor worse than other homes in similar areas, as all are misplaced with respect to the future growth of the city. Values are based on uses other than for homes, and public improvements are made to favor these uses.

When residence provisions are imposed in areas near business and factories, appeals for changes of use to lower categories are often granted, because of lack of protest against the change by property-owners. In Harlem, the zoning maps were made before Negroes took over the handsome residences classified as in single-family districts. These small areas are surrounded by commercial areas, and petitions for change of use have considerable force, especially when no vigorous protest is made by the home owners.

In Indianapolis, an area zoned for single-family houses, and built up with homes of wage-earners, has changed from white to colored. Industries are near by, but the district is made attractive by a desirable parkway. Speculative builders are proposing a change of classification to one giving the district over to the construction of multiple houses that yield higher rental returns, and thereby virtually excluding home owners.

Instances of lack of consideration for Negro homes in areas of changing uses are common. In Memphis, a street of good houses, largely owned by well-to-do colored families, lies near the edge of an area zoned for industry. It might easily have been stabilized as a residence street; but these families, to maintain as good homes as they now have, will eventually be obliged to move to new neighborhoods, and into houses costing from $5,000 to $15,000.

Zoning practice is still experimental and opinions as to the results may differ. In general, however, it is certain that suburban areas largely populated by Negroes have been given lower standards than those of similar white developments. The tendency is marked in districts under development by speculative builders interested in rental returns. It is usual to find districts built up with single-family houses put into apartment-house classification. It is also common to find the lowest provisions for area and height in these districts. Racial prejudices and slave-holding psychology are inherent in the treatment accorded an emergent race.

BUILDING CODES

Any adequate discussion of building codes would of necessity be technical. One tendency that affects Negroes is, however, to be noted here. It was a constantly recurring observation during this study that speculative builders in Negro sections frequently violated building codes without check from the city by not connecting with sewers where connection is required, by stinting on light- and air-space, and by the construction of inadequate fire-walls between adjoining houses.

VOLUNTEER ORGANIZATIONS

In the municipalities where the city government is not effective in alleviating housing-evils, interested private organizations can accomplish much toward the improving of housing and sanitation. Coöperation, the form of which varies with the needs, is a highly successful method of securing action by officials, of improving laws and ordinances, and of studying conditions to find remedies.

The Philadelphia Housing Association, and the Cincinnati Better Housing League, whose detailed studies were courteously made available for this report, are highly organized and efficient. An executive secretary, with a trained staff, carries on from year to year, developing programs. Both cities have large Negro colonies, and are actively at work on this phase of the problem. Reference has been made in the chapters on rents and migrants to the studies of the Philadelphia Housing Association.

The Cincinnati Better Housing League opened in 1926 the Michael M. Shoemaker Health Center in a part of the city where Negro health and housing are at their worst. Work is carried on in coöperation with all city departments, and with the Associated Charities, to cover family problems in all phases. A large three-story residence has been rebuilt and fitted up with offices, clinics, and model housekeeping-rooms. Only one trained worker visits a family, so there is no duplication of effort. Each worker has a definite district. The field work commenced with a housing-survey in which 2,500 cards were turned in. They will show home ownership, stability of population, white and colored families, rooming-houses, living-rooms over stores, income spent for rent, and general repair and sanitary conditions. On these cards as a basis, the work will be built up to establish normal and wholesome conditions.

In New York City, the Tenement House Committee of the Charity Organization Society has been for twenty-six years the active representative of citizens in law improvement and enforcement, coöperating closely with the city Tenement House Department.

In Chicago, virtually all organizations dealing with civic problems have active housing-committees which can be mobilized at need. Through the Department of Public Welfare a citizen's committee on housing has been appointed by the Mayor, with a first task of bettering the housing of small wage-earners.

In Gary, a survey sponsored by the Federation of Churches and the Interracial Committee developed the need of better ordinances and better enforcement in a rapidly growing city of mill-workers.

In Louisville, the Woman's City Club has done good volunteer work. Club women become responsible for a card-survey of an assigned district for reporting conditions. Reports and complaints are sorted by the secretary and taken up with proper city officials.

In Knoxville, the Free Colored Library made a card-survey of more than 3,100 colored families; and the report was printed by the city officials, leading to the correction of a considerable number of housing- and health-evils.

In Winston-Salem, through conferences and studies made by groups of white and colored leaders, a definite plan for development of housing, schools and recreation has been formulated.

Work can be done by citizen's organizations only as it is carefully based on accurate knowledge of conditions, and carried out continuously over a considerable number of years. Housing betterment is a year-by-year task, and not to be accomplished by waves of interest; and no amount of volunteer effort can do more than supplement the municipal health and building departments. As long as these departments do not function properly, so long will volunteer effort be more or less ineffective.

VISITING HOME-MAKERS

The generally used title of "Visiting Housekeepers" is a misnomer, as the workers so designated do little actual housekeeping. Their work is to gain the coöperation of families, landlords, civic and relief organizations, and city officials and institutions in bringing about better conditions, acting as liaison officers until the particular need is met. This type of service is of great practical value in helping colored families to learn how to live under city conditions.

From a memorandum [1] regarding this type of work in Cincinnati, the following data are taken:

> The Better Housing League of Cincinnati employs seven visiting housekeepers, four of whom are colored. A large per cent. of the houses occupied by Negroes are old and in bad condition. The work of the four housekeepers for the year 1925 is tabulated as follows:

> | | |
> |---|---|
> | 4,063 | family visits |
> | 294 | improvements in housekeeping |
> | 174 | families moved to better quarters |
> | 60 | cases of overcrowding eliminated |
> | 324 | first inspections of houses |
> | 1,260 | reinspections of houses |
> | 1,420 | conveniences installed |
> | 637 | nuisances removed |
> | 124 | houses with damp, dirty rooms vacated |
> | 7 | houses torn down |
> | 1,722 | repairs put in |
> | 2,112 | parts of houses cleaned |
> | 5,317 | rooms painted, whitewashed and papered |

> Under the new plan developed at the Shoemaker Center, three of the colored visiting housekeepers have been assigned to the Center, and the fourth will do work with families in other parts of the city, with assistance from the white visiting housekeepers.

The memorandum explains one method of coöperation as follows:

> While the housing survey was being made, it was found that in two particular localities there were many houses totally unfit for occupancy. The streets had never been paved, there were no sewers, and it was apparent that the district was valuable only for industrial uses. The houses were so dilapidated, and the locality so undesirable, that only persons accustomed to rough and sometimes questionable methods of living were attracted there.

> The Better Housing League discussed the whole matter with the Housing Bureau and the Building Commissioner (city of-

[1] Memorandum prepared for this study by Mr. Bleecker Marquette and Miss Ethel Ideson, of the Cincinnati Better Housing League.

ficials) after a careful inspection and decided that the houses were unfit, so orders were immediately issued on fifty-three houses. Six houses were ordered vacated until repaired, and the rest were condemned and ordered torn down.

The Better Housing League agreed to help find other more suitable living quarters for the families occupying the houses. Many of the owners protested the orders, and may have recourse to the courts. Some of the landlords are now evicting tenants, and two houses have been torn down. Six other houses have also been condemned and ordered torn down.

Dayton has a visiting home-maker service, sponsored and financed by the Junior League. Members bind themselves to earn the money for a budget of $4,000 to $5,000 to pay salaries of one colored and three white trained workers.

The colored worker is a college graduate, a former teacher, sympathetic and constructive. She has general instructions to help families out of difficulties, and to aid them in making adjustments to city conditions. Reports are made to her of sickness, neglect of children, family troubles, bad housing, desertion by fathers or mothers, and often of homesick families. Occasionally where there is sickness she puts the home in order; but in general friends and relatives can be found to help until the patient is well. She teaches housekeeping to ignorant, dirty mothers, so that the condition of the home will not discourage the wage-earning father and send the children to the streets. Sewing-classes, advice and help, and child-welfare tasks are a part of her duty.

Working with the sanitary inspector, she can cause changes to be made where there is insanitary and unhealthful housing. Their work has reduced the number of Dayton districts in which there are bad conditions of long standing to two, which is a small amount for an industrial city.

These, however, are only two cities out of eighteen. This kind of work could be well extended to many other places.

NEIGHBORHOOD ASSOCIATIONS

The aptitude of Negroes for organization has led them into forming several kinds of housing associations. Blocks and neighborhoods are organized for improvements carried out by family and city activities. One of the most successful and active was found in 136th Street, Harlem, in a block of handsome houses, most of which were owned by resident families. The tact and persistency of a well-trained woman have had much to do with its success.

Her family bought at a fair price, in the slump of 1919, a fine old house that had been through many hands, and that had been used as a rooming-house until it was badly run down. Thorough repairs were made, and the house was equipped with modern conveniences, as were a number of other houses in the block. In 1923-1924, business houses, tailor shops, and hair-dressing parlors commenced to creep down the block from Seventh Avenue, although restrictions in deeds to the properties so occupied limited their use to residence purposes only.

Mrs. G. wrote out a short invitation and left it personally with every family in the block. A meeting was held in her parlors and the block was organized. At the second meeting, $745 were collected to replace dead trees. All houses but six put out flower boxes. As the block ends on the west in the bluff of Morningside Park, a charming vista was created.

Well-organized, the association persuaded or forced owners to remove objectionable businesses and signs, carrying one case through the courts. Through coöperation with the street-cleaning department, garbage is regularly removed, and families take in the cans from the sidewalks promptly. Owners are encouraged to keep homes in repair, both outside and in. Details are looked after, such as the keeping of window shades even, the polishing of brass railings, keeping awnings clean, back yards in order, fences painted. The Board of Health coöperated to have broken fences torn down, and the Fire Department makes inspections.

A committee called by appointment on the Mayor, and as a result a comfort station costing $30,000 was located in Morningside Park on a site selected by the association.

Loud talking or excessive hilarity on the street is discouraged. Boys are kept by the police from playing ball and breaking windows. At times, vice creeps in, but it is promptly eliminated. Any residents who fall below the standards of the association are reminded of the rules.

Other block organizations like this one are being formed throughout the district, and the movement will be encouraged to spread all over Harlem.

In Morgan Park, Chicago, another type of local organization is made up of business men, professional men, and some city employees. Attention is given to municipal improvements in sewers, water, street-lights and paving, as well as improvement of property. The section is low, and even after street sewers were put in, water stood in cellars, and "frog land" was unsightly with stagnant pools. When the residents asked for a large intercepting sewer to drain this soggy land, the engineer of the local improvement board attended their meeting and tried to dissuade them on account of the heavy assessments, and because he believed that only real estate men were interested in the matter. After discussion, he recommended the construction of the sewer, with assessments spread as part of a general improvement. Later a paving-program was instituted with the aid of the ward alderman. One resident put it in words: "It used to be that the colored vote was counted before it was voted, but now there are enough influential leaders to stand up for rights and make a protest felt."

The Orange Mound Boosters, a live organization in one of the Memphis suburbs, has been organized sixteen months (in 1926) with a membership of one hundred and contacts with five thousand people. Its object is to "promote health, education, law and order, and the community spirit." Through coöperation with city officials, it has secured street-lights, improved roads, keeps the school up to standard, stands back of the colored postmaster of the branch office, gives advice and assistance in the purchase of homes, and is a general clearing-house for activities in the suburb. A similar association of women is formed to study civic problems.

In Woodlawn, Chicago, a white and colored coöperative group in a neighborhood association worked so successfully that there is now little for it to do. One of the most valuable results was a better understanding between the races.

These neighborhood organizations were found in only three of the eighteen cities.

MODEL HOUSE AND INDUSTRIAL PROJECTS

The housing-problem is so extensive, involving such vast capital, that philanthropic enterprises can do little more than demonstrate possibilities. Such demonstrations are, however, valuable, and usually create quite an interest in better housing, and develop methods whereby it can be obtained.

These are among the interesting experiments made in the early days of housing-reform, starting about 1900. It was felt by public-spirited citizens that model tenements and houses would materially influence the types and rental returns of housing developments. The principal contribution made by these projects is the accurate data that can be gathered from their records, which are valuable in housing legislation and in economic studies. The number of families housed is comparatively small, and the returns of 4 or 5 per cent. are not attractive to the average investor in property.

In the report on "Better Houses for Negro Homes," [2] the following data referring to work in New York are set down:

> About twenty years ago, the Phelps-Stokes family, because of their interest in Negro welfare, purchased stock (in the City and Suburban Homes Co.) to provide for the erection of five buildings to accommodate 175 colored families. These buildings are known as the Tuskegee and the Hampton Apartments in West 62nd and 63rd Streets. They are built from especially prepared plans which provide adequate light for every room. Hot water and steam are provided.
>
> Another illustration of "philanthropy on a business basis" is the erection by the Phipps Estate of New York of eight double apartment-houses on West 63rd Street, providing 162 two-, three-, and four-room apartments, built in 1907, and four buildings on West 64th Street, providing 184 similar apartments, built in 1911. The apartments are provided with steam, as well as hot and cold water, and are under careful supervision.

[2] *Better Houses for Negro Homes.* Prepared and published by The Commission on the Church and Race Relations, Federal Council of the Churches of Christ in America, September, 1925.

THE OCTAVIA HILL ASSOCIATION

The Octavia Hill Association, with offices at 64 Lombard Street, Philadelphia, states as its purpose: "An organization for improving the living-conditions of the poorer residence districts of Philadelphia."

While not directly concerned with Negroes, the association has 147 colored tenant families. Forty-seven families live in houses and tenements owned by the association, and 100 in managed properties.

The plan following is that of Miss Octavia Hill, carried on in the worst parts of London under the inspiration of John Ruskin. Improvement of old houses, bought outright, or managed as agents, and friendly contacts with tenants, is the basis of work. For many years this work was carried on by volunteers, returning only a small rate of earnings. Friendly rent collectors learned to know their families by weekly visits to collect rents, and often could help or advise them in family problems. The houses handled by the association were models of what can be done with old properties, by using care and thought.

The work has now been put on a profit basis, but retains all the friendly and social-service features. Some old houses have been sold to take advantage of rise in property, or because of changing uses, and others have been purchased. New houses have been built, with careful attention to construction and costs, with fair rentals based on values.

Rentals have been made uniform for similar houses in similar locations, and are on a parity with rentals for houses not owned or managed by the association, eliminating the philanthropic features of the original plan. Maintenance, however, is superior, and repairs are made promptly and well. If a yard hydrant gets out of repair, a sink costing about $32 is put in the kitchen and the rent is raised a dollar a month, paying for the improvement in three years. Other improvements are put in after consultation with the tenant, and are paid for in the same way.

Through experience, the association finds that Negro tenants are anxious to have good homes. Prompt payment of rent is secured through the friendly rent collectors, who have opportunity to make helpful suggestions. There is no arbitrary control of tenants, except as conditions become insanitary or unhealthful.

There are no one-room dwellings in the houses owned by the association. Nine two-room dwellings are located in a well-equipped, well-lighted tenement-house, and four in houses. The tendency is to maintain for tenants only three-, four- and five-room dwellings. In managed properties there are twenty-seven one-room and thirty-five two-room dwellings. During the housing-shortage, some room overcrowding has been tolerated.

The following table, furnished by the Octavia Hill Association of Philadelphia, shows the dwellings occupied by colored tenants, with the number of rooms and the ratio of owned and managed properties.

TABLE XXXIII—NEGRO HOMES IN PHILADELPHIA, OPERATED BY OCTAVIA HILL ASSOCIATION *

No. of Rooms	Owned Properties		Managed Properties		Totals
	Houses	Tenements	Houses	Tenements	
1	..	..	..	27	27
2	4	9	7	28	48
3	22	..	14	5	41
4	11	..	8	2	21
5	1	..	1	1	3
6	..	..	6	..	6
7	..	..	1	..	1

* Data furnished by the Octavia Hill Association, Philadelphia.

Of the twenty-seven one-room tenements, eleven have one tenant each, fifteen have two tenants, and one has three. The evils of using one room for cooking, sleeping, and family life, have already been discussed. The rent charged for dwellings was discussed in the chapter on rentals.

The Octavia Hill Association plan offers attractive work to any group interested in bettering housing conditions, and willing to assume the details of financing, management and repairs. Volunteer or paid friendly rent collectors can do a fine bit of social-service work, with an unforced method of approach to family needs. The financial management can be learned by experience, or entrusted to an experienced agent. The response of tenants to coöperation in improving their homes is delightfully told by Miss Octavia Hill and her coworkers in London, and by the reports of the American group.

The Whittier Center Housing Company of Philadelphia built seven two-family houses in 1916 and in 1920 purchased and renovated 32 one-family dwellings, which have been rented exclusively to Negroes. They contemplate additional operations.

THE CINCINNATI MODEL HOMES COMPANY

About 1912, Mr. Jacob G. Schmidlapp, a man of many enterprises, became impressed by the need of testing out plans for the housing of persons earning a low wage, and especially Negroes. Low-rent houses were scarce in Cincinnati, and the work of General Sternberg in the construction of large numbers of wage-earner homes in Washington, D. C., was attracting wide discussion.

The first experiments were tried by Mr. Schmidlapp with his own money invested; and when he had found a suitable type of dwelling, the company was formed and fostered by him until his death. The project was never considered a philanthropic one, but was devised to give a fair investment return. The project had the advantage of ready money for good sites, of building on a large scale with consequent economies, and of friendly management. The ordinary rules were enforced; but families were given opportunities for good community recreation, and wholesome home-life.

Building has been carried on as funds have permitted, and as increasing costs of construction have dictated. Rents have been raised to allow a gross return of 12.5 per cent., covering 2 per cent. for taxes, 2 for depreciation, 3.5 for maintenance and repairs, and 5 per cent. dividend to investors. It was estimated that of each dollar spent in 1922, 37.4 per cent. went for taxes (excluding income tax), 24 per cent. for maintenance and repairs, 21 per cent. for overhead charges, consisting of insurance, salary of superintendent, etc., 10.4 per cent. for water, and 7.2 per cent. for the running of a hotel.

The Model Homes Company has fifteen groups of houses, located in various parts of Cincinnati. Flats and houses are occupied by 224 Negro families. The tenants are steadily improving home conditions, and are satisfactory to the company. Studies by the association indicate that crime and mortality among its tenants are far below the averages for the city.

St. Philip's, a Negro Episcopal Church in Harlem, manages several hundred houses for a reasonable rental, indicating that churches also can be of service in model-house projects.

SOME TYPICAL INDUSTRIAL DEVELOPMENTS

The building of industrial towns in connection with various kinds of mills has been a marked development of the past ten years. A considerable number of these towns have been located in the South; and where Negro employees are used, houses have been built for them.

In *Better Houses for Negro Homes* the following instances are given:

> The Aluminum Company of America has made a special bid for colored workmen in its Alcoa, Tennessee, plant. The town of Alcoa, adjoining Maryville, has a population of about two-thirds white and one-third colored, located in separate communities. Between fifteen and twenty colored families are buying, most of them on the contract basis, homes built by the company. The houses are equipped with electric lights, water-supply and sewer connections. They have a large yard space, back and front, for vegetable gardens and flowers.
>
> Badin, North Carolina, is built around the aluminum plant of the Tallassee Power Company. The village for the Negro workmen and their families is on the north side of the plant, and is divided into two wards, each having its own ward leaders and organization. The village consists of three- and four-room cottages, each having electric lights, running water, and connection with sewer. The prospectus of the company setting forth the advantages for workmen states: "There is nothing in our scheme which tends towards philanthropy. Our business is the manu-

facture of pig aluminum but our policy is far-sighted enough to realize that, in order to obtain efficient results from the employees, they must be a contented people. In order to arrive at such a condition, they must be well housed, and the sanitary condition of their town must be as nearly perfect as science can make it. Our views have been more than justified by the results obtained."

The Youngstown Sheet and Tube Co. (Ohio) has built 299 houses of three and four rooms to house Negro workmen in East Youngstown. The houses were built for rental, but about 3 per cent. of them have been bought by their occupants. The company is ready to sell on the rent payment basis to any of their workmen who so desire.

The American Rolling Mill Company of Middletown, Ohio, has found it necessary to make housing provision for its colored employees. . . . A camp was first built consisting of dormitories for men, a dining-room and kitchen, washrooms and a recreation hall. . . . This type of housing did not satisfy the men who brought or wished to send for their families, and the company induced the Middletown Realty Company to provide homes. The houses, provided with baths, electric lights, cistern water, gardens or similar improvements, were sold on easy terms to the colored workmen. The development extends several blocks on both sides of two fine streets.

These efforts indicate that housing is improvable: (1) By the city, in providing better zoning protection for Negro neighborhoods, in supplying municipal improvements that will make the areas occupied by Negro home owners as good as any in town, and by the passage and enforcement of proper health and building ordinances; (2) by private organizations of home owners themselves for neighborhood improvement, and by organizations of interested community leaders which can be effective by furnishing visiting housekeeper service, by stimulating city officials to keep everlastingly on the job, and by making demonstrations in model houses and blocks; (3) by philanthropic foundations and individuals on an investment basis.

The fact disclosed by the experience of philanthropists that the providing of good homes for Negroes is a profitable business undertaking in cities, may lead to building-operations on a scale sufficient to aid materially in relieving the present bad conditions in many places, when that fact comes generally to the attention of investors.

The improvement has just begun, however, and much remains to be done in the way of extending and strengthening the organizations interested in housing. Especially is there need for intelligent and non-political organization of the city departments dealing with building and health.

PART III: SCHOOLS
By W. A. Daniel

Chapter X

NORTHERN TRENDS AND POLICIES

The relation of Negro schools to their community and to the public-school administration gives rise to special problems that ought to be better understood. These problems, rather than the technical educational questions, are dealt with in this report.

In each of the seven northern cities studied, an effort was made to ascertain the attitude of the boards of education toward the separation of Negro and white children in the schools.

The special problems arising as a result were considered; and the currents of opinion with respect to them in the colored communities were gauged as carefully as possible.

In the South, where separation is a fixed policy, the work was confined to a study of the results of this policy as shown by the comparative shortage of trained teachers in Negro schools, and by inadequacy and neglect of plant and equipment.

Migration and Adjustment

The rate of growth of the Negro population in northern cities is a matter of increasing importance to those who exercise supervisory authority over the public schools. In the northern cities included in this survey,[1] the rate of increase from 1910 to 1920 ranged from 58.9 per cent. in Philadelphia to 1283.6 per cent. in Gary, Indiana, as compared with an increase of the white population in the same cities ranging from 15.4 per cent. in Philadelphia to 205.1 per cent. in Gary, during the same period. Such a growth of Negro population injects new problems into the public-school system.

The Negro and white increase is reversed in the southern

[1] Buffalo, Chicago, Dayton, Gary, Indianapolis, New York and Philadelphia.

cities,[2] with the exception of Winston-Salem.[3] For this group the rate of increase of the Negro population (1910-1920) ranges from a loss of 12 per cent. in Lynchburg to a gain of 47.9 per cent. in Knoxville. The white population of each of these cities showed an increase, ranging from 6.2 per cent. in Louisville, to 131.7 per cent. in Knoxville.

All of the northern cities included in this survey have mixed schools, attended by white and colored pupils. There has been a steady increase in the number of colored pupils in mixed schools, owing not only to the volume of the Negro migration to northern cities, but also to the increasing tendency of the Negro population to become more widely distributed within these cities. There has also been a very rapid increase in the number of colored pupils attending, and graduating from, northern high schools, according to the principals of these schools. Separate statistics of enrollment are not kept, except in Indianapolis where plans are under way for a separate high school for Negro pupils. Table XXXIV presents a comparison of Negro and white enrollment in that city.

TABLE XXXIV—NEGRO AND WHITE ENROLLMENT IN INDIANAPOLIS HIGH SCHOOLS BY SEMESTERS (JANUARY, 1919, TO JUNE, 1924)

| | ENROLLMENT | |
Semester Ending	Negro	White
January, 1919	203	5,230
June, 1919	313	5,536
January, 1920	401	5,802
June, 1920	490	6,115
January, 1921	491	6,194
June, 1921	596	6,795
January, 1922	628	7,103
June, 1922	699	7,837
January, 1923	714	7,886
June, 1923	784	8,356
January, 1924	858	8,231
June, 1924	873 *	8,828 *

* Enrollment to March 31, 1924.

[2] Atlanta, Knoxville (Tennessee), Lexington (Kentucky), Louisville, Lynchburg (Virginia), Memphis, New Orleans, Richmond (Virginia), and Winston-Salem (North Carolina).

[3] Winston City and Salem Town were consolidated as Winston-Salem in 1913.

In six years the enrollment of colored pupils increased from 203 to 873, or 330 per cent., while the enrollment of white pupils increased from 5,230 to 8,828, or 68.8 per cent. Thus the rate of increase in the colored enrollment in high school was 4.2 times that of the white enrollment. The rate of increase in the colored population over a ten-year period was 1.8 times that of the white population. Moreover, of the northern cities included in this survey, Indianapolis had next to the lowest rate of increase in colored population and next to the highest rate of increase in white population.

The rapid increase in the number of colored pupils is not the only thing of importance. A large part of the increase is made up of children from the South where standards of public-school education for Negroes are poor; and these pupils are therefore seriously handicapped when they go North. In proportion to their numbers they constitute an unduly large percentage of the retarded [4] pupils in the public schools. A study was made of those south-side elementary schools in Chicago that are attended almost wholly by Negro pupils. It shows a high percentage of retardation, which is also characteristic of groups of similar schools in other cities.

TABLE XXXV—RETARDATION IN CHICAGO SOUTH-SIDE
SCHOOLS

| | RETARDED PUPILS | | | |
| Retardation | In Schools With Largest Negro Enrollment | | In Total City | |
	Number	Per Cent.	Number	Per Cent.
Total enrollment	19,602	100.0	329,878	100.0
2 years	2,822	14.4	28,974	8.7
3 years	1,486	7.6	11,202	3.4
4 years	769	3.9	4,357	1.3
5 years	519	2.6	3,004	.9

Children who by experience are old but whose formal training is that of the young, present a disciplinary, as well as overage, problem. The fact that they are regarded as a

[4] For the purposes of this study retarded and overage are used synonymously.

problem is itself a factor. It is quite evident that they need constant and systematic special instruction.

Another special phase of this general problem of migration and adjustment is the enforcement of the compulsory education laws. Not only are these laws more rigidly enforced among white children than among Negroes, but the school census data are more complete. The Negro newcomers elude detection by the school authorities more easily than do the natives of a city who are traceable by birth certificates; and more easily also than children from foreign lands, who may be traced by city authorities through immigration records. Some violators of the compulsory education laws are reported by their neighbors. But the neighborhoods that contain the most offenders are the kind in which this is least likely to occur; and it is almost wholly in the deteriorated, overcrowded neighborhoods that the newcomers from the South live. A good illustration of this type of neighborhood, or group of neighborhoods, is the area on Chicago's west side served by the Foster, Garfield, Smith and Walsh schools. In the neighborhood of one of these schools alone there were found to be thirty-five Negro children under sixteen who had not attended school since coming to Chicago, and who were unable to read or write.

For many of the migrants, the major need vocationally is reading and writing. Night-schools have contributed much toward increased personal and vocational skill. In all of the cities included in this survey many adult Negroes, recent arrivals from the South, were seen in the public night-schools; and they were mainly in the reading, writing and arithmetic classes.

But a more rapid adjustment of the migrants to their new environment would result if the benefits of the night-schools were more widely advertised among Negro groups and more widely extended. The newcomers to a northern city, whether Negroes or foreigners, are most in need of the night-school, and know least about the opportunities that are open to them. In Buffalo, advertisements of the night-schools are inserted in the daily papers and in foreign-language papers, for a week or two before the term begins.

Posters in two colors are distributed throughout the city, especially in offices and factories where large numbers of men are employed. Children in the day-school take home printed announcements of the courses to be offered in the evening-schools. Moving-picture houses have displayed stereopticon slides advertising these courses for a week previous to the opening of the schools. The pupils recorded in active attendance in the night-schools the preceding year receive personal invitations to return. These are mailed a few days before the term opens. Moreover, a colored man has been employed by the school board to stimulate a wider interest among colored people in attending night-school.

In Chicago, the colored branch of the Y.M.C.A. has addressed itself to this task by giving publicity to night-school work and stimulating the attendance.

DISTRIBUTION AND SEGREGATION

Some northern cities not only have schools attended by both white and colored pupils, but also separate schools, or separate rooms, for colored pupils. The distribution of the colored pupils between separate schools and mixed schools is not wholly determined by the number of colored pupils in a given area. It was found that some of the Negro areas of greatest density are served by mixed schools; while some of the separate schools for colored pupils are more accessible to white pupils than to colored pupils. Of the northern cities included in this survey, Philadelphia, Indianapolis, Gary, and Dayton have some form of separate accommodations for Negro pupils. New York, Chicago and Buffalo have no separate schools or separate rooms within schools.

PHILADELPHIA

For school purposes, Philadelphia is divided into ten administrative districts. Colored pupils are found in all of these districts. Of the 201 elementary schools (June, 1925) only thirty-two had no colored pupils. The distribution of the colored pupils, as indicated in the following table, shows that in the majority of schools, the colored enrollment was less than 5 per cent. of the total.

TABLE XXXVI—PERCENTAGE OF NEGROES IN PHILADELPHIA SCHOOLS

Proportion of Negroes	Number of Schools
100 per cent.	8
90 to 100 per cent.	0
80 to 90 per cent.	1
70 to 80 per cent.	1
60 to 70 per cent.	0
50 to 60 per cent.	4
40 to 50 per cent.	8
30 to 40 per cent.	12
20 to 30 per cent.	15
10 to 20 per cent.	16
5 to 10 per cent.	21
1 to 5 per cent.	41
Less than 1 per cent.	42
No Negro pupils	32

There are some colored pupils in all Philadelphia's senior high schools, and in all of the junior high schools with the exception of Stetson and Thomas. Colored pupils are also enrolled in the normal school. There are no separate colored schools above the elementary grades.

Although the number of colored pupils in each mixed school is small, more than two-thirds of the colored elementary pupils, 68.2 per cent., are in mixed schools. This represents an increase over 1923 and 1924 not only in the per cent. of colored pupils in mixed elementary schools, but also in absolute numbers; i.e., the total number of colored pupils has increased, but the number in separate schools has decreased. The number of colored pupils in separate schools in 1923 was 8,718; in 1924, 8,400; and in 1925, 7,755.

This increase in the number and per cent. of colored pupils in mixed schools is the result of the thinning out of the congested Negro districts as the Negro population has spread itself over the city. Six of the eight separate colored schools showed a smaller enrollment each year from 1923 to 1925.

INDIANAPOLIS

There is a growing tendency toward segregation in public schools of Indianapolis. The records do not show the number of colored pupils prior to 1918. Beginning with 1918, however, they show a steady increase in the proportion of colored pupils assigned to separate colored schools. In 1918 the separate Negro schools had 81.4 per cent. of the total Negro enrollment in the elementary grades; in 1920, 89.7 per cent.; in 1922, 90.7 per cent.; and in 1925, 93 per cent. The proportion of the colored enrollment in secondary and elementary grades of separate schools will be increased with the opening of a separate high school now in process of erection (1925-1926).

There are fifteen elementary schools for Negro pupils and twenty-one mixed schools. The remaining forty-six schools have no colored pupils; in some cases because no colored pupils live in the school district, in other cases because the colored pupils living in the district have been assigned to separate schools or mixed schools out of the district. As in Philadelphia, the number of colored pupils in each mixed school is small.

TABLE XXXVII—PERCENTAGE OF NEGROES IN INDIANAPOLIS SCHOOLS

Proportion of Negroes	Number of Schools
100 per cent.	15
15 to 20 per cent.	0
10 to 15 per cent.	2
5 to 10 per cent.	3
1 to 5 per cent.	13
Less than 1 per cent.	3
No Negro pupils	46

GARY

There has been a growing tendency toward segregation also in Gary. Technically there is only one separate school in Gary, the "Virginia Street School." From the standpoint of distribution, however, there are two other separate schools, the East Pulaski and the Roosevelt Annex, one of which has a Negro head teacher, while the other has a Negro assistant principal. The Virginia Street School has a colored principal. All of the pupils and teachers in these three schools are colored.

The Virginia Street School has decidedly the worst plant in the city. The other two are well housed.

DAYTON

Tendencies toward racial segregation in the public schools of Dayton were halted by a recent decision of the Supreme Court of Ohio.[5] This decision was in support of previous decisions by the Court of Appeals of Montgomery County, Ohio, that "the discretion of the board of education, while a broad discretion, does not permit a segregation purely on the ground of race or color," [6] and later that "there is no power in the board of education of the city school district of the city of Dayton, Ohio, to separate the child of relator and other colored children in the Garfield school district or to maintain a separate colored school or separate department of said school for colored children." At the time of this decision, December 24, 1925, the Garfield School was the only school with separate rooms for colored pupils. All of the colored pupils in this school were taught in separate classes by colored teachers.

During the school-year 1924-1925, however, 156 of the 392 colored pupils in the Willard school were formed into four separate classes taught by colored teachers. The mothers of two of the pupils assigned to the separate classes became plaintiffs in proceedings against the board of education in which no decision was ever handed down; but the separate classes were discontinued.

NEGRO OPINION

The opinion of Negroes regarding the advantages and disadvantages of segregation in the public schools is itself a

[5] No. 19,573 Supreme Court of Ohio. *The Board of Education of the School District of the City of Dayton, Ohio,* v. *State of Ohio, ex rel Earl Reese.*

[6] Decision rendered July 3, 1925.

factor in the situation.   There is a difference of opinion. Some advocate segregation, their main arguments being:

1. Colored children in mixed schools are often neglected, and, in some cases, mistreated by white teachers.

2. Separate schools provide positions for Negro teachers and principals in cities in which they are not employed in the mixed schools.

3. The employment of Negro teachers and principals is an incentive to the Negro boy and girl.

The opponents of segregation admit the force of these arguments, but feel that they are offset by other considerations; mainly, the following:

1. "Separate but equal accommodations" is a fiction.   Nowhere has segregation inspired the Negro with the hope of a square deal.

2. Segregation is, and is intended to be, symbolic of the Negro's unfitness to associate with white people on the assumption that he belongs to a lower order of beings.

3. One form of segregation hastens the adoption of other forms.

4. If Negroes and whites are to live together satisfactorily in America, the public schools should not neglect this phase of their avowed purpose to train children for future citizenship.

5. Segregation increases the distances children have to travel to school, in some cases making it necessary for them to pay carfare, and in some cases subjecting them to dangers and delays in crossing streets with heavy traffic.

NEGRO PUPILS IN MIXED SCHOOLS

Mention has already been made of the fact that sometimes Negro pupils are not allowed to attend the school nearest to their homes, but must attend separate or mixed schools some distance away.

This often happens in neighborhoods into which Negroes are moving, and when the neighborhood school, though having a mixed attendance, is attempting to keep the number of colored pupils to a minimum.   In a case of this kind the

white parents oppose the change of the school to one exclusively for Negroes because that would make it necessary
for white children to attend other schools at a distance.
Meanwhile there is a growing surplus of Negro children in
the neighborhood who are not admitted to the local school.

In cases of this kind it seems necessary to leave a certain
amount of latitude to the principal; but this policy sometimes
works hardship upon a principal who tries to be fair to all.
The principal of one of two neighboring schools in the path
of advancing Negro population refused to accept Negro
pupils, and sent them to a separate school some distance
away. The principal of the other school accepted those who
belonged to her district in spite of the protests of the Parent-
Teacher Association, and the school board upheld the principal. The situation became so tense, however, that the
school board decided to transfer the principal to another
part of the city. The parents were afraid that the school
would soon become a colored school if colored pupils were
admitted. They were moved also by a desire to check the
movement of Negroes into their neighborhood by forcing
them to go long distances to attend separate schools.

While this is characteristic of schools in changing neighborhoods, it is not limited to schools in neighborhoods into
which Negroes are moving. It is not at all uncommon for
a Negro pupil "belonging" to a mixed school by residence to
be asked by a white teacher or pupil: "Why don't you go to
the —— school *where you belong*?" The —— school is invariably a school attended wholly or almost wholly by Negro
pupils, and may be in another part of the city.

If the principal of the mixed school has this attitude, colored pupils are disposed of in summary fashion. As soon as
a colored pupil gives trouble he is transferred to a colored
school. Thus the principal of a given Negro school expects
to receive discipline-cases of colored children from certain
near-by mixed schools, while other mixed schools in his
neighborhood handle their own discipline-cases (white and
colored).

Just as a mixed school gets a reputation for accepting or
rejecting colored pupils, it also establishes a reputation for

its fairness or unfairness toward them. Objection is raised to the fact that some principals suspend colored pupils for certain offenses, but do not suspend white pupils for the same offenses.

The desire to be rid of colored pupils is not altogether a matter of race prejudice, as this term is generally understood; because in schools there is an emphasis on promotions, attendance and ratings of various kinds, and pupils likely to lower the "record" are not wanted.

There are, however, many rumors afloat in Negro communities concerning the policies and attitudes of different principals and teachers. Some of these reports are true and some are not; but the Negroes believe them and act accordingly. Often a parent's assumption of unfair treatment by principal or teacher precludes all possibility of understanding that the pupil may have been partly or wholly at fault. Pupils are quick to take advantage of a situation of this kind. On the other hand, a principal who has a "good" reputation among the colored patrons can do some things with impunity that another principal would not dare to attempt.

Seating arrangements in mixed schools differ widely; and often depend on the attitude of the teachers, some of whom feel that Negro children are mentally inferior to white children and, for this reason or for other reasons, should not be allowed to associate with the white pupils; while other teachers feel that they are entitled to the same consideration, or that they should be specially encouraged because they are handicapped. Colored pupils sometimes occupy only the front seats or the back seats; in some schools or rooms they are grouped on one side, or occupy alternate rows; sometimes they are seated without regard to race; or they share seats with white pupils, a method used regularly by one teacher for punishing white pupils. In one room a colored pupil is literally forced to take the back seat, in another room he is the president of his class and in another the editor of the paper, in another in charge of the tool room, while in another he is expected to do more than his share of menial tasks.

Overage Pupils

The fact that a very large proportion of the colored pupils are overage for their grade is often accepted as evidence of inferior mentality. The prevalence of this opinion is probably owing to the fact that under normal circumstances the number of white pupils classified as "overage" is virtually the same as the number who are making slow progress. This is not true of colored pupils, because many of them are from southern schools with poor standards, and because the early education of many was neglected entirely. The low educational background of their families, economic necessity which makes it necessary for both parents to work, frequent moving, and other factors handicap many of the Negro pupils.

Retardation caused by these handicaps should not be confused with retardation caused by failure of promotion under normal circumstances. As school records show the age of each pupil in each grade, principals and teachers can easily compare the records of white and of colored pupils. In the classrooms, on the playgrounds, and at assembly they also can see that many of the colored pupils are much older and larger than any of the white pupils in the school. The fact that many Negro pupils are overage is therefore brought prominently to their attention; and often it is accepted as proof of mental inferiority, especially by principals and teachers inclined to the belief, as many are, that Negroes are naturally backward. This mistake is avoided, however, when the principal is at pains to determine the *rate of progress,* as in Table XXXVIII, instead of drawing his conclusions entirely from the hidden symptoms of an age-grade table.

TABLE XXXVIII—OVERAGE AND SLOW-PROGRESS PUPILS IN ONE SCHOOL

CLASS OF PUPILS	WHITE		COLORED	
	Number	Per Cent.	Number	Per Cent.
Overage	109	44.8	447	70.9
Slow-progress	108	44.4	240	38.1

In this table all pupils whose rate of progress was less than the normal rate were counted as "slow-progress" pupils. For the white pupils there is a definite correlation between overage and slow progress; but for the colored pupils there is a clear contrast. Of the 109 white pupils who were overage, 108 were slow-progress pupils, while of 447 colored pupils who were overage, 240 were slow-progress pupils; thus the percentage of slow progress among the colored pupils is less than among the white pupils. This does not prove that the colored pupils were superior to the whites; but if the figures were reversed, the average principal of a mixed school, with the best of intentions toward colored people, would accept them as proof. The better showing of the colored pupils in this case was owing to the very large number of them who were overage, 70.9 per cent. Many in this group were merely *pedagogically retarded*, not *mentally deficient*, as is commonly assumed, and these tend to progress faster and to catch up with their normal grade. Wherever there are special overage classes composed entirely of pedagogically retarded pupils, there is a saving to the school board because of the number of extra promotions, as is shown in Table XXXIX.

TABLE XXXIX—NEGRO PROMOTIONS IN ONE
SEMESTER IN FOUR OVERAGE CLASSES

| Room | Number of Pupils Who Were Promoted | | | Total Semesters | Saving to the School Board in Semesters |
	2 Semesters	3 Semesters	4 Semesters		
1	4	4	2	28	18
2	5	0	0	10	5
3	9	5	3	45	28
4	15	2	2	44	25
Total	33	11	7	127	76

Unfortunately, there is a tendency to make these classes essentially a catch-all for the misfits in the regular grades, including subnormals and disciplinary cases. The problem is aggravated also if the special class is thought to be a device for introducing segregation. This was the contention of the colored people of Dayton, Ohio, in the Willard case.[7] The

7 See p. 180.

petition filed by attorneys for the plaintiffs in injunction proceedings against the school board seemed to rest mainly on
the point that whereas 156 colored pupils [8] were assigned to
four special classes for retarded pupils, no white pupils were
assigned to such classes, although there were retarded white
pupils in the regular grades.

Curricula and Extra-curricular Activities

Just as there are facts indicating a tendency in mixed
schools to have certain arrangements for colored pupils only,
there are other facts indicating a tendency to exclude colored
pupils from certain courses. This tendency in the schools
seems to be a reflection of the situation outside of the schools.
Thus, if it appears that colored pupils will probably have
great difficulty in finding employment at the completion of a
given course of study, or are likely to be seriously handicapped in getting the prescribed amount of practice during
the period of training, they are advised to try other courses;
and in some cases the "advice" assumes the proportions of a
requirement.

There are three types of courses to which this applies:
commercial courses, certain trade courses, and teacher-training courses, if it is felt that there are already enough Negro
graduates on the waiting list, or that the number of Negro
teachers in mixed schools is getting too large. The former
applies to cities with one or more separate schools, the latter
to cities that have no separate schools. Cities with some separate schools or separate rooms employ colored teachers for
these only. The openings for colored teachers in these cities
are, therefore, very limited, since the colored pupils are in
the minority and most of them are in mixed schools in all of
the northern cities studied except Gary and Indianapolis.
A few cities that have no separate schools employ colored
teachers in mixed schools.

Negro pupils of exceptional ability in any of the extra-
curricular activities of mixed schools are usually encouraged
to participate. The policy with reference to the other Negro

[8] There were 392 colored pupils in the school and 501 white pupils.

pupils varies according to the attitudes of those in charge of the activities. A wide range of colored participants was found—athletes, debaters, participants in plays and pageants, members of literary societies, monitors, marshals, cadet-officers of the R.O.T.C., workers in the library, in the office, on the school paper, class officers, officers of the "general organization" which supervises all student activities, etc. The holding power of extra-curricular activities is widely accepted. They are generally recognized, also, as one means of reducing the number of cases of discipline. The extent to which colored pupils are barred from participation in the extra-curricular activities of a given school is a fairly accurate measure of the extent to which they lack a sense of identification with that school. Moreover, a sense of identification with the school, as contrasted with a purely institutionalized relationship, goes far to reduce the elimination of pupils. One large high school allows Negro boys on all of its athletic teams except basketball; but bars them in basketball because there are too many good basketball players among the colored students. There is a wider representation in athletics than in other extra-curricular activities, and there are many Negro captains of athletic teams. As a rule, colored pupils are not barred from the semi-academic clubs, as, for example, the science club, the French club, etc. The "Arista" and other honor societies, some based mainly on scholarship, others including also additional qualifications, seldom discriminate against Negroes in electing members.

Use of Intelligence Tests

In addition to the overage of Negro pupils, the assumption that they are mentally inferior has contributed to the desire for separation. There are wide and important differences between individuals in native mental ability, and to determine these accurately would be of great value in educational administration. Recently a popular method of estimating these differences has been by the use of "intelligence tests"; and it is very commonly believed that native mental capacities are being measured by these "intelligence tests,"

As a matter of fact, the test results are determined by many factors besides the native mental ability of the pupils tested. A careful consideration must be given to such factors as language, physical condition, education, home environment, outside employment, freedom from interruptions, motivation, and different habits of thought. All of these considerations should suggest extreme caution in any attempt to draw conclusions concerning the relative intelligence of different pupils, or of different racial groups of pupils, on the basis of the "tests." A child of normal native ability will appear to be subnormal according to the "tests" if his hearing is defective, or if he has been inattentive or absent, or if he presents a disciplinary problem. Besides, his vocabulary and his motor reactions may be poor because of home conditions, particularly in the earlier years.

The groups whose ratings by intelligence testing are most affected by such factors as these are foreigners and Negro newcomers. The results from the tests given in the United States Army during the World War showed higher ratings for northern Negroes than for some white groups or for southern Negroes, indicating that the test-scores were affected by other factors than native mental ability. Changes in these factors are paralleled by changes of varying amounts in the test-scores.

It has been discovered that many Negro children from the South who made very low scores when they were first tested were tested with very different results after attending northern schools. Some cases were collected in this study showing increases and decreases of thirty or forty points between scores made soon after arrival in the North and scores on later tests. Thus, according to the assumptions that lie behind the mental tests, some gained and others lost one-third of the mental ability with which they were endowed at birth. Obviously, tests of this character are not reliable tests of native mental ability.

There are, however, some devotees of "intelligence testing" who admit that the tests now in use cannot be regarded as tests of native mental ability; but who assume that they do measure those native qualities which it is most important for schools to determine as indices of comparative probabilities of success in school and that these qualities, taken together, may be called "intelligence." Apparently these assumptions are incorrect:

> At first thought it would seem reasonable that since intelligence is an obvious asset of a teacher and since so much progress has been made in perfecting intelligence tests, the time has come to make use of these tests in connection with the examination given to those entering the teaching profession.
>
> In the recent examination for License Number One, it was thought that some light might be shed on this question by determining the correlation existing between the intelligence quotient of candidates and their standing in the written examination. It happened that the graduates of the New York Training School and the Maxwell Training School had been given group intelligence tests at their respective institutions, and it was decided to make use of the results of these tests, which were kindly made available by the principals of the training schools. The correlation between ranking in intelligence and ranking in the written test were calculated according to Pearson's formula with the following results: for one school the correlation was .42 and for the other .24. In other words the extent of agreement between standing in intelligence and success in the written examination is in the one case low and in the other insignificant.[9]

The popularity of "intelligence tests" is owing in part to the fact that they are comparatively new and are regarded as being therefore up-to-date, progressive steps. In the minds of many people they are not subject to critical judgment at all, but are believed in and defended. Contradictory cases are dismissed as "exceptions."

The following facts concerning twenty-seven colored pupils who failed their first semester in high school are quoted from a study made by the principal of the school, and show how contradictions are often brushed aside.

7 had Intelligence Quotients below 80.
3 entered two weeks or more late.
8 had absences amounting to t   weeks or more.
7 admitted practically no study outside of school.
9 showed very poor preparation.
12 showed an excessive amount of laziness, insubordination, foolishness, truancy, etc. One of these had a bad police record. All of these twelve, judging from their I. Q.'s and preparation had a chance to pass. One had an I. Q. of 107, another of 99 and another of 98.

[9] *Twenty-fifth Annual Report of the Superintendent of Schools, New York, 1923,* pp. 25-26.

Although fourteen passing pupils had lower intelligence quotients than the average for the twenty-seven failing pupils, it is asserted that "the intelligence quotients alone are enough to explain the major part of the failures." Moreover, "twelve, judging from their intelligence quotients and preparation, had a chance to pass," but failed because of "an excessive amount of laziness, insubordination, foolishness, truancy, etc." To these causes of failure for twelve pupils must be added other stated causes of failure for other pupils; late entrance, absences, "practically no study outside of school," very poor preparation and an excessive amount of outside work. In only seven of the twenty-seven cases was the intelligence quotient alone given as the cause of the failure when the causes of failure were enumerated.

Thus intelligence tests became a convenient means of proving the inferiority of Negro mentality and were made the excuse for establishing separate classes. However, the main fallacy of separating races on the basis of these individual tests lies in the fact that while there may be slight differences in average scores made by groups, there is always wide variation about the average, and the more able colored pupils test higher than the less able white pupils. The two groups overlap in intelligence.

Chapter XI

NORTHERN ENVIRONMENTAL FACTORS

Some of the problems that appear as school problems are in reality personal problems, family problems, or problems created in various ways by maladjustment. The ignorance of parents is a major factor, especially when it breeds indifference. In too many cases parents do not regard the education of their children as important enough to warrant the sacrifices necessary to insure the progress of the children in school. For example, it often happens that children are transferred from one school to another a week or two before the time of promotion because the family has moved, despite the possibility that the children will be handicapped in their school work as a result.

MOVING AND TRANSFER

Frequent moving is a major factor, partly for reasons beyond the control of the parents, and partly for reasons within their control. Nevertheless, frequent moving, by causing the frequent transfer of pupils from school to school, increases the educational and administrative burdens of the school system. Not only are the pupils who move affected, but also the pupils into whose classes they are transferred, unless the number of transferred pupils is very small in proportion to the total number of pupils in the class. The following was written by a principal of a school with enrollment 98 per cent. Negro:

> Last year we had 774 children take transfers during the year, and 475 were admitted by transfer. Our membership was 1,700. Only 54 per cent. of the children enrolled in September attended school throughout the year to June.

It would be incorrect to conclude that frequency of moving in itself indicates lack of interest in school affairs. One of the worst cases recorded in this study was that of a girl who had given her teacher three addresses in one week. The case is reported as follows:

> Found that family had lived in all three places, the mother said she had given up the rooms she had occupied, because of high rents. She seemed interested in having girl attend school although she is over seventeen and could be released if her services are needed at home.
>
> The mother was ill when call was made. She said she, with a grown son, had come to Chicago and had lived here the last six months. The son was willing to assume the responsibility of the family support in order that Katie might attend school. She had had no opportunity to do very much in the South and she at least wanted her to complete the grammar grades. Katie herself was present and seemed anxious to do what she could in school.

WORKING MOTHERS

Another important factor to be considered is the large number of Negro mothers who work away from home with the result that children oversleep, or go to school without proper food, or stay away entirely.

The following results were obtained in Chicago from a survey made by the principals of the south-side schools with the largest Negro enrollments:

There were 16,951 pupils present on the day when the count was made. It was found that 5,698, or 33.5 per cent. of the pupils, were left to themselves "either all the time or part of the time" because their parents worked, and that 4,904, or 29.5 per cent. of the pupils, did "not eat their breakfasts or lunches or both at home."

Sometimes when it is hard for men to find employment and wages are low, women of the wage-earning class can still get jobs at good wages. The cases of widows, deserted mothers, unmarried mothers, and otherwise unsupported mothers, add a considerable number to the list of women who work irrespective of the condition of the labor market for men. To these must also be added the cases of mothers who work because the wages of the fathers are not sufficient to meet the needs of the home, and of others who want to supplement their husbands' earnings even though it is not necessary for them to do so. It was shown in the chapter on rent that the high ratio of rent to the family income makes it necessary for both parents in many families to work.

A principal of a mixed school prepared the following table giving some comparative statistics on occupation of Negro and white parents. Ninety per cent. of the white mothers were housekeeping, as contrasted with 58 per cent. of the Negro mothers.

TABLE XL—OCCUPATION OF MOTHERS OF 317 PUPILS, GRADES 5-8

Occupation	Number		Per Cent.	
	White	Negro	White	Negro
Professional	1	1	1	1
Business	4	0	3	0
Skilled labor...............	5	20	4	11
Unskilled labor.............	0	5	0	3
Domestic service	2	48	2	27
Housekeeping	111	103	90	58
Total	123	177	100	100

In Chicago, 47.7 per cent. of the Negro women "twenty years of age and over" are gainfully employed, as contrasted with 34.5 per cent. of the native white women of native parentage for the same age-group.

The regular absence of the mother from the home almost always means unfavorable home conditions; and, if there are children in school, a part of the burden is shifted there, as in the following case:

> Called to see the mother who said she found it very difficult to get away from her work, but would make arrangements to come to the school a little later. The father has deserted the family, and since the mother is the only support, she says she must keep regularly employed. . . . Found later, in talking with the principal, that the children from this family had always been a problem in the school.
>
> The mother seemed willing to coöperate, but because she was away from home every day, seemed unable to keep the girls under her control. M— herself has given trouble on several occasions and it had been thought once that she would have to be taken care of in the parental school; but the teacher was willing to give her another trial, as the mother tried so hard to manage her properly.

Employment of Pupils

It is also true that a large number of pupils are employed. Some are self-supporting. In some cases parents want their children to work, although they know that the school work will suffer. On the other hand, there are many cases in which the parents are willing to make every necessary sacrifice to the end that their children may have a better chance. This case is illustrative:

> After talking with the mother, Visiting Teacher was convinced that the boy was overtaxing himself. The mother said he had a job in the morning before school time, would leave home at 6.30 and work until 11.30, and then would spend his time from 12.15 to 4.30 in the school. After school he returns to his place of employment and works from 5 P.M. until 8.30 and 9 at night. Mother said that this is done to help out the family, since only the father is employed and his wages are not adequate to provide for the family.
>
> Visiting Teacher explained to her that since the boy was over sixteen, he could be released from school and take regular employment. This, however, she did not want done, saying that none of her children had ever had a chance to get any education in the South and she wanted this boy to continue in school as long as he was willing to go. She said she would be willing to make the sacrifice and keep him there even if he had to stop work.

Poverty and Crowding

It frequently happens that the economic strain is so great that the quality and quantity of food, clothing and shelter are below any acceptable standard. A mother wrote the following to a teacher:

> Arther hasn't no clothes to wear. He has on all the clothes he got, and I have not a penny to buy soap. He can come to school with his face and hands clean, but his clothes he cannot do any better. I sent him to the county agent for shoes the third time and they won't give him no shoes. Mrs. —— promised to give him some clothes and she has not brought them yet and the shoes he got on now he found them in the alley.

In the following case the mother is dead. The father and children are living with a cousin. The oldest daughter has been reported as showing delinquent tendencies:

Another visit was made to the home of the cousin later. She feels very strongly that the children, especially the girls, need more supervision. Feels too that the father is not helping them to form right habits. According to her, two of the girls, B—, age fourteen, another child, age twelve, and a brother, age sixteen, all occupy the same bed. Mr. P— occupies a bed with a younger son and daughter. Mr. P— said that the family was at present occupying one large room, but the landlord had promised that he would rent him another room as soon as it is vacant.

Numbers of these cases showing the pressure of environment upon Negro pupils are in the hands of visiting teachers and truant officers.

The following case is too long to be reproduced here in full, but the essential facts of crowding, illness, and irregular attendance are culled from a long record revealing a type of health and housing problem which, with the rapid urbanization of the population, is becoming to an increasing extent also a school problem.

The immediate family consisted of a mother, father and eight children. In addition to these there was also a grandmother and grandfather and four children belonging to a sister who lived in another part of the city. There were only four rooms in the apartment. . . . When she kept complaining of colds and a cough which hung on, Visiting Teacher suggested that the child be taken to the dispensary for examination.

Mr. T— thought this was not necessary since the doctor was prescribing for her. The father had also brought home some cough medicine which he was using. . . . Mrs. T— finally decided to let Visiting Teacher take J— and K— (both of whom had been irregular in attendance because of illness) to the M.T.S. dispensary for examination.

The physician pronounced J— an advanced case of pulmonary tuberculosis, K— an incipient case and recommended that both children be taken to Oak Forest. Said he considered the case very urgent, and would make special arrangements to have them placed as soon as possible. [In the meantime the father, mother and children had moved to a new address.] The family at this new address was occupying one room in a basement and the cooking was done across the hall in a kitchen that was used by two other families who occupied rooms in the basement.

The Gang

Another phenomenon of city life that is becoming a more and more important school problem is the Negro gang. The gangs have brought no new problems to the Negro schools;

they have simply aggravated some of the existing problems—truancy, home-work, monitors, hold-ups, fighting, loitering, stealing and disorder in the classroom, particularly in the absence of the teacher. The pupil who is outstanding and recognized at school on any other basis than that which the gangs prescribe is likely to become a marked man. The gangs, like other mobs, want mediocrity and conformity. Like other mobs, they arrogate to themselves the "duty" of regulating affairs that have been officially and properly delegated to others. It was found, therefore, that the gangs like to "beat up" the monitors, so that all who do not resign will be ready to take orders from them. Another favorite performance is to "hold up" pupils for their lunches or lunch money and dare them to report it.

It is impossible to determine the extent to which gangs exert an influence upon the schools. The impression gained in this survey, however, was that the type of behavior which the gang represents is more extensive than is generally supposed. It was found, however, that some of the principals were keenly aware of the true nature of the problem of the gang and knew how to deal with it.

Coöperation with Parents

Very few of the parents visit the school except when sent for by a principal or teacher. Some do not know that they may visit the school, and some are indifferent and careless. The conception parents have of the school and "the teacher," as well as related concepts, largely determine their conception of their own "duty." The following note, the second note from this parent, was received by a teacher who had requested the mother to come in person as the signature on the first note looked suspicious:

> Yes, I wrote you a note to give you for I did not know what she did and far as me coming over I ain't coming for your all is spose to make them mind.

On the other hand, the lack of closer coöperation between the Negro parents and the schools is not wholly a matter of negligence. Attention has already been called to the much larger proportion of Negro mothers than of white mothers who work. In many cases loss of time from work means a real hardship. Then, too, some principals discourage visits unless the parents have been sent for. It is also a matter of common knowledge that many white people, school principals not excepted, want to deal with Negroes of whatever age as if they were children. Finally, where the principals leave the interviewing of parents to an assistant or clerk, the cases are usually disposed of in a summary manner without adequate consideration of the problems involved.

Visiting Teachers

The most satisfactory means of approach to the problem of closer coöperation between parents and school has been through the visiting teacher. The special field of the visiting teacher has been to handle the cases of children who are unadjusted to their school, home or community life.

> Such children include those who have fallen below standard in scholarship, but who are not subnormal; those whose conduct is below standard and who more or less show tendencies to delinquency; the average who are restless in the classroom, counting the days until they go to work; those who, finding it necessary to go to work, need advice; the adolescent; the indescribable, who are always in need of counsel; the precocious and the gifted children who do not find full scope for their interest and abilities; and those whose home conditions are so adverse that they need special supervision or guidance.[1]

These are some of the many problems of adjustment that are outside of the strictly "educational" work of the public schools, but which are, nevertheless, of great importance in relation to the larger problem of making the schools function most effectively. The following cases indicate something of the value of the work of the visiting teacher:

> Visiting Teacher asked to make visit here, as the girl had been absent since March 24th. She was having trouble with her eyes and was sent home by the school doctor. Had later returned but was not admitted. The principal was anxious to know whether or not the girl's eyes were receiving treatment.

[1] *The Visiting Teacher;* pamphlet issued by the National Committee on Visiting Teachers, p. 3.

Called at the home and found that the mother was only using home remedies. This child's eyes were still in bad condition. After much persuasion she agreed to allow her to be taken to dispensary and Visiting Teacher went with her. Secured a card and saw that she was entered as a patient. The mother promised to follow up dispensary visits. A call was made later to the home, and it was found that the girl had been attending the dispensary. She was helped so much by the treatment that the school doctor later admitted her.

The Visiting Teacher was told of a new little boy in the neighborhood whose hearing had been so impaired by an injury he received as a baby that his parents decided it would do no good to send him to school. The Visiting Teacher told them of the wonderful results obtained by sending children to the special rooms for the hard-of-hearing.

Later a child-study examination was arranged and a permit secured for the parents to place the child in a special division. He has now been in attendance these two years, during which time medical attention has been given and the teacher reports that the child is making wonderful progress.

The following case is that of a recent arrival in the North from a small southern town:

Not accustomed to the work of a big city school and being too confused to express herself intelligently when taking the preliminary test for grading, she made such a poor showing that she was placed in the special room for overage retarded children. In order to get even for what she considered injustice, F— decided to make no effort to do the work given her because, as she confided to the Visiting Teacher, she had already done work much more difficult and doing it over was simply a waste of time.

This attitude of mind soon had its effect on her behavior in the room and she came to the Visiting Teacher as a conduct case. A visit was made to the mother, who was employed during the day and had not taken the time to follow up the matter of the child's grade in school. Samples of work done in another school were brought to the teacher . . . and the child was allowed to take another test. The result was so good that she was regraded and she is now doing very successful work with a class two grades higher than the one in which she was placed.

The following letter from a principal presents, in part, the case of a ten-year-old girl, whose father has deserted the family. Her mother is working and the girl "is left quite too much to her own devices."

I'm anxious for any information and advice you can give me in regard to H—. Last week she took sixteen dollars from a locked drawer in her teacher's desk. Once before she stole her pitch-pipe and she has been suspected of various minor thefts—all since coming here the middle of April. She is an attractive little miss of ten, and according both to her teacher and the Child Study Examiner (who has just examined her) she is of at least average brightness.

But she has these bad habits of taking what doesn't belong to her, and then of lying about it, as well as of lying at other times, when, as the examiner puts it, "it isn't necessary." The home conditions are bad. The father left the family January first and since then the mother and four children have been living in a seven-room flat with two other colored families. They have the two small bedrooms off the kitchen. The mother works so H— is left quite too much to her own devices. The family came up here from Mississippi two years ago and have lived in several different places since then, so that the children haven't had a chance to progress in school as they should.

Besides, H— has been sick with tuberculosis, her mother says. (I have written M.T.S. for a report on her health.) She seems pretty well now, however, so what is worrying me principally is her morals. Her teacher is greatly interested in her, is watching her carefully and sends H— with a report to me once a week. (If she is good she is to get a picture of a bird as a little reward.)

Then I have talked frankly with Mrs. —— with whom her mother lives and she promises to do what she can for her. I have also interested one of the leading girls in 8 B. in her and she is acting as a "Big Sister" to H—. And as soon as I get reports from all the agencies registered on the family, I shall have another talk with the mother. I can also lend H— books to read and that project seems to please her.

But what I should like would be to find some club or class in this neighborhood which she could join to keep her busy some of the days between 3.15 and supper time. Do you know of any such in this region? ——, I understand, has no classes for the colored and I don't know of any other society that does in this neighborhood. Could the Urban League help in such a situation? Or can you suggest any other person or organization that could?

"Outside" Organizations

A large number of pupils stop school to go to work soon after they reach the age at which they can legally do so. With some it is a matter of necessity, with others it is a matter of a lack of interest or of foresight on the part of parent or pupil. This, in turn, is owing to a lack of a sufficient incentive as contrasted with some of the more attractive and immediately obtainable ends to be gained by with-drawing from school to go to work.

Attention has already been called to the fact that the school environment itself is not always one of stimulation and encouragement. What is needed is an outside force strong enough and extensive enough to offset the counter forces that directly or indirectly create the impression that children, especially Negro children, "ought not to waste too much time in school; they ought to go to work." A person assuming this attitude in a given case almost invariably means that any more time in school would be "too much time."

Some progress has already been made toward a solution of this problem. An unpublished report on the Negro in the public schools of Dayton says that "the per cent. of students dropping out of high school has for the past five years decreased more than 75 per cent. Part of this is due to the interest shown students by the educational commit-tees organized at the Y.M.C.A. in 1920 and also largely to the campaign conducted annually by the Theta Lambda Chapter of the Alpha Phi Alpha Fraternity."

The growth of cities, and the processes of urbanization of the population, increase the number and intensity of the out-of-school influences that affect the school. In addition, the policy of building large schools in the place of small and scattered units is gaining wide acceptance in the inter-est of a better classification and promotional program. These factors tend to create a situation in which the relation-ships between parents and school principals and superin-tendents are increasingly impersonal. This situation may be desirable or dangerous according to how it is met. It is too often met by various uncoördinated and conflicting efforts by groups seeking notoriety, with results that confuse or mislead the school authorities. There is great need for constant and constructive contacts between the school au-thorities and the colored people; and it is highly important that these contacts be of a thoroughly representative character.

Chapter XII

SOUTHERN ADMINISTRATION AND ORGANIZATION

School funds are not adequate to meet the needs either in the North or in the South. The South, however, is not only poorer than the North but also less disposed to distribute such funds as are available according to the school population. The Negro schools are a secondary consideration. In comparison with schools for white children they have fewer seats in proportion to the school population, more pupils per teacher, more double sessions, fewer teachers, poorer salaries, fewer and smaller playgrounds, and less adequate provision for the health and comfort of pupils and teachers. They also have few, if any, of the "extras," such as libraries, lunch-rooms, auditoriums and gymnasiums; and the courses of study in the high schools and normal schools are more restricted. In practice, the policy toward the Negro schools is based on a feeling that less care and attention must suffice.

The cities that show the greatest contrasts between the white schools and the colored schools in such items as those mentioned above are not in all cases the cities that show the greatest contrasts between them in current expenditures. The differences are owing mainly to long periods of neglect of the colored schools. The recent comparatively substantial efforts to improve both the white and the colored schools still leave the colored schools far behind the others, which also need to be further improved to bring them up to the best educational and physical standards.

FINANCES

Some cities also need to improve their financial systems. One city still has three sets of figures; one for local consumption, one for the state report, and one for its report to the United States Bureau of Education. The following statistics are not given for the sake of comparisons with statistics in other reports, because per capita expenditures for public school purposes are usually reported on the basis of attendance or of enrollment. It is obvious, however, that comparisons of the per capita expenditures for white and for colored public schools in the South on this basis do not do justice to the facts, since attendance and enrollment are conditioned by the amount of money spent for teachers, supervision, buildings, equipment, attendance-enforcement, and other items that determine the efficiency of the public-school system. Moreover, a larger proportion of the school-dollar is spent for "instruction" in one city than in another; and so also for the other items of expenditure. The following comparisons are based on the amount spent per child of school age, according to the latest school census, and represent a composite compilation for four cities:

Item of Expense	White	Negro
Capital investment	$172.64	$61.59
Current expenses	48.96	29.16

"Capital Investment," as used here, includes the value of school-sites, buildings, equipment, and "permanent improvements." The figures in the above table are based on the value of the school property in Louisville, Richmond, Winston-Salem and Memphis. "Current Expenses," as used here, includes the cost of instruction, operation and maintenance. The figures in the above table are based on the costs of these items in Louisville, Richmond, Lexington and Memphis.

Table XLI shows the comparative costs in different grades of schools in two cities.

Often when the Negro's vote has been needed to pass a bond issue, there has been a more equitable distribution of the funds obtained by the sale of the bonds than there has been of the current school funds. This is owing to the fact that in the southern cities studied, and in the South generally, the Negroes have almost no voice in the city gov-

TABLE XLI—PER CAPITA CURRENT EXPENSES (BASED ON AVERAGE ATTENDANCE)

	White	*Negro*
Louisville		
Normal schools	$172.04	$68.72
High schools	98.41	88.92
Elementary schools	55.66	47.91
Special schools	129.58	107.63
Kindergartens	53.77	51.89
Night-schools	18.99	9.29
New Orleans *		
High schools	$109.51	$71.43
Elementary schools	59.18	36.03
Night-schools	15.28	8.09

* This does not include either the F. T. Nicholls school, of secondary grade, which offers industrial courses for white girls, with an average cost per pupil of $189.09, or the white normal school, with an average cost per pupil of $173.66, making a total cost per white pupil for the whole city of $63.09; for colored pupils, $34.82.

ernment, and are not in a position to defend the interests of the Negro pupils. It is therefore difficult for a superintendent of schools in a southern city to obtain fair treatment for the colored constituency.

STANDARDS

The most logical and effective procedure would seem to be for the superintendent of schools to secure the adoption of definite standards for the city. The best educational practice requires the development of standards for the size and location of sites for schools; for the planning and erection of school buildings; for the heating, lighting, ventilation, sanitary arrangements, etc., of schools; for upkeep and repairs; for the janitorial service; for the size, condition and equipment of playgrounds; for the size of classes, for the length of the school day; for the education and compensation of the administrative and teaching staff; for the courses of study and the promotion of pupils; and for the keeping of financial and educational records.

Even the cities in which different and inferior standards

have been adopted for the Negro schools show improvements over cities with undefined standards. This is especially noticeable in the education and experience required of teachers, and in the salary schedules. There are still teachers in Negro elementary schools who themselves have not completed the elementary grades. In some cases it is still possible for such teachers to get themselves appointed, particularly if they can get a letter from some influential white person in the city. One woman who was appointed principal says that her letter read as follows: "I do not know Mary, but I believe she has the right spirit." One man who had been a waiter in a hotel secured the following recommendation from the manager of the hotel: "I do not know how much James knows, but he has been a mighty good boy."

Although there are many people who secured their appointments in this way, it is becoming increasingly difficult to secure an appointment on this basis, owing to the adoption of minimum standards for appointments to the elementary schools where the abuse was the greatest. The difficulty now is in the adoption of the correspondingly higher standards of eligibility for appointments to the high schools and normal schools. With reference to schools of all grades, the best practice requires that appointments made as exceptions to the adopted standard be not permanent appointments, otherwise they would, in effect, lower the standard. Moreover, appointees without regular rank and pay would find it necessary to measure up to the standards of the system or be forced out as soon as there were enough qualified applicants. This applies especially to principalships and to teaching positions in the high schools and normal schools. Present practice offers but feeble incentive for elementary teachers to qualify for these positions.

But the needs of the situation are not met merely by the fixing and enforcing of standards.

TEACHERS' PAY AND CERTIFICATION

Suitable salary increases help to maintain standards. "Provision should be made for increasing a teacher's position on the salary schedule at any time she secures additional training of one-fourth or more of a year." [1]

North Carolina has adopted this policy. As a result there were, in 1926, more than 1,700 colored teachers in summer-school courses of college grade, as contrasted with eight in South Carolina.

Successful teaching experience also merits consideration in the working out of the salary-scale. The placing of appointments and of increases in salary on an impersonal basis goes far to remove from the public mind suspicions of petty graft and other abuses, and gives the teaching profession a higher standing than it has when a system of personal bargaining is in vogue.

The personnel of the teaching staff is the most important factor in determining the efficiency of schools; and the problem of securing good teachers is largely a question of money. Nevertheless, some of the southern cities pay the janitors of schools more than the teachers; and this in no case means that the janitors are overpaid. It is therefore not at all uncommon for pupils, as well as for parents, to feel that nothing is to be gained by "getting an education." Moreover, many Negro teachers are forced to spend their vacations in domestic service or hotel work, and some find it necessary to do manual labor even during the school term, to supplement their meager salaries.

The schedule of salaries in Lexington provides a minimum of $1,000 for white elementary teachers, and a maximum of $900 for colored elementary teachers. The minimum for white high-school teachers is $1,400, while the maximum for colored high-school teachers is $1,200. White teachers receive $35 additional pay for summer-school work, and Negro teachers $20. The annual increment for white teachers is $50, for Negro teachers $25.

In Memphis, the minimum salary for white elementary teachers is $1,000, and the maximum is $1,600. The minimum for the colored elementary teachers holding certificates

<hr>

[1] *Report of the Survey of the Public School System of Atlanta, Ga.* Made by the Division of Field Studies, Institute of Educational Research, Teachers College, Columbia University, New York City, 1922, Vol. II, p. 187.

is $720, and the maximum is $1,020. In the high schools, the white teachers receive a minimum of $1,400 and a maximum of $1,920; the colored teachers a minimum of $1,020 and a maximum of $1,680.

In New Orleans, the minimum salary for white elementary teachers is $1,200. The maximum is $1,750 for teachers without degrees, with an additional $150 for holders of the bachelor's degree, and an additional $150 for holders of the master's degree, or a maximum of $2,150. The minimum salary for the colored elementary teachers is $1,000. The maximum is $1,550 for teachers without degrees. Negro teachers holding degrees formerly received additional pay as indicated above for the whites, but this has been discontinued.

In the high schools, white teachers receive a minimum of $1,400 and a maximum of $3,300 (holders of the bachelor's degree). Colored high-school teachers with the bachelor's degree receive from $1,100 to $2,300.

The following is a consolidated table, showing the distribution of white and of Negro teachers in the designated salary-classes for four southern cities: Winston-Salem, Knoxville, Lexington, and Richmond:

TABLE XLII—TEACHERS' SALARIES, IN FOUR CITIES

Range	Normal and High Schools				Elementary and Junior High School				Total
	White		Negro		White		Negro		
	M	F	M	F	M	F	M	F	
$500 to $600....	..	..	..	..	..	2	..	8	10
600 to 700....	..	..	..	4	..	2	1	34	41
700 to 800....	..	..	..	4	..	3	1	128	136
800 to 900....	..	..	5	15	..	5	..	76	101
900 to 1,000....	..	..	5	5	..	73	2	27	112
1,000 to 1,300....	1	43	8	14	1	583	17	75	742
1,300 to 1,600....	6	44	10	2	6	267	4	2	341
1,600 to 2,000....	28	58	1	..	17	212	2	..	318
2,000 to 2,500....	29	50	2	..	8	76	..	..	165
2,500 to 3,000....	3	2	..	..	12	2	..	..	19
3,000 and over...	5	..	..	..	18	1	..	..	24
Total	72	197	31	44	62	1,226	27	350	2,009

In the normal schools and high schools only 20 per cent. of the Negro teachers are above the $1,000 to $1,300 range, which is the minimum for whites; and over half are below the minimum for whites. In the elementary and junior high schools, less than 1 per cent. of the white teachers, and almost two-thirds of the Negro teachers, 65.8 per cent., receive less than $900.

The system of certifying teachers in one state is not strictly comparable to the system in another. In the nomenclature, and in the requirements for the various grades of certificates, there are differences that make comparisons among cities in different states of little or no practical value. For the purposes of this study, therefore, a special classification of teachers in different cities was made on the basis of the certificates held. According to this method, teachers are placed in four corresponding, though perhaps not exactly equivalent, classes. Therefore the use of *A, B, C* and *D* in the following table is not a rating, but merely a designation.

TABLE XLIII—PERCENTAGE OF TEACHERS BY CLASS OF CERTIFICATE *

Class	Normal and High Schools		Elementary and Junior High Schools	
	White	*Negro*	*White*	*Negro*
A	70.4	45.0	13.5	4.9
B	24.9	38.5	51.4	43.4
C	1.5	7.7	21.7	19.9
D	3.2	8.8	13.4	31.8
Total	100.0	100.0	100.0	100.0

* The cities represented in this table are Richmond, Winston-Salem, Knoxville, and Memphis. Holders of "College Professional" and "College" certificates in Richmond are designated *A* in the above table; special certificates of college grade and "Normal Professional" certificates are designated as *B;* "Elementary Professional" and "Elementary" certificates are designated as *C;* and "Special" and "First Grade" certificates are designated as *D*. Holders of *A, B,* and *C* certificates in Winston-Salem are designated *A, B* and *C* respectively in the above table, and holders of the "A Elementary" and "B Elementary" certificates are designated *D*. According to the nomenclature and requirements in Knoxville, holders of the "Professional" certificate are designated as *A* in the above table; the "First Grade" certificate as *B;* the "Second Grade" certificate as *C*, and the "Temporary" certificate as *D*. College graduates in the Memphis system are listed above as *A;* those who have had "partial college" training as *B;* "normal graduates" as *C*, and all others as *D*.

These cities, taken together, constitute a fair average for the southern cities included in this survey. Louisville would rank higher than the average indicated here for Negro teachers. All of the teachers of academic subjects in the high school are college graduates; and there are eleven elementary teachers and principals with earned credits equivalent to four years of work above high school. The records, however, show amazingly poor preparation for some of the elementary principals, and for the normal-school faculty.

LOWER STANDARDS FOR HIGH SCHOOLS

As the schools for colored pupils become higher in grade the standards become relatively lower. In such items as salaries of teachers, preparation of teachers, courses of study, and laboratory and literary facilities, the contrasts between the Negro and the white high schools are greater than the contrasts between the Negro and the white elementary schools. In addition, the colored elementary schools are not all overcrowded, and all of them have the same number of grades as the white elementary schools of the same city (seven or eight years). On the other hand, all of the colored high-school buildings are badly crowded and some do not have four-year courses.

Richmond did not begin to develop a good Negro high school until 1916-1917, and did not have a modern high-school building for colored pupils until 1922-1923. This building contains 962 seats, had an enrollment in its second year of 1,032, and in 1925-1926 of 1,196.

Lynchburg did not have a four-year high school for Negro pupils until 1920-1921, and did not have a modern high-school building for them until 1923-1924. There was crowding in this building, owing to the fact that some classes of the sixth and the seventh grades were also taught here.

The Negro "industrial high school" of Charleston is an eleven-grade school adjoining the city dump heap.

There was no public high school for colored pupils in Atlanta until 1923-1924. It was built to accommodate 1,000 pupils, but 1,565 enrolled on the opening day. The enrollment for 1926 was 2,215. This school became a four-year high school in 1926-1927.

Lexington had its Negro high-school classes in one of the elementary schools until 1922, when a modern high-school building was erected, which was overcrowded the first year.

The high-school classes in Knoxville are being crowded out by elementary classes that overflow into a neighboring church, and into the basement of the colored library several blocks away. Instead of erecting a much-needed high-school building and abandoning the old one to elementary classes, the school authorities have been waiting for two opposing Negro factions to settle their differences in regard to a site for the building.

In Memphis, the colored high school has been housed for the past sixteen years in a building that was abandoned by a white elementary school sixteen years ago. The modern building in course of erection when the survey was made will accommodate about 900 pupils, according to the superintendent of schools. Memphis has never had a four-year public high school for colored pupils, because of crowded conditions at the old school. If the fourth year was added in 1926-1927, as was planned, the new building will have been badly crowded the first year. The net enrollment (February 28, 1926) was 849. The net enrollment of the first-year class was 403. Assuming that as large a class entered the following year (a larger one was expected), the net enrollment would be about 1,252, even if none who completed the three-year course in previous years returned.

In New Orleans, the three-year colored high school is housed in a building that was erected in 1883 as a white elementary school. It became a colored elementary school about fifteen years ago and one year of high-school work was added in 1916-1917, the first public high-school work for Negroes in that city. An additional grade was added each year, making a four-year high school in 1919-1920. It was reduced to a three-year high school in 1922-1923. It is estimated that about one-fourth of the three-year graduates take the fourth year in the high-school departments of the local denominational and independent colleges.

In addition to being crowded, therefore, most of the Negro high schools have been housed for a long time in old buildings that were not adapted to the needs of a high school; and when new buildings have been erected, they have invariably been too small. Furthermore, there is a tendency to "mark time" for a long period preceding the erection of a new building, on the grounds that the occupancy of the old building is a temporary arrangement. A *bona fide* temporary arrangement, however, need not interfere with the purchase of movable equipment such as lockers, laboratory apparatus and chemicals, books for the library, maps for the classrooms, desks, chairs, clocks and tables. And when the "temporary" arrangement extends over any considerable period, the health and comfort of the teachers and pupils require that necessary repairs be made to the heating plant, that necessary electrical fixtures be installed, especially for the dark halls and stairways characteristic of some of the old-style buildings, and that sanitary toilets be built.

TEACHER-TRAINING STANDARDS

No cities south of Washington have Negro normal schools that measure up to the standards of accrediting agencies in this field. The training of the teachers assigned to the training of Negro teachers, and the facilities at their disposal, do not entitle these schools to consideration as professional normal schools.

Yet all of the cities with normal schools, and some that offer no training above the high school, prefer their own graduates as teachers. A policy of inbreeding is cheap and convenient; but it does not produce the best results. It is strongly advocated, however, by a majority of the citizens. This policy is by no means confined to the colored schools nor to the South. The following conclusions and recommendations [2] prepared by a group of educational experts after a survey of the public schools of Philadelphia apply also to most of the cities included in this survey, especially the southern cities.

[2] Report of the Survey of the Public Schools of Philadelphia, by the Pennsylvania State Department of Instruction, Philadelphia, 1922, Book 3, pp. 177-178.

Two conclusions seem to resolve themselves from this study:

1. Through a practice pursued for many years of providing the entire supply of new teachers annually from the ranks of the graduates of the local normal schools and through a tradition which dictates that preference shall always be given to members of the teaching force of the local school system when vacancies occur or new positions are created, a system of inbreeding has developed which has practically isolated the Philadelphia school system from contact with other systems of public education.

Recommendations:

1. Definite steps should be taken to provide a flow of trained teachers into Philadelphia from outside and sufficient elasticity should be introduced into the machinery for the filling of vacancies and new positions that there may be attracted to these positions the most competent people obtainable regardless of whether or not they are already members of the Philadelphia teaching force.

2. The school authorities of Philadelphia, and particularly the superintendent's office, should address themselves at once to the problem of organizing and providing a plan of teacher training in service which shall be under the control of the school authorities and which shall be designed specifically to further the several objectives of the school system and to see that adequate incentives and opportunities are presented to the teaching force to undertake this work under favorable and attractive conditions.

Addenda:

1. Although undoubtedly the administrative and supervisory staff in Philadelphia have some academic knowledge of other school systems through reading and occasional visits, it is the contention of the Survey that this by no means provided the freshness of viewpoint and diversity of experience which is generally considered necessary to the health of every growing organization. It is not contended that Philadelphia lacks competent people within her own school system, but simply that the practically unbroken practice of supplying her administrative positions from within has deprived her of the services of leaders in other school systems, who without necessarily possessing any greater native competence, would have brought to the system a new basis of experience and a new angle of vision which would have been beneficial.

Of the southern cities included in this survey, Winston-Salem is an outstanding exception to this policy. Almost two-thirds of the colored teachers, or 65.4 per cent., and three-fourths of the white teachers, 75.7 per cent., are not from Winston-Salem. They come from various sections of the country. The plan for annual visits to be made to the colored schools and colleges by the superintendent of schools or the assistant superintendent is highly recommended. First of all it results in a large number of qualified applicants. Moreover, it makes possible a better appraisal of the relative worth of various applicants by interviewing them, seeing their records, and conferring with deans and teachers who have known the students intimately during their school careers.

For teachers of industrial subjects, Hampton, Tuskegee and some of the other schools for training industrial teachers, can be relied upon to sift through their lists of graduates and former students and recommend suitable prospects with various degrees of experience.

INDUSTRIAL TRAINING

It is generally believed that the so-called industrial education in the public high schools for Negroes in the South is a makeshift. The opportunities for first-hand observation afforded by this survey tend to confirm this impression. In the first place, teaching industrial subjects is more expensive than teaching academic subjects. It requires a larger outlay for equipment, raw materials, and teachers than the teaching of academic subjects does, and fewer pupils can be taught in the same space and time. Moreover, the high schools are so crowded with the classes in regular subjects required for accrediting that there is no room for more than a minimum amount of industrial training.

There is also a strong undercurrent of suspicion on the part of parents and pupils that the encouragement of industrial training will mean curtailment of other parts of the curriculum to the end that colored pupils will be denied access to subjects that are included as a matter of course in white high schools. This attitude is traceable to the fact that such changes have been made, and to the belief that the industrial work is not on as high a plane as the academic work.

The real choice of colored pupils is probably well indicated, however, by the subject-enrollment of colored pupils in the high schools of Indianapolis, where conditions more nearly approach those of a southern city than do the conditions in any other northern city included in this study; and where there are a wider range of subjects than in the Negro high schools of the South, and industrial courses of higher standard.

The following table is based upon a total pupil-enrollment of 859 and a total subject-enrollment of 3,271 in the Indianapolis high schools:

TABLE XLIV—ENROLLMENT BY SUBJECTS IN INDIANAPOLIS HIGH SCHOOLS

Subject	Subject-Enrollment	Per Cent. of Total Subject-Enrollment	Per Cent. of Pupils Enrolled
English	843	26	98
Mathematics	656	20	76
History	438	13	51
Latin	265	8	31
Modern languages.........	188	6	22
Science	186	6	22
Music	166	5	19
Domestic art..............	142	4	17
Domestic science	32	1	4
Commercial	116	4	14
Art	99	3	12
General shop..............	70	2	8
Auto repair...............	36	1	5
Mechanical drawing.......	34	1	4
Total	3,271	100	100

There is a noticeable avoidance of the industrial subjects. Domestic science (cooking) ranks lowest in the proportion of pupils enrolled, with only 3.7 per cent.; mechanical drawing second, with only 3.95 per cent.; auto-repair third, with only 4.9 per cent.; and general shop fourth, with 8.14 per cent. On the other hand, at the top of the list there are English, with 98.14 per cent.; mathematics, with 76.36; history, with 50.98; and Latin with 30.84; modern languages, science and art constitute an intermediate group. It is the general testimony of the principals of the northern high schools visited that most of the Negro pupils are inclined to avoid the industrial subjects. On the other hand, it is quite evident that some of the principals feel that it is their duty to guide as many Negro pupils toward industrial courses as possible.[3]

Some of the industrial teachers are evidently fitted by training and experience for far wider service than they can render in their present positions in the southern high schools for Negroes, and are discouraged by their limited opportunities; but this is the exception rather than the rule. The combined literary and technical training of most of the industrial teachers is much less than the literary training of the average teachers of academic subjects in the high schools.

Up to this point the discussion has been of the technical courses, or trade-work, of high-school grade. Turning now to the elementary schools, it must be said that the problem is of a different character. The industrial work of elementary grade, commonly called "manual training," has a different objective and a different method. The objective here is merely to secure "skill with the hands." The work therefore includes a little wood work, a little basketry, a little paper-cutting, and similar activities.

Only in the upper grades of Negro schools is industrial work taught by special teachers. This type of work is similar to that which has already been described for the high school, and is taught in the upper elementary grades that are included in the junior high school, in accordance with the present tendency in the organization of public-school systems. But in the elementary school proper, the classroom teachers teach the industrial work also. A beginning has been made toward providing so-called industrial supervisors; but, at the present stage of its development, this arrangement is very unsatisfactory. This is owing to the comparatively low educational standards and low salaries of the supervisors, who hold what is essentially a teacher-training position that requires high literary, technical-industrial, and technical-educational preparation.

---

[3] Nevertheless, as is pointed out in the discussion of the schools in the North, there are certain industrial courses from which Negro pupils are virtually barred.

DIFFERENTIATION OF INSTRUCTION

If the needs of the Negro school population are to be served adequately, there must be a more highly differentiated system of instruction than that now characteristic of the southern cities. In the cities studied, the best work has been done in the departmentalization of the upper elementary grades, and in organizing a system of coaching for ungraded, nutrition, and open-air classes. But efforts in this direction must be considerably extended to meet the needs. The range of subjects taught in the Negro high schools is very limited; and there are no continuation, vocational, or junior high schools for Negro pupils as there are for white pupils. The lack of kindergartens is indicated in Table XLV.

TABLE XLV—KINDERGARTENS IN EIGHT SOUTHERN CITIES

City	White	Negro
Atlanta	40	0
Lexington	8	1
Louisville	42	7
Lynchburg	5	0
Memphis	0	0
New Orleans	46	0
Richmond	21	0
Winston-Salem	0	0

Only Lexington and Louisville have colored kindergartens, and these do not meet the needs of the colored population. According to the school census taken during the month of April, 1925, there were 4,876 white children and 4,819 colored children in Lexington, with eight kindergartens for white children as against one for the colored. About the same time, March 1, 1925, there were 27,199 white elementary and high-school pupils in Louisville and 6,377 colored, a ratio of 4.3 to 1.0; but there were forty-two white kindergartens as against seven colored, a ratio of 6 to 1. "Studies have shown that where kindergartens are maintained there is less retardation, overage and elimination from school in the elementary school than in those cities where kindergartens are not provided"; [4] and all of these are known to be major problems for the colored schools.

TABLE XLVI—STATUS OF PUPILS IN FOUR SOUTHERN CITIES *

Class of Pupil	White %	Negro %
Normal	57.5	43.8
Overage	34.7	49.4
Underage	7.8	6.8
Total	100.0	100.0

* Data for Winston-Salem, Lynchburg, Knoxville and Louisville.

Table XLVI shows that almost half of the colored pupils and more than a third of the whites are overage. This is a consolidated table based on age-grade tables for Winston-Salem, Lynchburg, Knoxville and Louisville.

The problem of elimination in the elementary and high schools is indicated by the distribution of the enrollment. In computing the percentages in Table XLVII, Richmond is substituted for Louisville in the above list of cities, because Louisville has an eight-year elementary school, while Richmond has one with a seven-year course as have the other three cities.

TABLE XLVII—PERCENTAGE OF THE ENROLLMENT BY GRADE IN FOUR SOUTHERN CITIES *

Grade	White	Negro
I	14	21
2	13	14
3	12	13
4	12	13
5	11	10
6	10	8
7	8	8
8	7	7
9	6	3
10	4	2
11	3	1
Total	100	100

* Data for Winston-Salem, Lynchburg, Knoxville and Richmond.

[4] *Report of the Survey of the Public School System of Atlanta, Ga.,* made by the Division of Field Studies, Institute of Educational Research, Teachers College, Columbia University, New York, 1922, Vol. II, p. 141.

ATTENDANCE LAWS

A major problem for the Negro schools, which also is related to retardation and elimination, arises out of the lax enforcement of attendance laws. As compared with the white schools, the truant-officer service is slighted. It would seem that the reverse would be the case, as a much larger proportion of the Negro mothers than of white mothers are employed, thus necessitating more outside supervision of the Negro children to insure proper attendance. Certainly the Negro schools have a poorer attendance rate than the white schools.

| | RATIO OF ATTENDANCE TO ENROLLMENT | |
Grade of School	White %	Negro %
High school	89.6	87.9
Elementary school	85.2	82.2

If the attendance laws were enforced, however, the present facilities for housing colored pupils would have to be substantially increased, as there is already considerable overcrowding; and it is believed that disinclination to improve facilities accounts in part for laxity in enforcing attendance laws, including the issuance of work-permits. Moreover, there are some cases of failure to record absences, the purpose of the omission being to give a particular school or room a better record than it should have. Pupils are sometimes counted as being "present" merely because their absences are considered excusable.

The greater difficulty of enforcing the attendance law among colored pupils than among white pupils is owing in part to the greater crowding in the colored schools, which makes it necessary to hold double sessions and, in Atlanta, triple sessions. The prevalence in the South of the part-time sessions, whether double or single, in Negro schools, causes a large number of children to be out of school at all hours of the day, making it difficult for truant officers and neighbors who might report non-attendance to determine whether children seen away from school are offenders or not.

VOLUNTEER AID TO PUBLIC SCHOOLS

The desire on the part of white and of colored principals, and of parent-teacher associations, to raise the standards of comfort and efficiency of their schools by raising money to buy needed equipment is to be commended. Cases were observed in connection with some of the colored schools, however, in which this willingness had been imposed upon. Heating, lighting, and repairing of school buildings are necessary items of operation and upkeep; and it may be questioned whether it is a wise policy for principals and parent-teacher associations to provide money for these purposes. Money is frequently raised under such auspices to purchase land adjoining school property to provide play-space for the pupils. Sometimes the ground purchased is for building a school; sometimes a hall, a church, or an old dwelling-house is furnished "rent free" to the school board, which is satisfied to continue a makeshift arrangement of this kind indefinitely without planning to erect a suitable building for school purposes. Another result of a heavy money-raising program is that it makes some of the principals and teachers too dependent upon the good-will of certain patrons whose children must not be disciplined or denied promotion on the same basis as other children. As a rule, preparation for the various forms of entertainment resorted to as means of raising money takes the principal and some of the teachers and pupils for a time from what is ordinarily considered the work of a school.

Chapter XIII

SOUTHERN BUILDINGS AND EQUIPMENT

In the last chapter it was shown that the per capita investment for sites, buildings, equipment and "permanent improvements" for colored schools in four southern cities was little more than one-third as much as for white schools. It was not possible within the limitations of the present study to obtain more detailed data of an exact and tabulable character as to buildings and equipment. To have attempted to do so would have involved the rating by scale of the physical equipment of both white and colored schools in the cities investigated—in itself an elaborate study. It was felt, therefore, that the essential facts in the situation would be adequately covered by presenting the observations of a trained investigator who personally visited all of the colored and many of the white schools in the cities under discussion.

Most of the school buildings for colored pupils were found to be old and in poor condition, whether by comparison with accepted standards or with the white schools of the neighborhoods. Usually when Negroes had taken over white neighborhoods they had fallen heir to their predecessors' schools, although exceptional cases were found of white schools surrounded by colored residents or abandoned for school purposes.

In the building program for colored schools, lack of prevision was evident. Ninety per cent. of the new elementary schools, and all of the new high schools visited in the course of this survey, were built too small in the first place. With one or two exceptions, the buildings were over-run with pupils the first year, necessitating the holding of classes in rooms designed for cafeterias, libraries, teachers' rest-rooms, auditoriums, halls, and principals' offices. The use of such rooms means improvised blackboards and unsatisfactory disposition of cloaks and hats, which usually have to be put on front seats, on a bench, or on the floor. The best educational and financial policy requires that buildings be built to meet future, as well as present, needs; and in the case of white schools, at least an attempt is made to adhere to this policy.

Furthermore, various so-called temporary arrangements had frequently been allowed to exist for a very long time. "Portables" for the white schools are regarded as acceptable for temporary use only. For the Negro schools they are often multiplied indefinitely after a Negro neighborhood has grown large enough to warrant the erection of a modern school building.

With the annexation of new territory, county schools that are below city standards are added to the city school system. Almost invariably the probability of extending the city limits has been discussed for several years; and the county officials are inclined to neglect the school buildings involved, on the ground that the city will not reimburse them sufficiently to justify additional outlay. When the annexation is actually made, the outlying white districts receive attention first, while some sort of temporary arrangement is effected for the colored. What usually happens in such cases is that the older and bigger children then go "in town" to the larger and better, but already overcrowded, schools, which keeps the enrollment of the outlying schools small in proportion to the population of the area. Thus the temporary arrangement of a rented store or church is allowed to remain indefinitely, pending the enrollment of a larger number of pupils.

This kind of temporary arrangement for colored children is not limited, however, to the outlying sections, nor to rented stores and churches. The use of dwelling-houses is common; and instances were found of the use of a lodge-hall, a hospital, the loft of a fire-engine house, and the basement of a library. Most of this kind of property in use for school purposes was in a very dilapidated condition, and some of it had even been condemned by health and sanitary inspectors; but the property was cheap and, for that reason, considered highly desirable as a means of relieving the congestion of the regular school buildings. Two such buildings actually "fell in" during the school year of this survey. Virtually none of these makeshift schools had play-space. Where church buildings were used for schools there was sometimes an arrangement with the school board which did not allow the use of the electric lights, but which did include a provision that the church would be vacated whenever it might be needed for funerals.

SANITATION

The toilet facilities for these makeshift arrangements, as well as for many of the old school buildings, were usually limited and insanitary. Nearly always they compared unfavorably with white schools in regard to privacy, heating, lighting, ventilation, cleanliness and repair. Except in the new buildings, there were usually no separate toilets for teachers. In many places where the installation of water-flushed toilets would not have been difficult, none had been put in. The practice of boarding-up toilets, instead of making prompt repairs, was partly accountable for the limited number in proportion to the school enrollment. The following from the surveyor's report is fairly typical of the neglect of the old and overcrowded school building. The enrollment of this school was 1,233 at the time of the survey.

> Girls' basement. Eight water-closets, but five are boarded-up, making three usable. The principal and janitor said that a report was made each of the five times, but that nothing had been done about it.

EQUIPMENT

The equipment of the colored schools was found to be far behind that of the white schools. Adequate provisions for health and comfort, for heating, lighting and ventilation, and adequate toilets, drinking-fountains, cloak-rooms, etc., were found only in the newest buildings; and even the new buildings for colored pupils were sometimes equipped with old heating-plants, desks, manual-training equipment, cooking-room equipment, etc., taken over from white schools that had received new equipment. The unfinished condition of some of the new buildings was also apparent, although they had been in use two or three years. Knobs had not been put on the doors, and many doors that should have had glass in them had none; teachers' desks were lacking; electrical fixtures were installed but not connected; walls were unplastered; plumbing was incomplete; and other items were left unfinished.

The educational equipment, especially of the colored high schools, also revealed serious deficiencies as compared with the white schools. The equipment of libraries and laboratories was particularly poor, some of the latter having no water or gas connections.

The colored schools of Winston-Salem compared very favorably with the colored schools of southern cities generally. The following statement from a report of the Winston-Salem superintendent of schools, referring to the colored schools, is therefore applicable to the colored schools of all the southern cities visited:

> The materials of instruction are somewhat meager. Some schools have apparatus for visual instruction; others do not. The maps for history and geography are inadequate. There is a dearth of supplementary reading material. There are practically no libraries. This lack of equipment tends to make the instruction more of a textbook nature. A wider range of material, if used by the teacher, will put more interest into the work.[1]

CROWDING

As has been seen, the problem of excess enrollment in the Negro schools was met in part by providing makeshift classrooms in cafeteria, library, principal's office or hallway, as well as by the makeshift use of churches, dwelling-houses, lodge-halls, etc. Partly also it was met by double and triple sessions, and by crowding in pupils beyond the normal capacity of the classrooms. While overcrowding of classrooms is in most cities not confined to Negro schools, the practice was far more common, and conditions were a good

[1] *Tenth Annual Report of the Public Schools of the City of Winston-Salem, North Carolina*, p. 64.

deal worse, in the Negro than in the white schools of the southern cities studied. Desks were pushed against the walls, making access to blackboards and windows difficult; aisles were narrowed or eliminated altogether; two pupils were placed in single seats and three in double seats, while others were seated on chairs, benches and window-sills. Even then some of the pupils had to remain standing or sit on the floor. The seat-crowding was paralleled by class-crowding, *i.e.*, two or more classes recited in the same room at the same time.

Besides its educational and disciplinary disadvantages, overcrowding of this kind is unhealthy and unsafe. Several children were hurt in a fire-drill on the day one school was being surveyed. A real fire might prove disastrous.

Playgrounds

With the exception of Winston-Salem, none of the southern cities included in this survey was found to have adequate play-space for its colored pupils. Almost uniformly the Negro schools were at a disadvantage in this respect as compared with the white. Streets and alleys were often the only available playgrounds. Where play-space was available, insufficient attention had sometimes been given to surfacing it so as to provide free drainage and to minimize injuries from falls. The recreation section of this report emphasizes the need of more attention to the possibilities of schools as recreation centers.

Location of Site

In the nature of the case it was not to be expected that the sites for Negro schools would be as desirable as those for white schools. With all allowances for differences in neighborhoods made, however, the sites for colored schools seemed at times to have been selected with less judgment and foresight than should have been exercised. The original land purchase was inadequate, and the rise in property values caused by the coming of a school made impossible the acquiring of additional space. Many of the schools adjoined buildings that obstructed light and air; others were undesirable on account of their proximity to railroads, coalyards, factories or sawmills. Some were situated in alleys. Some were difficult of access in bad weather, owing to absence of sidewalks and even of streets.

Finally, it was not found that due consideration had been given to the probable results of various environmental factors upon the children who must attend a given school. The value of the available lands seemed to be almost the only consideration in locating a school for colored pupils.

Bond Issues

To correct these defects, which have been accumulating in Negro public-school plants for many years, large outlays of money are necessary. In nearly every city this money can be supplied only by the issuing of bonds. Recently money so raised in several southern cities has been very fairly divided between white and colored schools; but so much needed to be done before the bonds were issued that hardly more than a start has been made in supplying the deficiencies of the Negro schools. What more is done will depend largely upon the recognition by boards of education, and by the voting public, of the many urgent needs of Negro schools, and of their just claim to a fair share of money devoted to education.

PART IV: RECREATION

By Henry J. McGuinn

Chapter XIV

RECREATIONAL NEEDS

As there was known to be a great deal of delinquency among Negro children in overcrowded areas of large cities, an effort was made in this study to obtain data on the subject, and to ascertain how important a contributing cause the lack of wholesome recreation for the young people in these areas was believed to be by judges of children's courts and welfare workers acquainted with conditions and accustomed to dealing with juvenile delinquency cases.

The figures in Table XLVIII indicate that Negro children contribute a disproportionately large number of cases to city juvenile courts.

TABLE XLVIII—JUVENILE DELINQUENCY IN SEVEN CITIES

	Estimated Negroes in Total Population %	Negroes in Total Juvenile Cases %
Richmond (average 1921-24)	31.5	41.0
Chicago (1925)	5.0	16.0
Indianapolis (1925)	12.0	35.0
Gary (1925)	14.0	41.0
Dayton (1923)	6.0	27.0
Memphis (1925)	31.0	48.0
Charleston (1925)	47.0	75.0

Data gathered in this study from the records of the juvenile courts confirm the opinion of other students that during adolescence, the period of greatest emotional stress, the child is most likely to be the victim of social maladjustment. The records of the Cook County Juvenile Court, Chicago, for the year 1923, show that 3,072 of the 3,316 cases in which boys were involved, and 680 of the 886 cases involving girls, were those of children between the ages of eleven and sixteen, both groups reaching their peak in the sixteenth year. Similar data collected in Knoxville showed a marked concentration between the ages of twelve and fifteen. While age-data had not been collected for the city of Richmond, the judge of the juvenile court ventured the opinion that most of the cases brought before him represented the age-groupings between thirteen and seventeen years. The Report of the Children's Court of New York City (1923) shows that of a total 2,078 cases, 1,825 were those of children ten years of age and above. The fourteen-year-old group represented the peak in this instance. The significance of the above facts is important so far as all children are concerned, but especially important with reference to the Negro group because, as has been shown in this report, municipalities rarely provide play-areas that are adequate for the needs of adolescent Negro youth.

Causes of Delinquency

Judges and court workers, without exception, mentioned the economic factor as perhaps the chief contributing cause of excessive delinquency among Negro children. Low wages and the consequent inability of the father to support the family result in both parents going out to work, so that neither can be at home when the children should be sent to school. As the children return home before their parents do, and have little systematized recreation to attract their attention, they drift into trouble.

A second factor is the broken family. Court officials in at least five cities pointed to the fact that husbands regard loosely their marriage ties, desert their wives, and throw the responsibility of bread-winning upon the mothers who therefore have little time to devote to their children.

Lack of supervised recreation during the absence of parents was mentioned by court officials of Indianapolis, Charleston, Memphis, Richmond, and Louisville. In commenting on this situation one official said that cases of delinquency are much more frequent in Louisville in winter than in summer when the playgrounds are open, a fact that should cause the city to develop a year-around recreational program. The Director of the Bureau of Social Service of Charleston said that the older Negro boys who come into court present a very real problem. If a lack of healthy emotional outlet is the basic trouble, it is most unfortunate that there is no organization that offers these recreational opportunities. The only playground in Charleston is visited largely by younger children, and the older boys are likely to start trouble. Efforts to form Boy Scout troops have been blocked by the local scoutmaster. At present there is a club of 100 boys who have come under the jurisdiction of the court. The Negro welfare worker in Charleston has received some aid from a man interested in the work, and a club for under-privileged boys seems to be in the process of realization.

The court officials in Chicago were inclined to regard the large number of Negro delinquents as the result of maladjustment caused by the migration of the Negro. The court had similar experiences during the Polish and Irish influxes. One of the white probation officers mentioned a fact, which was also brought out in Charleston, that the percentage figures reflect to some extent the tendency on the part of the police to arrest Negroes more frequently than they arrest others.

Social workers were inclined to feel that a lack of recreational facilities on the south side, as well as the leniency of the court in dealing with offenders, helped to explain the situation. A Negro politician's son, who leads a group of disorderly boys, rules them by sheer bravado, and seems to know in advance that he will be dismissed without trial if arrested.

Recreation of a poor type was mentioned in four instances. A dance hall in Richmond, and another in Dayton, were condemned on the ground that they afforded chance meeting places for girls and men and boys bent on immoral purposes. In Charleston and Louisville, western pictures and crude vaudeville were mentioned as detrimental influences in the lives of young boys and girls. This is in keeping with the findings of authorities on the subject who stated that the fighting, shooting and stealing emphasized in western pictures is often found to be the basis of criminalistic imagery that affects young people.

There was a general lack of reference to "fundamental race differences" as a reason for Negro delinquency. One judge spoke of a "lack of inhibition," a process which he felt to be developed as a result of long contact with civilization; while another found an explanation in the fact that Negroes were wanting in "the traditions of Puritan morality which we have known for three hundred years." Most of the officials agreed that the explanation of a child's behavior is to be found in reactions to environment. In some of the southern cities, notably Memphis, Charleston, and Richmond, the effort to deal with the maladjustment of Negro children in an understanding manner is notable and commendable.

It appears that Negro children fight more frequently than white children, both on and off the school grounds. This would seem to call for stricter discipline in the school yards, and for regulation of dismissal to prevent children jostling one another. Better policing of Negro neighborhoods is also a necessity. The chief purpose should be to keep children from fighting, not to arrest them.

While there are many contributing causes to delinquency other than lack of wholesome recreation, there can be no doubt that well-planned and effective recreational and character-building agencies can be effective in reducing delinquency.

As real, yet more difficult to picture concretely, is the need for wholesome recreation to contribute to the physical and mental hygiene of the race. The studies are yet to be made measuring exactly the extent to which the bodily and mental development of Negroes is retarded by lack of directed play and organized athletics.

Chapter XV

MUNICIPAL FACILITIES

In the large cities, certain recreational activities for the young are provided and supervised by the municipalities themselves; others are provided by voluntary organizations like the Y.M.C.A.; still others are left to the initiative of individuals and groups whose sole objective too often is profit, and who carry on, in many cases, with little or no official supervision. In this chapter the recreational facilities provided by the cities will be considered; and those provided for Negro neighborhoods will be compared, to some extent, with those for white neighborhoods.

Parks

The facilities of the large parks in Philadelphia, New York, Buffalo, Chicago and Gary are accessible to Negroes. Important exceptions are in Buffalo, Chicago and Gary, in parks that have bathing-beaches. Here, where there is particularly likely to be friction, some type of separation is practiced. The director of the Colored Settlement House in Gary reports that a beach was recently set aside by the city for the use of Negroes.

Bathing-beaches in Chicago are still the scenes of friction. At the beach at Jackson Park, a park policeman would not stop young white men from interfering with Negroes. His attitude was that Negroes should go back to 33rd Street where they belonged. His removal was finally secured as a result of a protest of representative Negroes. Under the city plan, a beach will be developed at 35th Street, but it will not be ready for two years.

In Dayton, Negroes may rent the cottage at Hills and Dales Park. They are assigned Mondays for the use of tennis courts and dance pavilions. Island Park has a bathing-beach, the facilities of which are not available to them. When the children from Linden Center were carried to this park two years ago for a picnic, they were denied the use of the bath-house for changing their clothes and were sent up the river to bathe in dangerously swift and muddy water.

Indianapolis, Lexington, Louisville, Knoxville, Memphis and Atlanta have separate parks for Negroes. With the exception of the park at Lexington, the parks supplied Negroes were found to be below the standard of those for white people in the same cities.

This disparity in standards is noticeable with respect to both size and equipment. The parks for Negroes are uniformly smaller in number and in acreage than those for white people. At least one or two for white people in each city are equipped with ball diamonds, swimming-pools, concert facilities, and sometimes with golf links and more elaborate features. In many instances the park for Negroes is a piece of bare ground provided with no facilities or attractions.

Only four cities, Indianapolis, Louisville, New Orleans, and Atlanta have swimming-pools for Negroes, and these have been built very recently.

Negro parks are also often inadequately supervised by the police, with the result that rowdy patrons or unscrupulous concessioners create an atmosphere that citizens of the better class desire to avoid. The value of the park to reputable Negroes is therefore destroyed.

Parks properly equipped undoubtedly provide the kind of activities of which young adults and adolescents are very much in need, particularly the young Negroes; but parks that lack athletic fields, dancing facilities, swimming-pools, music and even shade, as some do, will not attract the young people.

The general custom in the South is to make separate provision for Negroes; and separate parks and expensive equipment undoubtedly cause a drain on the city treasury. But Negroes are taxpayers and have just claims on the recreational facilities of the city. Where they are excluded from the parks in the general system, special provision is a matter to which city-planners ought to give increasing attention.

PLAYGROUNDS

Philadelphia, New York, Buffalo, Gary, and Chicago are officially committed to the position that the playgrounds and recreation centers are open to all people in a neighborhood. As a matter of fact, however, some form of separation is observable in Philadelphia, Chicago, and Gary. The large north-side Negro settlement in Philadelphia, in the Thirty-second ward, is not provided by the city with facilities for play, as the neighboring grounds, Fairfield, Penrose, Mill Creek, Francisville, and Athletic Center do not welcome Negroes. In Gary, playgrounds are connected with the schools; and as there is some separation in the schools there is also separation in the matter of facilities for play. The swimming-pools of Gary are used on Monday and Thursday nights by Negroes.

In general, Negro playgrounds are less numerous, smaller, poorer in equipment and less adequately supervised than playgrounds for white children in the same city.

Table XLIX shows the comparative number of playgrounds for the two groups in several cities.

TABLE XLIX—NUMBER OF PLAYGROUNDS IN TEN CITIES

City	White	Negro
Indianapolis	38	16
Dayton	19	2
Louisville	16	6
New Orleans	17	1
Charleston	4	1
Memphis	16	2
Richmond	13	9
Atlanta	21	3
Knoxville	11	2
Lynchburg	8	3

PROGRAMS

Wide variation was found in the type of program offered. In the main it is noticeable that there is a distinct tendency away from games and gymnastics involving the use of apparatus, and a marked tendency in all of the cities studied toward free play.

The programs offered young children are decidedly more attractive than programs offered preadolescent boys and girls. This does not mean that elaborate programs of cities such as Philadelphia, Gary, Chicago and Winston-Salem are not an improvement over the programs of most of the cities studied. It is undoubtedly true that these programs are more attractive, and for that reason secure a larger degree of participation on the part of the children using the grounds. What is implied is that such an agency as the Playground and Recreation Association of America is helping to vitalize the programs of smaller cities to the extent that a fairly good generalized idea of the playground needs of small children has filtered through to most of the cities.

With respect to the play-needs of preadolescent and adolescent boys and girls, the same condition does not obtain. The reason for this is not far to seek. Programs in most instances are not provided because, so far as the needs of Negro youths are concerned, most of the cities studied have not yet supplied adequate play-space for this group of boys and girls.

Philadelphia, Gary, Chicago, and Winston-Salem have done most to supply this need, though even in Chicago it is noticeable that the south side still is in need of large recreation parks. Memphis may reasonably claim to have done something in this direction in providing a diamond and an auditorium at Church's Park.

One who has seen the teams of older boys and girls at work on the athletic field, who has watched them at work in gymnasiums and clubrooms, or who has listened to their laughter as they engage in social and rhythmic dances, must be convinced that the athletic field and the recreation centers can be developed into strong agencies for the social control of these young people at a time when newly awakened impulses make for maladaptation.

It cannot be too strongly urged, therefore, that Richmond, Lynchburg, Knoxville, Louisville, Lexington, New Orleans,

Atlanta, and Charleston, as well as Buffalo, New York and Indianapolis make efforts to provide the much-needed space and supervision for the play of adolescents.

One of the chief difficulties is that in some of the cities the program is seasonal. Thus in Buffalo, work is done with the adolescent group at Memorial Chapel in the fall, winter and spring. The gymnasium of the 133rd Street bathhouse in New York is used by groups of older boys and girls in the fall, winter and spring. The athletic programs of the high schools in Lexington, Knoxville, and Louisville meet the needs of some members of this group during winter. During other seasons there is a general dearth of after-school activities. There is a decided need in these communities for live recreational activities that will employ the leisure time of the children and offset the ill effects of poor commercial recreation throughout the year.

The following program of the Bureau of Recreation of the Department of Education, City of Chicago, 1924, shows the varied activities for men and boys, and for girls and young women, which a well-regulated recreational system offers its young people.

> For the boys and men: harmonica contest, barber shop quartet contest, pet shows, playground rodeo, knot hole club, playground circus, snow modeling, whittling contest, radio contest, skating, wrestling tournament, top contest, local playground and volley ball leagues, baseball pitching, horseshoe pitching tournament, track and field, Defense Test Day athletics, Chicago Olympic track and field, marbles tournament, pushmobile races, stilts contest, playground ball, volley ball, diabolo contest, soccer football, efficiency tests. For girls: valentine making, radio construction, poster drawing, clean-up week, play festival, folk dances contest and the festival, doll show, playground mardi gras, sand craft, lantern parade, circus (girls), ukulele contest, jackstone contest, O'Leary contest, top tournament, playground ball, volley ball, efficiency test, apparatus contest, Defense Day contest, Girls' Day in recreation.

PERSONNEL

The emphasis at present laid upon free play in the scheme of playground organization makes increasing demands upon those who are to lead in play. The interest of the child is

involved here. Both intelligence and personality are required in the leader.

Directors of recreation bureaus have difficulty in getting
competently trained play-leaders for work among Negro
children. Directors in Chicago, Gary, Indianapolis and
Winston-Salem stressed this fact. Most of them were willing to acknowledge that salaries are at present too small to
attract the best men. The need of trained leadership should
turn the attention of the young men and women of athletic
ability to the courses in this work that some of the best
schools of physical education are offering.

Ernest T. Atwell, Field Director of the Bureau of Recreation of the Colored Community Service, Department of
Parks and Playgrounds and Recreation Association of
America, summarized the condition of Negro recreation in
1923 in a statement that is practically true also of conditions
in 1926.

Writing in *Opportunity* for May, 1923, he said:

> We should not overlook the handicap of not having play-space
> or playgrounds where colored people live. The need almost over-
> shadowing the other activities is a recreational program that can
> be both educational and cultural, such as the inclusion of and
> participation in community service, dramatic and literary activi-
> ties that for a large mass of adults will be the only attractive
> phase of the recreational field.
> These latter activities are phases of social life which colored
> people are greatly in need of. Except for a limited and favored
> group, social recreation is largely of the commercial and un-
> wholesome type, or to say the least conducted in an atmosphere
> of moral haze.

Since the effectiveness of playgrounds is largely determined by the quality of leadership provided, it will be seen
from the following typical examples that this essential item
is often neglected in Negro recreation:

Louisville: Colored instructors constitute a force of only
six out of a total of fifty-four in the city. This is only
one supervisor of play for each colored ground as against
two for every white ground, and four and five on the two
largest.

Lexington: Spends $500 of its $3,000 budget on colored
playgrounds.

Charleston: Spends $360 out of $8,975 on colored playgrounds.

Lynchburg: The following budget for personnel is provided in Lynchburg's recreational program:

1 General supervisor, annually................	$1,200
1 Athletic director, annually..................	1,080
3 White playground directors, 3 mo., monthly...	65
1 Colored playground director, 3 mo., monthly..	50
3 White play leaders, 9 mo., monthly..........	25
1 Colored leader, 9 mo., monthly.............	20

In Winston-Salem alone of the southern cities studied, the administration announced a policy of paying trained colored supervisors the same as white supervisors.

LIBRARIES

Libraries in Philadelphia, New York, Buffalo, Chicago, Gary, Indianapolis, and Dayton are open to all citizens of the neighborhoods in which branches are located. The probable explanation of this fact is that the relationships are largely impersonal. In Lexington and Richmond, a portion of the reading-room space is reserved for colored people. They have access to the shelves under a system that conforms to southern tradition. Louisville, Knoxville, Memphis, New Orleans, Atlanta, and Lynchburg provide separate branches for Negroes. Charleston has no colored branch, and Winston-Salem no library for white or colored.

The testimony of librarians indicates that Negroes appreciate the advantages of libraries and use them rather freely, especially if the librarian has a program that extends the service out into the community and interests the people.

Table L summarizes library facilities as far as statistics could be obtained for the cities visited.

In the main, branch libraries that can obtain books from the central library, even though inadequate in themselves, may be made to serve the needs of the community. Most cities have the largest number of volumes in the central library, and justice can be done to all patrons only when the books in the main library are available on requisition

TABLE L—LIBRARIES FOR NEGROES

City	Volumes	Av. Monthly Circulation
Richmond		
City Branch......................	1,800	*
Lynchburg	2,050 ‡	1,200
Philadelphia		
Wanamaker Branch †.............	19,000 ‡	*
Wareton Branch †................	11,000 ‡	*
New York		
135th St. Branch †...............	‡	12,000
Indianapolis	5,926 ‡	5,000
Louisville §	25,000 ‡	10,000
Knoxville	6,000 ‡	2,300
Atlanta	5,600	2,140

* Not available.
† Branch not confined to colored patronage but largely used by colored.
‡ Additional books may be drawn from central library.
§ Two branches combined.

through the branches, or are accessible at the main building. Memphis, New Orleans, and Atlanta are behind other cities in this respect.

Half of the branch libraries visited were found to be wanting in that feature of library work devoted to making the service available at all. Programs like that of the 135th Street branch in New York City might well be studied by all cities. This branch has story-hours, free public lectures by outstanding men and women, and a forum. It is developing a reference library on Negro literature, and places on exhibit the work of Negro artists and sculptors.

The question was often asked the investigator: What can we do to improve the colored library? Two suggestions seem of practical value for branch libraries. First, the best possible librarian should be obtained, no matter where from; a librarian of adequate training who knows how to carry the library to the people through the children's story-hour, through work in the schools, and finally through lectures and forums that have as their objective the creating of love of good literature. Poor pay and poor service usually go hand in hand, and it is not reasonable to expect a person without adequate training to do a first-class job.

The good use made of the libraries that are efficiently

reaching out into the community indicates that institutions of this kind may become important factors in the development of wholesome use of leisure time and in the spread of literary culture in colored neighborhoods. Cities should therefore develop a library program that will serve the Negro neighborhoods.

Chapter XVI

ORGANIZATIONS

To some extent the inadequate facilities in public recreation for young people are supplemented by private recreational and character-building organizations such as the Young Men's and Young Women's Christian Associations, by institutional churches, clubs and settlement homes.

Y.M.C.A.

PHYSICAL EQUIPMENT

Of the cities included in this study, Philadelphia, New York, Chicago, Indianapolis and Atlanta have modern Y.M.C.A. buildings, equipped with lobbies, clubrooms, game-rooms, gymnasiums and swimming-pools. Buffalo has set aside $150,000 for a new building, $36,497 of which was raised by the Negro population. In Dayton, a $150,000 building is to be erected for the use of Negro youth. The trustees of the central association have pledged themselves to erect the Negro building first.

It is important to note in this connection that these buildings represent the combined effort of Negro citizens, the entire community, and in four instances the encouraging philanthropy of Julius Rosenwald. In December, 1910, Mr. Rosenwald offered $25,000 to every city that would raise $75,000 for a building for men and boys of the Negro race. More than a dozen cities have already availed themselves of the offer and erected buildings.

The rapid increase in the Negro population of New York, Philadelphia and Chicago, and the establishment of Negro neighborhoods in new areas, have rendered it virtually impossible for the present buildings in these cities to serve their entire communities. Thus the West 135th Street branch, which was built over ten years ago for a population of 50,000, is to-day attempting to serve a population of more than 100,000. As a consequence, the boys' department has had to take over space intended for educational work, and still it is necessary to limit the work done to 150 boys. Obviously there is need here for a new building devoted almost entirely to the use of boys and younger men. The fact that the dormitory is crowded to capacity would also suggest the need of more space to care for these men.

There is particular need of a colored branch in North Philadelphia. This section of the city is the most neglected of any part of Philadelphia in which large groups of Negroes live. Here and in West Philadelphia the new Negro neighborhoods are growing most rapidly. A like expansion of program and facilities to include the colored population of West Philadelphia is also a necessity. The building occupied by the Louisville association is old and in a bad state of repair. The roof of the gymnasium leaks, and there is no provision for heating the swimming-pool during the winter. The central association was expected to put on a drive for a new building soon. The colored men's branch owns the land on which the present building is located—a plot 707 x 710 feet. It is centrally located, and a new building here would make it possible to increase the effectiveness of the program.

The building in Indianapolis, while adequate for the needs of the community, should have a general cleaning and overhauling. A very fine program is put over by this association.

The building in which the Hunton branch is located in Gary, is a small, converted private building that is inadequate from every point of view for the needs of the growing community. A modern building and a more attractive program might do much to interest the large number of men who work at the mills. Dormitory space is particularly needed.

The building and gymnasium in New Orleans are far from adequate for the needs of the 46,919 men and boys in that city. Dormitory space, for example, is limited to seven rooms; and there is hardly space for all the club and educational activities. The gymnasium is 85 x 37 feet, and has four showers. The association proper has seven rooms in which to conduct its activities. There are six members on the staff. During the summer a camp was maintained at Waveland, Mississippi, for ten days. Gulfside, the resort for Negroes which is used by the Y.M.C.A., is being developed by a group of men who hope to make of it a resort for religious conferences similar to the white resort at Silver Bay.

The leaders of the community chest recognize the fact that facilities for both white and colored associations are inadequate, and hope to start a building drive for both associations within two years.

A vigorous attempt is being made to rehabilitate the Butler Street branch in Atlanta. The central association is giving $2,000 toward the reconditioning of the building. This branch association demonstrates more clearly perhaps than any other one studied, the handicap under which an organization in need of financial help suffers. The organization had practically ceased to function. Much credit is due the regional secretary, who has not only labored zealously with his own racial group but even more assiduously in pleading the cause of the association with the central association in Atlanta.

The building and property of the association in Charleston are at present both idle. The building has been closed for two years, and is at present in such a bad state of repair that a new building will almost be necessary before the work can be undertaken. There is a fine lot here, 150 x 300 feet, which might very well serve as a splendid athletic field for the boys and young men in Charleston if it were properly equipped.

The building at Lynchburg is rented; and while it is not adequate for the needs of the town, an intensive use of the game-rooms and other present facilities might go far toward making this association useful in the community life.

Two associations, that in Lexington and the one in Winston-Salem, are operating on a no-equipment basis. The work in Lexington is mainly confined to Hi-Y Clubs among schoolboys. Winston-Salem has a paid secretary who not only carries the work to the high-school group but who has carried religious and medical instruction and a physical education program to men who work in the city's numerous factories. In one of the factories, the white and colored volley-ball teams play against each other, and a most friendly spirit exists despite the fact that the Negro team has won by far the larger number of games.

This association formerly had quarters in an old school building which it had equipped with gymnasium, showers and classrooms. The building was finally burned after two incendiary attempts had failed. The community chest supports the work of the association liberally.

ORGANIZATION

Y.M.C.A.'s in the South do not as a rule compare favorably with the associations in northern cities. One of the main reasons for this is that southern associations on the whole are independent branches and not parts of the municipal Y.M.C.A. system as in the North. Again many people in northern cities have been interested in the welfare of the Negro neighborhoods and have contributed liberally to the funds that have gone into the buildings of the colored branches. Some of the cities in the South are changing their attitude and helping to support Negro work. Thus the community chest of New Orleans has helped to make possible the Dryade Street branch, some $6,980 of the annual budget coming from this source. This year the central branch of Atlanta is paying $2,000 for the reconditioning of the Butler Street building.

Economic stability is the first great need of most of the southern associations. The central organizations should therefore seek to establish closely knit branch relationships that will, as in northern cities, give the branch the benefit of its financial support and expert advice. Such financial support as is given should aim to make the branches help support themselves rather than help to pauperize them.

The Y.W.C.A. has helped its colored branches very substantially by underwriting the secretaries' salaries. In almost every instance the branches also receive some support from the community chest. When one remembers that Negroes in the South receive low wages, the need for financial support for social agencies that work among them is the more apparent.

In Knoxville and in Memphis there is need of coöperative effort that will look to the establishment of branches for the use of Negro youth. Commercial recreation in both of these cities is of poor quality, and there should be an effort of some kind to offer the masses something better.

The branches in a few cities, notably those in Chicago, Indianapolis, and Winston-Salem, are doing a splendid work in the industrial field. The association at Dayton carries speakers to various factories; but it is not yet doing very much to provide recreation for the men who work in the factories. The secretary has been able to influence them to join the association, but has so far not been able to get many of them to take advantage of the activities. Other cities studied also neglect this important feature of the program.

A man who has had wide experience as an industrial secretary states that he found the men with whom he worked of the opinion that the Y.M.C.A. is a white-collar organization. The feeling can be broken down when the association carries the program to the workers.

Most of the dormitories are much used by the student element, those of the Indianapolis and the Philadelphia associations to less extent, however, than those of the New York and Chicago associations. The Indianapolis association is probably more used as a domicile by working men than any other association building. While the rent per room, which as a rule varies from $3.50 to $4.50 a week, seems high and out of the reach of many laboring men, it ought to be kept in mind that the facilities are better than those provided in private homes for the same rental. As the larger associations rely upon the rental of rooms as a means of income for keeping the work going, a larger share of the upkeep of the associations will have to be borne by public philanthropy before rates can be materially lowered.

A member of the national council, in commenting on membership fees, admitted that they were perhaps a little high for men and boys of the under-privileged classes. The Boys' Work secretary of the central association of Richmond believed they were high for the poorer white boys in his city. He said, however, that a way is usually found to help the boy who really wants to use the association; and he felt that so far as Negroes generally were concerned, it was a good thing to have a fee high enough to make them believe they are helping to support their own organization. The fee for the use of physical privileges for men in Philadelphia is $10, for boys, $5. The New York association has a social membership fee of $5. The fee, including gymnasium and social privileges for young men from 18 to 21, is $8; for boys, $5; and men, $10. The Dayton association has at present a membership fee of $1 for boys, and $2 for men. It uses the Masonic Hall as a gymnasium. One hundred and four boys, exclusive of Scouts, use the central association's camp for two weeks at a cost of $1 a day. The present fee in Buffalo is the same as that of Dayton; but with the coming of the new building it will be $5 for boys and $10 for men. These fees are typical of the contrast between associations with, and those without, modern buildings.

Most of the associations visited attempt the three-fold program of the Y.M.C.A. In those associations that have modern buildings, the tendency toward institutionalization is quite marked; and often it happens that there is greater emphasis on the physical and recreational aspect of the work than upon religious education. Some of the associations, notably the 135th Street branch in New York City, do good work in the field of Bible study; but there are few forums of the kind that one finds highly developed in Chicago, Indianapolis, and New York City.

It is difficult to imagine an institution that serves so large a number of people in so many effective ways as does the Wabash Avenue branch of the Y.M.C.A., Chicago.

The Sunday afternoon forums in Indianapolis are particularly fine. The association brings to the community many of the best speakers in the country, and thereby attracts a large following of people of both sexes.

Y.W.C.A.

Only two of the cities studied have modern buildings in which to conduct their Y.W.C.A. work; in fact, the outstanding handicap of the women's associations is the lack of equipment for carrying on a recreational program. The associations in Lynchburg, Richmond, Indianapolis, Dayton, Knoxville, Atlanta, and Charleston are all in need of gymnasiums and swimming-pools. Some of the small buildings used by the associations are kept spotlessly clean and attractive. The secretaries in many instances show great ingenuity in the use to which they put rented halls and small school gymnasiums for purposes of physical education, despite the fact that the physical equipment is often inadequate.

Two cities, Buffalo and New Orleans, have no branches for Negro girls. The girls in New Orleans are at present using the facilities of the Y.M.C.A., and there is great need of a special girls' branch.

The Indiana Avenue branch of the Y.W.C.A. in Chicago has woefully inadequate space and physical equipment. It boards and lodges girls in its limited quarters for $6 a week; but its building, which is valued at $20,000, is small and unattractive.

FINANCE

Aside from the question of physical equipment, the Y.W.C.A.'s were generally found to operate on a much firmer financial basis than that of the Y.M.C.A.'s. This was not only because the central associations (white) have, as a rule, pledged themselves to pay the salaries of the secretaries, but also because a portion of the budget is provided by the community chest, except in New York and Chicago. This support relieves the secretaries of much financial worry, and leaves them free to devote themselves entirely to their work.

INDUSTRIAL PROGRAM

Because of the general lack of dormitory facilities, the associations find it difficult to reach the industrial girl effectively. A second handicap is the lack of an industrial secretary. At least three associations reported that they had more calls for work than they were able to fill because there was no one to establish contact between the girl and the work.

The Lynchburg and Indianapolis associations are doing a fine work among the factory girls. The Lynchburg association carries its programs to these girls, and has a portable outfit with which it serves them meals twice a week at a reasonable price. The secretary spends four nights a week with girls employed in factories and in domestic service. The Indianapolis association has a membership of 600 and reaches, through clubs, approximately 700 girls who are not in the Girl Reserve Clubs. The association secretary was able, by means of talks and lectures, to reduce so greatly the labor turnover in a glove factory employing Negro girls that the firm has built a new plant with a capacity of 500 in which only Negro girls will be employed.

Many of the branches of the Y.W.C.A. are doing splendid work among employed girls. It appears certain that Negro girls will find work in increasing numbers in the industrial field, where there are great moral hazards, especially because many girls so employed live in isolation after working hours. There will be a growing need, therefore, for the services the "Y" can render.

GIRL RESERVE CLUBS

In general the work the "Y" is doing with girls in both the Girl Reserve Clubs and the high-school groups is most interesting and helpful. Reports show that most of the city associations, especially those in the smaller places, have as many Girl Reserves as they have other members. Thus the Phyllis Wheatly branch in Lexington touches 150 girls weekly through these clubs, and only 120 members through other activities. The Indianapolis association has a membership of 600, but reaches 500 girls weekly in the Girl Reserve Clubs and the twelve public-school groups. Of the 250 people using the Dayton association, 90 belong to girls' clubs. The Knoxville association has a membership of 135, and a group of 125 girls in its clubs. The same condition is true of the Richmond, Louisville, and Lynchburg associations.

Given adequate physical facilities, the program is sufficiently elastic to reach even a larger number of girls; but, as the secretaries point out, the lack of gymnasiums and swimming-pools is a very real handicap.

The work of the Y.W.C.A. is in special need of strengthening and development in Chicago, Lexington, Memphis and Charleston. The organization in Memphis is little more than a paper organization. Lack of coöperation on the part of the women themselves, because of rivalry among the federated clubs, is in part responsible. The Charleston association now has a paid secretary for the first time in two years.

The improving of the work of the Y.W.C.A., and especially of the Y.M.C.A., should be in the main in the fields of personnel, equipment and finance, and in close coördination between the branches and central associations.

In most instances, the people heading the work are conscientious and trained for their work. Wherever they are not, the national council appears anxious and willing to make a change. First-class men and women can be attracted, as a rule, only by salaries that insure a comfortable living; and money for better salaries is often lacking.

Boy Scouts and Girl Scouts

The extent to which Negro girls are touched by the Girl Scout movement in the cities studied is so small as to be of little importance. The Manhattan Council reports eight troops with a minimum of seventy-two girls. There are a few colored troops in Philadelphia.

Taken as a whole, the number of Boy Scouts found was also limited. There are eight troops in Manhattan which include 447 boys, about 387 of whom are uniformed. The scoutmaster in charge of this group reports that various social clubs that have degenerated almost into street gangs have made it difficult to attract the boys in large numbers.

It is doubtless true that the effort on the part of the Manhattan Council to organize one-fifth of the boys in the Borough will reach the Negro boys in larger numbers than heretofore.

In Buffalo, there are two troops of forty boys each, and a group of junior scouts, a mixed troop of fifty.

In Chicago, the colored division of Scouts is directly supervised by a Negro leader. At the time of the collection of these figures it contained 680 boys and was in the midst of a drive to send the figure over the 1,000 mark.

Dayton has approximately forty boys in the "Y" troop.

The largest organization of Scouts in the South was found in Louisville, where some 550 boys are included in the movement. The colored division is under the leadership of a white man who was formerly a minister, and who devotes all of his time to this work.

The chief difficulty encountered by the Scout organization in its effort to enlist large numbers of Negro boys in the South arises from the charter requirement that the consent of troops already existing in the neighborhood must be obtained before new troops can be formed. Groups of Negro boys who wished to organize in Atlanta, Charleston and Richmond found it impossible to do so because the local organizations were unwilling to allow Negroes to use the title and uniform.

A scoutmaster in Memphis said that white boys would not stand the presence of Negro boys in scout uniforms, and that violence would result from an attempt to organize them.

Boys' Clubs

Very few boys' clubs, except those of the associations and the Boy Scouts, were discovered during this study.

Wissahicon Boys' Club in Germantown, Pennsylvania, employs two directors and six part-time workers, and has an average daily attendance of 125. It is the only club for Negroes that is a member of the Boys' Club Federation of America. It was organized twenty-two years ago, and for a number of years represented an effort of the Philadelphia

Friends to provide a club for under-privileged Negro boys. They provided the club with its present building, which is valued at $40,000. The building contains a large gymnasium, a pool room, radio room, library, carpentry shop, shoe-repairing shop, room for sign painting, a kitchen, and a dining-room which is nicely furnished by one of the downtown merchants.

The membership fees for the club are small: one dollar for men and fifty cents for boys. The club prides itself on the fact that no boy is ever turned away because of a lack of funds.

The activities include radio and library hour; classes in shoe-repairing, cooking, chair-carving, fancy-work, hammock-making and show-card lettering. The director states in his annual report that the object of these vocational classes "is not to furnish finished tradesmen but to find out the talents that the boy may possess and help him to find and discover himself."

The athletic program includes basketball, baseball, football and swimming, all of which are taught by competent instructors. There is a band of forty-two pieces to interest the boys and older men, while an effort is made through community movies and supervised dances to interest the entire community.

A fine feature of the work for the boys is a camp at Norwood, a twenty-seven acre plot of land with a lake for swimming, an athletic field, and a well-equipped playground. The camp is virtually self-supporting, since the boys raise enough in their garden to pay for their board and lodging.

The club has been very successful in competitions, and at the Pittsburgh convention of the Boys' Club Federation, won five first, one second, and two third prizes.

The Benezet House, 917 Walnut Street, Philadelphia, is attempting a somewhat similar program among the boys and girls of one of Philadelphia's slums. The Benezet House grew out of a Friends' Sunday school that aimed at reaching a group of people who seldom attend church. A day-nursery was next developed which is now well supervised by two graduate nurses. There are sewing-classes, cooking-classes, classes in basketry and fancy-work for girls, a play-hour from 4.30 to 5.30 for the midgets, a class in carpentry for the boys, and athletic clubs under the leadership of a Negro track and athletic star from the University of Michigan. The average attendance is 600. The organization employs a staff of eight paid workers and works on a budget of $12,000.

The Western Community House, on South Street, operates on a budget of $4,495.66. A staff of four workers, aside from furnishing meals and fuel for the needy in the community, promotes a settlement-house program among Negroes and for the Whitesmith community. The community classes are divided on racial lines. A special attempt is made to offer girls a recreational and industrial program that will offset bad neighborhood influences. The attendance here is 560 a week.

In New York, the Children's Aid Society has a large boys' club at Lexington Avenue and 127th Street which is devoted chiefly to recreational work among under-privileged boys and young men. It is at present attempting a small work among colored boys, and allows them to use the roof gymnasium, and an indoor gymnasium that is fitted with a prize ring, a punching bag and a wrestling mat. The boys also use the lockers and showers every day from 3.30 to 5.30. Two Negro college boys have charge of the work and supervise the indoor baseball, basketball, boxing, wrestling and full play of a group of fifty preadolescent and adolescent boys. This club has a membership total, white and colored, of 1,800, and operates on a budget of $18,000. It is destined to become more largely colored because of the movement of Negroes into this neighborhood.

There is need in Harlem of a well-established club of this nature that will serve a larger number of boys and girls of the under-privileged classes.

The club of the South Side Boys' Foundation on Michigan Avenue at Thirty-ninth Street, in Chicago, was opened May 15, 1925, with a building and equipment estimated to be worth about $75,000. The building is the gift of men who felt that something ought to be done for the under-privileged boys who were a constant source of trouble along a part of Grand Boulevard.

The Foundation is operated on a budget of $10,000 and, to insure its permanent operation for at least five years, those backing the movement plan to undertake a five-year budget.

The building contains a good gymnasium, a billiard-room, a bowling alley, and a room for small games. The director is paid by the Foundation. Two physical instructors are furnished by the Board of Education, while the surgeon general of the Rapid Transit Company has charge of the physical standards and first-aid work.

The Foundation goes into the churches and schools and organizes boys' clubs which are federated as they are brought into the organization. An attempt is also made to organize boys who have passed through the Juvenile Court. No attempt is made to destroy the boys' gang, but instead to transform the gang into a useful organization. It is proposed to add to the present equipment a building for vocational guidance with the hope that classes in tailoring, printing, auto mechanics, etc., may further orientate these boys.

Some of the gangs that use the club represent the rougher element. Few attempts are made to preach goodness to these boys, the idea being to bring play into their lives. Thirty of the boys are members of the Boys' Cadet Club, an organization recognized by the United States Government.

The workers in the Juvenile Court in Charleston are attempting to form a club to help boys who are brought into court. The absence of a Y.M.C.A. for Negroes, and of a community center in the city of Charleston, makes the work of rehabilitating these boys very difficult. The playground, which is the only place to which they may be directed, is not large enough for the organized games of adolescents, and they therefore use the apparatus with the small children. Conflict often results, and there are sometimes clashes with the law.

A clubhouse, which is to be located on the river, will be

rented. The Relief Circle, a group of Negroes, has promised to equip the house. Trained workers will not be available immediately because of a lack of finances; but at the
time this study was made two volunteer workers were at
work drilling the boys and forming a band and glee club.

In this connection it should be noted that the Boy Scouts
of Charleston refused to accept these Negro boys after 100
of them had been organized by the welfare workers, the
scoutmaster suggesting that they call themselves the Brownie
Club. He was unwilling that they should be called "Scouts"
because of the feeling that the presence of Negro Scouts
would hinder him in his work with white boys.

It cannot be too strongly urged that in most of the cities
studied a very effective and necessary work can be accomplished among the under-privileged. This group is not
easily reached by the Y.M.C.A., because the boys who
compose the group do not feel at home among those who
occupy the next social level, and many of them do not have
the money for dues.

Churches

Except in New York, Chicago and Memphis, the work of
the churches in the recreational field was found to be very
limited. Several of the churches in Manhattan, New York
City, have well-organized recreational programs. The St.
Philip's Parish House has a rather elaborate recreational
program which is supervised by an ably trained social
worker from the University of Chicago and Columbia, an
athlete who made a distinguished record for himself during
his school career.

There are 480 girls who use the parish house, 120 of
whom, between the ages of eight and eighteen, are organized
in club-groups. The program of each club is the result of
its own planning and includes educational, recreational, religious and service features. The recreational activities include paddle tennis, basketball, theater guilds, bazaars, plays
and community sings. There are 370 boys and men enrolled

in six different clubs, with programs that include Scout programs, pool, billiards, cards, basketball, cross-country runs, painting, choral club and sketching.

The St. Philip's Episcopal Church is one of the wealthiest Negro churches in America. The parish house is valued at $50,000 and contains equipment valued at $5,200. The social workers are paid by the church.

The Abyssinian Baptist Church is a community church that includes in its program, in addition to church services, a week-day school of religion, that gives courses recognized by Columbia University, and a daily vacation Bible school in the summer.

The church owns a gymnasium which contains 3,000 square feet of space and is very well equipped. The physical director is a former college coach and athlete. The gymnasium is used by 200 different people every week and has a total weekly attendance of about 500. In the summer, the daily vacation Bible school had an average daily attendance of 300 children. Supervised recreation is a feature of this program.

The Salem A.M.E. Church has one of the finest athletic clubs in Harlem, and has sent members as far west as San Francisco to compete in games.

St. Mark's Catholic Church has a dance hall which is frequently used by West Indian groups. The gymnasium is largely used for basketball.

St. Cyprian's Parish House is connected with St. Cyprian's Chapel, and is managed by the New York Protestant Episcopal City Mission Society. It is the outstanding social center among the seven blocks of poorer-class Negroes who live between 59th and 65th Streets in the Columbus Hill district of Manhattan.

This section was formerly noted for its rough character, but now represents the area nearest the poverty line to which the poorer migrants flock.

Social dances are given at the parish house twice a week. The fees for these dances vary from twenty-five to fifty cents a person. Large groups attend, and it is difficult to maintain order. A playground with a social worker in charge is open to the colored children of the neighborhood. It is suited to the needs of smaller children and equipped with a sand pile, and for basketball and croquet.

This organization has girls' clubs which attract between 150 and 200 girls, and gymnasium classes and basketball for 200 boys. A paid social worker and two volunteers from Columbia assist in this work. The services of a physician and a dentist have been secured, and a clinic for a limited number of cases will be opened at the parish house. The budget of $12,000 a year serves a neighborhood of 7,000 colored people.

The Urban League is also attempting a recreational work on a small scale in the Columbus Hill neighborhood in New York. There are girls' clubs in esthetic dancing, in art, needle-work and physical education. A boys' club organized around the idea of the Big Brother movement is under the leadership of a student from Union Theological Seminary. Altogether about 150 young people are reached by this program every week. The boys and girls use the gymnasium of the Ethical Culture Society for their games and exercises. The club-work is all attempted on an intensive rather than an extensive basis.

An interesting illustration of coöperative recreational activities on the part of churches is found in the Union Sunday School Athletic Association of Chicago. This organization is composed of twenty of Chicago's largest Sunday schools. The present organization is an outgrowth of incidents that occurred twenty years ago. The Negro Sunday schools formerly belonged to the Cook County Sunday School Association. After a colored Sunday school had won the championship for three successive years, the Cook County Association attempted to form a colored division. The Negro schools revolted against the idea and withdrew to form a league of their own.

Baseball and bowling are the Negro sports fostered by the association. Basketball has never been a marked success because of a lack of gymnasium space. The association also fosters tennis. There were 300 baseball players on these Sunday-school teams last year and 50 on bowling teams.

The bowling teams use the alley of the Catholic Club, a white organization at 41st Street and Michigan Avenue.

The girls in the Sunday schools are anxious to play basketball but are handicapped by a lack of gymnasium space. Two churches, Bethel and Mt. Olivet Baptist, did good work with the girls' teams. Mt. Olivet has a gymnasium. Bethel had a well-equipped gymnasium before the church was burned.

There is an annual fee of $2 for each Sunday school and a forfeit fee of $5. Each player pays twenty-five cents. The individual Sunday schools are responsible for fitting their own teams. Members of league teams are not allowed to play professional ball.

As the Negro church is still the organization that touches the masses of the people, an organization of this kind represents a fascinating possibility for all of the cities studied. The Chicago organization is interdenominational and has been a means of promoting a liberal and tolerant attitude on the part of young people.

At least two attempts on the part of churches in southern cities to undertake community features were noted. The Tabernacle Baptist Church of Memphis has almost completed its new $150,000 edifice. A gymnasium, swimming-pool, and rooms for art and industrial equipment are integral parts of the building.

The swimming-pool, approximately 75x25 feet, is already in use and attracts 150 daily during the summer months. The pastor is responsible for the statement that groups of boys and young men who are ordinarily classed as loafers use the pool in large numbers, and through it are sometimes brought under the influence of the church. Lectures on hygiene and health are given to all of the young people using the pool.

The People's Community Church Center of New Orleans is attempting something in the line of recreation. Aside from a baby clinic, a community school with an attendance of 130, and an employment bureau, a Girl Reserve Club with forty-five members and a junior auxiliary with forty have been organized. These young people put on community pageants and include physical exercise and dramatics in their program. The center was instrumental in influencing 100 girls to attend the Y.W.C.A. conference at Waveland, Mississippi. The great needs of this organization at present are a physical director and a properly equipped gymnasium.

Bishop R. E. Jones has projected an interesting recreational program for the Methodist church which is located near the Dryades branch of the Carnegie Library. The church is at present purchasing an entire block on which to build a modern community center and swimming-pool.

It is evident from the foregoing descriptions that a variety of unrelated small efforts are undertaken by most private organizations, which are usually doing good work with limited equipment and personnel, and which are in great need of finances for expansion. As they are for the most part localized in some one institution, they reach only a fraction of the people in need of leisure-time employment.

Chapter XVII

COMMERCIAL RECREATION

THEATERS

The theater offers a form of recreation that strongly appeals to the keen dramatic sense of Negroes. The findings of this study indicate, however, that Negroes of all classes are limited in their opportunity to enjoy plays of the best kind. Those who go to theaters find obstacles placed in their way in a majority of the cities and are often humiliated.

Many of the better-class Negro citizens in most of the cities studied said they could not reconcile themselves to side-entrances, alley-entrances and Jim Crow balconies, and therefore did not go to the theater. In New York, Buffalo, Gary and Chicago, there was little complaint against most of the large down-town theaters; but it was stated that in some places Negroes were subjected to special treatment that tended to keep them away. They are seldom afforded the opportunity to see the best the country has to offer under circumstances that make for happiness and contentment.

CIVIL RIGHTS CASES

Several states have civil rights laws that make separation in theaters punishable by fine. This law contains in substance the following principle:

> Any person who shall deny to any citizen by reason of race, creed or color, the full enjoyment of any accommodations, advantages, facilities or privileges of theaters or music halls or shall incite such denial, shall for every such offense forfeit and pay a sum not less than $100 or more than $500 to the person aggrieved thereby to be recovered in a court of competent jurisdiction in the county (in which) said offense was committed.

The mere existence of a civil rights bill does not mean in every case that separation of the races will not be attempted. Houses that treat Negroes with the greatest liberality are those that are not located in neighborhoods in which Negroes live in large numbers.

An aggrieved individual going before the court in which he is pitted against a corporation is often at a serious disadvantage. For example, the proprietor of a theater is not liable where it is shown that he, personally, had not authorized the exclusion of the plaintiff, but that the plaintiff was excluded by an employee in violation of the rules of a theater that customarily permits Negroes to enjoy accommodations therein. (*Thomas* v. *Williams* [1905] 48 Misc. 615 mem., 95 N. Y. 592.)

Refusal to sell or furnish theater seats to colored persons, when they have been sold to previous purchasers, is not in violation of this section. (*Hull* v. *Eighty-sixth Street Amusement Company* [1913], 144 N. Y. S. 318.)

Refusal to allow a colored person to occupy in a theater a seat she has purchased is a discrimination because of color, and it is immaterial that a seat is offered in another part of the theater. (*Joyner* v. *Moore-Wiggins Co.* [1912], 152 App. Div. 266, 136 N. Y. S. 578, affirmed 1914 [211] N. Y. 522.)

Most of the theater cases have been lost or settled out of court. A New York Negro attorney cited the following procedure as illustrating the manner in which the plaintiff's case is lost:

> Recently, I attended the trial of a theater case, and as usual the plaintiffs lost. It was the usual set of circumstances where a colored fellow and his girl purchased orchestra tickets, and when they presented the tickets the usher refused to seat them. They immediately called for the manager and a gentleman who said he was the manager appeared and informed them that they could not sit in the orchestra as there were no seats, but as they saw several vacant seats they decided to bring suit.
>
> At the trial the defense counsel had the manager of the theater stand and asked the plaintiff if he was the person with whom he talked on the date in question, to which the plaintiff quickly replied in the negative. Later the defense had this same man testify that he was manager at the time and had no trouble or knew of no trouble with colored patrons.
>
> In other words, the person to whom the plaintiff talked was not the manager and the case was thrown out. It has been the tendency of theaters to defend upon the grounds that the cor-

poration has always given instructions not to discriminate and to treat all persons alike. The employee of the theater always admits that he has received such instructions and the case against the theater is lost. The only remedy is against the employee.

Enough has been said to indicate that the process of litigation involves certain complications that operate to the disadvantage of the plaintiff; and that while the law helps to establish the status of the Negro in these cases it is rather easily circumvented.

This report is based on information gained through interviews and by direct observation, and represents an attempt to indicate some of the attitudes and problems encountered by Negroes who wish to attend the theater.

It will be noted that little is said with reference to the Negroes' attendance upon the more expensive type of show, such as is to be found on Broadway. It is true that at present Negroes do not attend those shows in large numbers, a fact that is explained by the cost of admission. The results of a study made by the Russell Sage Foundation in 1916 indicate that working masses of any race constitute about 2 per cent. of the audiences in these theaters. As this average has doubtless changed little or not at all since then, it seemed best to confine the study to those theaters that attract Negroes in fairly large numbers, although cases that illustrate restrictive practices have been included in some instances.

A study of 112 different theaters in the seventeen cities covered in this survey reveals four policies with reference to the admission of Negro patrons. Under one policy Negroes are sold seats anywhere in the house and their freedom of choice is limited only by their willingness to pay the price demanded. Under another, there is a surreptitious practice of some form of separation. Managers, while disavowing any attempt at separation, have nevertheless quiet and effective means of grouping Negro patrons in the first balcony, in the very first rows of the orchestra, or in undesirable seats in the rear of the house. Throughout the South, and to some extent in Indianapolis, separation is openly practiced. Negro patrons are confined to the gallery, or to a part of it, and may not purchase seats in other sections of the house. A fourth policy is that of exclusion. This is not general among theaters and vaudeville houses, but is the rule among the better-class moving-picture houses in the southern cities studied.

MIXED AUDIENCES

In certain areas, such as the theater district that has 125th Street in New York as its center, and the area at 63rd Street and Cottage Grove in Chicago, where the number of Negroes in the neighborhood might make it profitable to accommodate them, some form of separation is likely to be surreptitiously attempted. Several methods of effecting this objective are employed.

In houses that sell the purchaser the use of a particular seat, certain blocks of tickets are sold to Negroes, so that they automatically find themselves in one section of the house.

Some theaters sell general admission to the orchestra, or the balcony, and make no attempt to sell patrons a particular seat by number. In such houses a patron is entitled to occupy any vacant seat in the section of the house for which the ticket is purchased. Houses of this type wishing to limit the freedom of Negro patrons have the ushers direct them to seats that are undesirable because of their nearness to the stage, to seats in the rear of the orchestra, or along certain outside aisles of the orchestra. A final and favorite method is to try to direct Negro patrons to the balcony. Often when Negroes question the authority of the usher in these matters, attempts are made to engage them in argument and to make them participants in unpleasant scenes.

The investigator, when in company with a law student, saw the head usher in one of the big vaudeville houses on 125th Street in New York City attempt to send to the balcony two Negroes who had bought orchestra seats. When these Negroes insisted that they did not buy tickets for the balcony, the assistant manager was called and the men were engaged in lively argument for fully five minutes. The law student informed the young men of their rights, and suggested that they keep their tickets. After this, no effort was made to prevent them occupying the seats to which their tickets entitled them.

The manager of a large moving-picture house that is owned by the same circuit, when questioned with reference to the treatment accorded Negroes, said:

> We try to keep Negroes upstairs in the balconies. They can smoke up there and feel more at home among themselves. That is the psychology of it, and besides they have their own theaters uptown.

One of the theaters in Buffalo, which was pointed out by Negro citizens as attempting segregation, is also a member of this circuit.

The manager of a very low-grade burlesque house in New York City said, "We do not court Negro patronage. When they come we try to send them to the balconies."

One of the owners of a widely known burlesque circuit spoke in high terms of the four all-colored shows, and the eighteen other colored acts that are on his circuit. He asserted that his house did not segregate, and that Negroes themselves resented a statement in one of the Negro weeklies, which charged that his house practiced discrimination. Several Negroes were seen in the orchestra, but the marked concentration of others on one side of the first balcony did not seem to bear out the assertions as to non-segregation.

If there is a large demand for seats when a colored show plays on Broadway, the ticket office is likely to sell Negroes seats in certain blocks in the balcony. The Secretary of the Harlem Branch of the Urban League has been asked by Negroes to protest when the attempts at segregation have been marked.

In Chicago, the Secretary of the National Association for the Advancement of Colored People mentioned several cases which his organization had taken up with the manager of a down-town motion-picture house that aims to seat Negroes as near the screen as possible. Suits have been brought by Negroes against two Chicago theaters.

A Negro physician received a judgment of $2,000. He

had refused to be directed to any particular part of the house, had attempted to take a vacant seat to which his ticket entitled him, and had been beaten over the head with a flashlight by an usher. The verdict was rendered on a charge of assault.

Most of the down-town houses in Chicago are regarded by Negroes as fair in their treatment.

In Gary, most of the theaters are liberal. Two houses were singled out by intelligent Negroes as attempting to seat Negroes as near the front as possible.

The third policy is to allow Negroes to occupy seats in the gallery only. Whether the gallery is especially for Negroes or a part of it given over to their use, the policy is generally the same, *i.e.,* to give them seats by themselves.

Moving-picture houses in Indianapolis, except those in colored neighborhoods, exclude Negroes; while the vaudeville houses and legitimate theaters with one exception segregate them. There is a civil rights bill in Indiana; but apparently Negroes have not made vigorous efforts to test cases under it.

In Dayton, the down-town moving-picture and vaudeville houses exclude Negroes.

Exclusion, the fourth method, is largely practiced by moving-picture houses all over the South. Vaudeville houses and legitimate theaters usually provide gallery accommodations. Now and then a moving-picture house that is hard hit by competition changes its policy and provides gallery accommodations. This is the case of a moving-picture house in Lexington which did not admit Negroes until a large house opened three blocks away. The second balcony contains loges now open to Negroes. It is easily one of the best appointed galleries open to them in the South.

GALLERIES

There are certain valid objections to the mere physical accommodations that are provided for theater-going Negroes. One of these is the location of the entrance to the gallery. In Louisville, the entrances to the second balconies are located on dark alleys, one of them being on an alley behind the theater almost half a block from the street. Vaudeville houses in Atlanta and Memphis have entrances similarly located, the only difference being that the alleys are well lighted and that concrete walks are provided. In Lexington, one of the vaudeville houses has its entrance in the rear of the building and almost facing the city jail. Some of the newer houses will provide separate entrances for Negroes and will have their entrances on a side street, or, as in two instances in Charleston, two in Lexington and one in Richmond, will have the entrances for Negroes facing the same street as the other entrances.

Alley and rear entrances are particularly offensive to Negroes, who feel that they are provided to increase the humiliation to which the Jim Crow gallery subjects them.

Some theaters accommodate white and colored people in the second balcony, and both races sometimes use the same entrance; but in four or five instances the side-entrance is for Negroes only.

The physical condition of the galleries tends to improve with the type of the house. In the newer houses, which are of concrete and steel construction, the galleries have good lighting, ventilation, and sanitary facilities and are kept clean.

Only two theaters were found that provide loge seats for gallery patrons, one of which was in Lexington. In New Orleans a large $2,000,000 house has a balcony for Negroes which is fitted with loge seats, rest-rooms and a smoking-room. The balcony in one of the large New Orleans vaudeville houses is well appointed physically and equipped with aisle lamps built in the concrete steps. All over the city there are neighborhood moving-picture houses that have clean, well-lighted balconies for Negroes.

In at least three theaters in New Orleans, however, sanitary conditions are bad. In one in which first-class stock companies appear, the men's toilet opens directly on the balcony. The evening the writer was there water was flowing into the balcony from this toilet. In two other theaters toilets were in such bad condition that the hallways leading to the galleries were offensive.

A large room which opens on the balcony of one of the cheap moving-picture houses is filled with dust-covered brooms, mops, old pieces of staging and dusty rubbish. There is no door to this room, and in its present state it is a menace to the health of patrons.

In the older houses, galleries are poorly lighted and poorly ventilated. Houses that are cooled by small electric fans often have no fans in the gallery. A vaudeville house in Lynchburg which is fitted throughout with fans, failed to operate those in the gallery on a hot night. Since the heated air rises, it is easy to understand that galleries are very uncomfortable in hot weather if they are not artificially cooled.

The seating arrangement is a very uncomfortable feature of some second balconies. Long wooden benches are built so close together that patrons are forced to sit through shows in cramped and uncomfortable positions. This was the case in at least a dozen theaters included in this study.

The question of exits is largely taken care of by fire ordinances and insurance laws which aim to reduce the fire hazard. A burlesque house in 125th Street, New York City, and a theater in Charleston are so constructed that it would be difficult for persons in the second balcony to get out of the building quickly. Most second balconies are built in tiers, and the aisles contain steep steps, which increase the need of good lighting in the galleries.

Plays of the kind produced on Broadway can be seen only in the larger down-town houses. Usually the last few rows in the gallery are provided for Negroes, though they are sometimes sold reserved seats in two or three front rows. Accommodations vary all the way from the entire gallery to fifty seats, as in Louisville and Dayton.

Two or three back rows in the balcony are provided for Negroes when the large musical recitals are given in city auditoriums. When the Chicago Civic Opera appeared in Memphis a hundred seats in the gallery of the City Auditorium were set aside for Negroes. It was not deemed a sufficient precaution to sell Negroes seats in a solid block to themselves. A black curtain three or four feet high was run between the white and the colored patrons.

Negroes regarded the black curtain as a needless affront, though one Negro woman is alleged to have suggested this device as a means of protection against insult.

NEIGHBORHOOD SHOW-HOUSES

The neighborhood houses in the areas in which Negroes live, except in New York, Chicago and New Orleans, usually afford a kind of show decidedly inferior to those to be seen elsewhere in the same cities. Only in the very poores, sections of the three cities named is the old, lurid moving-picture shown in a converted store where cheap and tawdry vaudeville is also provided for ignorant audiences.

In New York City most of the moving-picture houses are well lighted and offer first-run pictures and good music. A fair charge to make against most of these houses is that in winter they are overheated and not as well ventilated as they might be. The lighting of some of the older houses is decidedly poor.

The nineteen theaters and moving-picture houses in the Harlem area show a seating capacity of 39,332. Few sections of New York City, when the down-town theater district is excluded, are thought by competent managers to be better supplied with theaters. These include twelve moving-picture houses, four vaudeville houses, two burlesque shows and one legitimate theater. With two exceptions, they are owned by white men. One moving-picture house owned by a Negro does a large business.

The colored neighborhood houses in Chicago are not so numerous. Twelve have a total seating capacity of 10,473. Two of the large moving-picture houses, one of which is owned by a Negro, have large colored orchestras; and many patrons admitted that the music was for them a most attractive feature. One large moving-picture house has a clientele that is perhaps 35 per cent. white. One of the houses that feature Negro vaudeville offers shows that are very crude.

In Buffalo and Gary, both races attend the same houses to such an extent that any attempt at neighborhood classification would have little meaning. According to the Buffalo survey of 1925, there are sixty-nine theaters of all descriptions in the city with a total seating capacity of 39,332, which represents a ratio of one seat for every twelve persons in the city's population.

In the South, and to some extent in Indianapolis, conditions are different. The six Indianapolis houses that cater solely to Negroes have a total seating capacity of 3,000. Three of these are in a fair state of repair and offer good pictures and fair music for the prices charged. The remaining three are poorly ventilated, the very low ceilings making it almost impossible to keep a fresh current of air in circulation; and the exits are far apart.

One of these three is exceptionally low-grade, and rats from a near-by canal are frequent visitors. The pictures at a vaudeville house are the same as those shown uptown; but many of the vaudeville acts are of such a character that representative citizens do not regularly attend. The manager admitted that some of the shows "were rotten," but said they represented the run of the colored circuit and were the best he could get.

In Dayton, the nine thousand Negro citizens have very poor theater facilities. None of the down-town vaudeville or moving-picture houses admit them. A burlesque show and the legitimate theater do provide gallery accommodations. There are two moving-picture houses in colored neighborhoods. One seats about 250 people, pictures are of the cheapest western type and the music is very poor. A police officer is responsible for the statement that even in the summer the air is so foul that it is difficult to see how patrons are able to sit through a show. Another moving-picture house is clean and well ventilated, but poorly lighted. Petting parties of a rather unseemly nature are so general that the manager is kept busy trying to break them up.

Negroes in this town constantly referred to the fact that they have little commercial recreation that can be considered interesting. Crowds of young men frequent the squalid pool rooms and stand listening to old mechanical pianos in cheap soft-drink stands.

Louisville has fine theaters owned and operated by Negroes. Three of these are splendidly equipped and run a mixture of first, and second-run pictures. A large moving-picture house in the heart of the Negro district has gallery accommodations for Negroes and does a good business. Western pictures and sensational society dramas are usually shown here.

The colored vaudeville house is long and narrow, and its only exit is at one end. It takes between fifteen and twenty minutes for a full audience to get out. The vaudeville is generally crude and not infrequently vulgar. Western pictures, lurid serials, and an occasional society drama complete the program. This house draws large groups of the children of the poor and "the ne'er-do-wells." Many people who regard the Jim Crow balcony as an evil go here rather than deprive themselves altogether.

A mixed house that draws Negroes from the east end of the town has white vaudeville that is possibly still more crude. Officers of the Juvenile Court point to this house as one that contributes greatly to the delinquency of both colored and white boys.

The moving-picture house for Negroes in Knoxville is poorly ventilated. The pictures are largely of the western type, and thrilling dramas that appeal to the masses. An attempt was made to run a better show at higher prices, but the house was not well supported and closed after running about a year. An attempt is now being made there to educate the masses by the gradual use of better pictures.

Two of the theaters in Memphis that cater to Negroes are well appointed and well ventilated. The colored vaudeville shown at one varies from good to bad according as the acts that go around the circuit are good or bad. The third, a moving-picture house, is a stuffy, poorly ventilated place where low-grade, blood-and-thunder shows are given.

The colored vaudeville theaters in Atlanta, Winston-Salem, Richmond, and Philadelphia are of the same general type. Most of the managers said that it is next to impossible to get shows that are consistently clean and wholesome. Three managers also said they had found it necessary to discharge certain troops because of the crudity and sensualness of their shows. A fourth manager, who operates a chain of moving-picture houses, said that he had long since quit the vaudeville business because he felt that he could not maintain his self-respect and continue to offer the type of shows that were on the circuit.

In no city, perhaps, are there more daring performances than those in one house in Philadelphia. The principal comedian, who performs here almost the year around, is a past master at portraying the old razor-slashing Negro who has virtually disappeared from the stage. Both in the language employed and the general suggestiveness of the jokes, the show, which has points of real merit here and there, is geared to the taste of the lowest strata of society.

Colored moving-picture houses of the better type usually have first-run pictures that are shown in some instances as soon as the principal white moving-picture house has shown them.

The cheaper houses, such as two small ones in Atlanta, three of the small ones in Indianapolis, and small places in Dayton and Memphis, are so dirty and poorly ventilated that they are a menace to health. The shows are largely of the western type that creates bad examples for young children.

It is evident that Negro vaudeville is generally in need of enrichment, which means in turn that actors more highly trained and more talented must be secured. The music in all of the houses, and particularly in the moving-picture houses, should be improved.

DANCE HALLS

Dance halls and pool rooms are popular in Negro communities and, whether under Negro or white ownership, are highly commercialized. The evidence gathered in this study indicates that they are far less adequately supervised by city authorities than are similar establishments for white people, while at the same time the pressure of colored public opinion is not sufficiently strong to check some of the evils associated with this type of recreation. The better-class Negroes are inclined to express a merely negative disapproval by avoiding the commercial recreation halls, and the ministers are for the most part so uncompromising in their opposition to all dancing that they are not in a position to work for better supervision of the commercial dance halls.

The pages that follow represent an attempt by the investigator to record his first-hand impressions of conditions as he found them in a large number of places of commercial recreation in both northern and southern cities.[1]

HALLS AND EQUIPMENT

A majority of the halls in which dances are given are clean, well lighted, and well ventilated, providing the windows are kept open. In the larger cities the halls and casinos are spacious, accommodating three or four thousand people. In some instances the same halls are used by white clubs for dancing.

In New Orleans, Philadelphia, and Lexington, white men operate three well-constructed halls built over garages. Roof-gardens, which are extensively used for dancing, have been constructed over the buildings of fraternal organizations in Louisville, Memphis, and New Orleans. The one in New Orleans is spacious and its lighting effect is beautiful and visible from quite a distance. A number of other fraternal organizations and social clubs own smaller halls, and almost invariably they are profitable investments.

That some halls are poorly ventilated is often the fault of patrons who insist on excluding the fresh air. If halls are properly heated this is not necessary. The larger halls and casinos often become clouded with tobacco smoke during the intermission.

[1] Since so many character interpretations of Negro life are drawn from the cabaret and the crude dance hall, it is important to emphasize that there is a group of colored people with a social life all their own whose recreation is as decorous as could be found anywhere.

The defect in ventilation found most frequently resulted from placing all the windows on one side of the hall. It takes no great exercise of the imagination to realize the condition when two or three hundred people are crowded into one of these halls that is from 60 to 100 feet long, with all windows on a twenty-five-foot front.

In only one instance was the floor of a dance hall dirty; but in this case it was fairly covered with saliva. Men half drunk were spitting freely.

Poor sanitary facilities were noted in a number of halls. One in Memphis has a single toilet for the use of both sexes, and one in Knoxville has a men's room that is merely a corner partitioned off with burlap and containing only an ordinary sink. A second hall in Memphis has toilets located a block away, and as a result the young people disregard the proprieties and use the back yard as a urinal.

CONDUCT

At subscription dances the conduct is usually good except, of course, when a few extreme couples gain admission. The character of these dances depends much on the sponsoring organization. The same hall may have a well-ordered crowd one evening and dancers and dancing of a low kind the next. It is at the entirely public dance that the conduct is most shocking. All in all, possibly less than 25 per cent. of the dancing seen at subscription dances was bad.

The subscription dance of the Debs Club at St. Peter Clavers, in Philadelphia, is one of the most commendable found. It is given by a group of young people to provide clean dances. Admission is by card and only those whose references have been found satisfactory receive cards. Any one whose conduct is at all objectionable is required to leave and thereafter is denied admission. The chief objective of this group is to furnish wholesome recreation for the large number of young college people who spend week-ends in Philadelphia. The attendance varies from 900 to 1,600.

Three of the large benefit dances in Chicago were well ordered. In fact the dances in that city show the effect of the numerous dancing schools. At the better-class pay-dances extreme couples are very exceptional. The music is also good and there was a noticeable absence of drinking. In only one instance was the dance marred by a fight.

In Gary, dancing is allowed in the public schools, dancing classes are formed, and supervised dancing has a place in the school carnivals. Representative citizens feel that this keeps the young people out of the pay-dances at the public halls. Thus in every city there were dances quite above the ordinary; but the other side of the picture is not so encouraging.

The dances that attract servants and laborers were of a different class. All too frequently these groups are not reached by social organizations, do not feel at home at the subscription dances, and resort to the public hall where denizens of the underworld make them welcome.

In places of this kind, drunkenness, bootlegging, prostitutes in search of men, and men in search of easy prey, are frequently seen. The dances are often sensual, and the motions of the dancers most suggestive and objectionable. Unseemly conduct in at least two halls was abetted by the turning out of all the lights except a spot light, in order that the "people might have a good time."

A large hall in Philadelphia was found to be frequented by young Negro prostitutes who danced chiefly with foreigners. Money was seen to pass between one of the men and the manager as the price of securing a girl. No attempt to suppress lewd dancing was made. Two women fought in the hall over a man, and continued the fight in the street with bottles. One of the girls confessed to a long police record. A large group of well-behaved young people who had recently moved into the city were present in this obviously degrading atmosphere.

Another spacious hall, which has the reputation of good order at most times, was the scene of a public masquerade dance. The costumes worn by most of the girls were very scant and easily rivaled those of the bathing beauties. Much of the dancing was extremely lewd. There was much boisterousness and hilarity during the intermission. The boys slapped the girls on their bare legs, hugged some, petted others, and approached most of them in daring language. Four men came in drunk. The ages varied from fifteen to twenty-one.

A third hall was the scene of much drinking, fighting and sensual dancing. The fourth was small, and the young people clapped, whooped and gave vent to their feelings during the Charleston contest in a way that would have made a passerby think that the building was being wrecked. The dances here are reported to be characterized by drinking and fighting at times. Liquor was not seen on the place, but a restaurant across the street did a suspiciously flourishing business.

A dance given by a club in New York was very wet, the boys having had "good stuff" imported from Canada. Men having a surplus supply acted as bootleggers for others. The dancing of 60 per cent. of the couples was obviously based on erotic thrill. One man confessed that he had landed a woman during the dancing that he had been trying to "make" for over a year.

An election-night dance was quite spirited. At least 10 per cent. of the people drank liquor from bottles and hip-flasks. Many minors were present when the dance closed at two in the morning. The dancing in the majority of the cases was fairly modest, but no effort was made to suppress the conduct of extreme couples. The special officer present centered his entire attention on maintaining order. The men's room was littered with whiskey bottles and boys were seen making up a pot to buy a quart across the street. Several of the boys lost from $2 to $10 to card sharks who operated at the dance.

A large Chinese restaurant in New York has dancing as an added attraction. The crowd, which was preponderantly colored, contained at least half a dozen white girls and about the same number of white men. The dancing of some of the couples was extreme and very unconventional, both races being equally at fault. Most of the colored men present escorted their own company. In one case an older woman whose language and actions marked her as a pros-

titute, was put out because of vile language used in alterca-
tion with a colored girl. A note sent by a colored man to
the white woman was the cause of the disturbance.

During the summer, Negroes in Buffalo use the dance
pavilions at the amusement beaches in common with other
groups. There has been some friction at these beaches, but
workers at the welfare bureau feel that it is abating. Public
dances in some of the down-town halls are very rough.

The regular pay-dances at some of the Chicago halls are
constantly investigated by the Juvenile Protective Association, which has a capable colored worker. Her report indicates that 80 per cent. of the young people attending are
below eighteen years of age. The report said: "The young
people were dancing with abandon. There was no restraint
in the manner in which the girls were held or the type of
lateral and longitudinal movement. There was a great deal
of promiscuous petting while the dancing was in progress,
and on a number of occasions it seemed proper for the girl
to kiss the man at the end of the dance." The attitude of
the manager when brought into court was interesting. He
stated that he considered dancing as a sublimation of the
sex instinct. When reminded by the officer that the report
indicated that as conducted in his hall, it was rather a stimulant, he replied, "If the long-haired reformers would mind
their own business and break up the brothels rather than
interfering with my private business, all concerned would be
better off."

The language used to describe this dance would also apply
to one visited by the investigator. Young men and women
were searched for guns, knives, and razors before they were
permitted to enter. Reasonable precautions were taken to
prevent fighting and noisy conduct; but no attempt was
made to suppress the dancing of "the stationary," nor the
vulgar examples of young prostitutes, some of whom spared
no pains in their efforts to get young men to follow them.

A fourth hall in Chicago is one of the worst public dance
halls. It is the rendezvous of pickpockets and denizens of
the underworld. The Secretary of the Y.M.C.A. stated
that young men living in the dormitory who visit this hall

are often lured to houses of prostitution and robbed of their money.

Union Park, on the west side, conducts weekly dances that are strictly supervised to counteract the influences of the bad dance hall in the community. The supervisor says that a dance at a near-by settlement house was broken up by an envious gang of older boys who shot out windows and lights before the police could arrive and stripped several of the girls of their clothing.

Two of the public dances in Indianapolis presented an interesting contrast. A subscription dance given by a social club was characterized by loud laughter and a spirit of play, but the general behavior and the character of the dancing were unimpeachable. On the following night a dance given by an orchestra became wild and sensual.

The probation officer in Dayton said that the dance hall was responsible for the trouble of many of the unmarried mothers under her care. The city has a supervisor, but this does not prevent gross irregularities at the dance halls.

A new dance hall in Lexington is beautifully decorated and very spacious. Working girls, high-school girls, demimondes and young men of all strata were there when the investigator visited it. There seemed to be much drinking by both men and women, and five or six young girls between sixteen and eighteen years of age left the hall intoxicated. Much of the dancing became orgiastic as the evening progressed. The men's room contained about forty empty whiskey bottles, and the floor was littered with them. Liquor was sold over the confectionery counter. The drinking of corn liquor, the general prevalence of drunkenness, the familiar conduct of the couples, and the vulgar types of dancing permitted, made this a most unsuitable place for the many young boys and girls who attended. It was said that the hall was owned by two white men influential in politics; and a Negro manager was operating it.

A dance given by an orchestra in Louisville was characterized by drinking, and on the part of many couples by close and unseemly dancing. At a barn-dance given by a high-school group, undesirable characters were present. In at least six instances the high-school boys were bootlegging corn whiskey at $2 a pint. Five boys grouped themselves in a corner outside the hall and drank a quart to the tune of "How Dry I Am." The men's room was littered with empty bottles. While most of the couples behaved well, a few were extreme. A colored policewoman made some attempt to supervise the dances, but she was not free to give full time to it.

Several halls in Memphis were of a very low type. The regular public dances at two of them are operated by a Negro politician. A crowd in one numbered about 600, and was a mixture of boys and girls of the teen ages with women who appeared hard and rough. When the lights were all extinguished except a spotlight, and the crowd danced the "mess around" to the tune of "Shake That Thing," the dancing was extremely sensual. To add to the low atmosphere, a singer would occasionally intone a verse reeking with suggestion. Some of the most extreme couples pivoted on one spot and gyrated their closely pressed bodies from their knees up. A policeman who ordered the lights turned on was told by the politician to "let the people alone and let them have a good time." The officer replied, "They are your own race, and if that is the way you feel about it go ahead; but it is a d—n shame."

Outside the hall men and women drank from the same bottle, and staged petting parties in their automobiles. Three girls were engaged in a heated argument over a stolen watch and indulged in much profanity. In front of the hall a girl lifted both feet from the ground as she hugged her friend and announced her intentions in such loud language that even the boy protested. A garage owner in the rear of this hall complains that groups often crash the door and use his garage as an assignation house.

A dance at another Memphis hall was equally objectionable. Servant girls, boys and hardened characters made up the group. Two or three boys displayed bottles of liquor and were followed around by half-intoxicated girls pleading for a drink.

In New Orleans, two of the halls were quite objectionable.

One either dispenses liquor or pays no attention to those who do. On the night visited, six young men were intoxicated. The dancing of fully a third of the couples was extremely close. One young man threw away all attempt to mask his feelings and handled his partner in such a rough and vulgar manner that she slapped his face. A quarrel grew out of this incident and a group left in bad humor. Some of the dancers were obviously poor migrants from the country, others prostitutes and men of the world.

New Orleans requires white halls to hire a supervisor and keep uniformed police on hand during the dance. Colored halls are required to have uniformed police present; but they are only ordered to suppress fighting and to eject dancers who are considered objectionable by the management.

The public dances in Atlanta are often of a questionable type. The best hall in the town is frequented by the better class of people only when special dances are given. The dances on the whole are quite decent though they become wild during the spotlight numbers. At the dance attended, four boys during the intermission turned their partners over their knees and spanked them. There was much petting and kissing. Three persons were intoxicated when they came in. One was thrown out for disorder. A schoolboy who regularly attends these dances says that he has purchased liquor at the soda fountain. Of approximately a hundred girls present, three-fourths were between sixteen and eighteen years of age. Many were orderly, but the language of at least twenty indicated that they were much interested in landing men.

Charleston has a hall in which fighting and drinking are so common that the police refer to it as "The Bucket of Blood." The owner of a dance hall at a local picnic-ground said that there is much drinking and fighting when excursions come to town.

Pay-dances in the small park at Winston-Salem are rough, and there is much drinking and fighting. At another place, two white owners sublet to colored groups. They keep the concessions, and it is said that liquor is sold freely. A club that sometimes meets there has to pay $30 rent instead of $20 in order to insure a decent dance. When this payment is made the concessions are not operated.

CABARETS

There is little to say about cabarets that has not already been said about dance halls, except that a tough cabaret is probably tougher than a tough dance hall. Colored neighborhoods studied were found to have cabarets distributed as follows among five of the cities: New York, 15; Chicago, 6, of which 2 were padlocked at the time of visit; Indianapolis, 2; Buffalo, 2; New Orleans, 2. These places were widely different in character. One cabaret in Chicago has a supervisor who suppresses all forms of sensual dancing; liquor is not sold there; and even the slightly intoxicated are discouraged from remaining. Only members of the same party are partners in the dancing, and the entertainment is snappy, with good music.

Another employs a supervisor who was seen constantly to turn her back on couples dancing immodestly. Men and women were admitted without escorts and danced promiscuously with chance partners. Prostitutes were present and used the waiters to reach unaccompanied men. The investigator was told that he might talk to one of the girls if he would pay fifty cents for the introduction. The waiter, when offered money for a drink, said there was none on the place, but offered to slip outside and purchase it.

The large number of cabarets in New York make it possible to find all grades from high-class places of amusement to those that are meeting places for pickpockets, prostitutes and confidence men.

The two cabarets in Buffalo are poorly regulated with reference to soliciting and the type of dancing allowed. One, however, makes an effort to preserve the outward appearance of decency.

In Indianapolis and New Orleans, no attempt is made at regulation. The waiters at one of the cabarets in Indianapolis told the investigator he could get anything he wanted to drink and that there were girls around who were looking for a pleasant evening. The entertainer was a very crude dancer and rather of the rough-house type who "mourned her blues." Four officers of the law drank large glasses of a liquid greatly resembling liquor which was openly given them by the manager.

In cabarets in New Orleans, liquor was sold on the premises just as in the days before prohibition, and prostitutes were easily available. Fully 60 per cent. of the dancing was objectionable. One of the entertainers was exceptionally crude, and the climax of her act was to prostrate herself on the floor and do a stomach dance.

The fact of racial intermingling has often been played up as an objection to the cabaret. A much more valid objection is that the unsupervised cabarets are sluiceways through which vice pours into the community. In the better-class places, there is little actual intermingling; but in some there is an evident attempt to make them meeting places for white men and colored girls.

Pool Rooms

All cities studied have regulations covering the admission of minors to pool rooms. These regulations are sometimes very laxly enforced, as in Richmond, where the Judge of the Juvenile Court says that offenders are occasionally brought into his court after infrequent raids. Enforcement is even more lax in Memphis.

Dayton, of all the cities studied, has the strictest regulation. Two of the cities, Charleston and Winston-Salem, do not license colored pool rooms; but each has a men's club where there is gambling at dice, poker, and pool.

Among some patrons of pool rooms, gambling is the rule rather than the exception. In only three of the eleven pool rooms in Richmond did there seem to be any effort to suppress gambling. One of the remaining eight dispenses liquor, and has a reputation for fighting and shooting scrapes. In New York City, a few managers attempt to regulate gambling by confining it to certain tables. Gam-

bling in a number of rooms in Philadelphia is not sup-
pressed. The investigator was asked to hold stakes for one
group who seemed to belong to the class of pool sharks that
loaf all winter and live off inexperienced players who as-
semble on Saturday night in search of a good time.

Buffalo, Lexington, and Louisville have pool rooms located in the same building with other gambling dens. A
social investigator in Buffalo traced much of the poverty
among Negroes to games of chance, and indicated that two
of the rooms are operated by a Negro with political power.
A room in which a cold-blooded murder was committed is
still operating. Poker, dice, race-horse booking, bootlegging,
and in one instance prostitution, were associated with these
places.

Three pool rooms in Memphis are overrun with bootleggers and late on Saturday night prostitutes go into these
rooms in search of men and boys. One room which bears
the name pool room has one table used for poker, one for
dice games and a counter at which both men and women
are served with liquor.

Indianapolis has two fairly decent rooms, but the remaining eight are largely of the bootleg-dive type. From a con-
versation overheard in one of these it appears that a crime
committed the night before had been planned there.

Two of the twenty pool rooms visited in New Orleans
were clean and well regulated. The remaining eighteen were
dives of the lowest type. Each had its bar over which
liquor was sold, its special room for poker and dice, and a
small dance floor with mechanical music for the convenience
of men and prostitutes who infest the places. Houses of
prostitution are connected with these pool rooms in many instances, and one hall has a dark room into which a man buying a pint of liquor may take a girl without extra charge. A
dance hall connected with one of these rooms has been the
scene of three fatal cutting and shooting scrapes in as many
months. The girls who compete in the dancing contests here
dance in the nude.

Of approximately 150 pool rooms visited, less than 20 per
cent. are owned by Negroes. Often these are the best in

town. This is owing in a measure to the vigilance of the police in supervising Negro owners, and to the fact that the Negro owner is in close touch with the community and responsive to pressure. The others are operated purely for exploitation.

Comparisons in the field of morals are futile; but it must be borne in mind that a similar investigation of white dives would probably reveal conditions as shocking. The striking fact revealed by this investigation is that, owing to the almost criminal lack of supervision by the community, it is probably much easier in Negro places to "get away with" roughness and vulgarity.

Another difference in the situation of the white and the Negro groups is the degree to which different classes mix in the colored places of amusement. There are white dens that are the hangouts for pickpockets, prostitutes and their ilk; but the respectable working classes do not go there frequently. In the colored community, however, lack of wholesome recreation often leads the servant girl and workingman into these dens of vice and crime. In these circumstances it is not strange that the Negro crime-rate in cities is far higher than that in the country and that poverty and social maladjustment take such a heavy toll.

In commercial recreation, the city is seen at its worst. The migrants, settled in segregated areas, are neglected and exploited.

Appendix

The data on condition and equipment of dwellings were compiled from an examination of 12,123 house-cards. Of these 1,400 were filled out under the direct supervision of the staff and 10,723 were gathered from other surveys which were made at or about the same time as this study, and which were recorded on cards comparable to the one used in this study. The data from other studies were derived as follows: Philadelphia, Studies of the Housing Association; New York, Tenement House Department; Chicago, Studies of the Department of Welfare and the Urban League; Louisville, Urban League; Knoxville, Study by Librarian; Dallas, Study by Interracial Committee. The card is printed herewith, together with the instructions issued to enumerators.

It is felt that since these 12,123 cards were scattered in seventeen cities, and in representative neighborhoods within these cities, they are fairly typical of housing conditions in large and medium-size cities. A certain amount of bias toward the better class of houses arose from the use of volunteer workers, but this is at a minimum. The fact that about 30 per cent. of the cards represent dwellings of home owners indicates that slightly more cards for this class were included in the sample than the class constitutes in the total number of families. This, however, does not invalidate any comparisons between owners and renters, nor does it affect conclusions based on rental dwellings alone.

In detail, the method of apportioning these cards was as follows: The city was divided into representative districts. Negro population in these districts was computed from census enumeration district figures. A group of colored women was asked to volunteer for the enumeration, and in each city a number of earnest and interested women were assembled. After the proportion of cards had been assigned to districts, according to the proportion of the total population within the district, each volunteer worker was assigned a small section of four or five city blocks and was asked to secure twenty to twenty-five cards within that section. They were cautioned to apportion their cards to good and bad, front and alley dwellings in about the same proportion that such dwellings formed of the total number of dwellings in the section.

HOUSE CARD

FILL OUT ONE CARD FOR EACH FAMILY
Answer each question with a Check Mark or number inserted in the blank column

A City _____ B Section _____ Class _____

Street _____ Number _____ Investigator _____

D. Occupied By
   White Owner 51
   Colored Owner 52
   White Renter 61
   Colored Renter 62

1. Owned By
   White ....
   Colored ....
   Unknown ....

2. How many years has occupant lived in this house.................... 7

3. Weekly Rent Paid (in dollars)....................

4. Number in Family—Total....................
   Over 15 years old....................
   Under 15 years old....................

5. Number of lodgers.................... 12

6. Number of Rooms—Total.................... 13
   Number of Bedrooms.................... 14

7. Separate Living Room?
   Yes 151
   No 152

8. Separate Kitchen,
   Yes 161
   No 162

9. Bathtub
   Yes 171
   No 172

10. Inside Repairs
    Good 181
    Fair 182
    Bad 183

11. Inside Condition
    a. Furniture old ....
       Furniture new ....
    b. Floor
       Swept 191
       Unswept 192
    c. Windows
       Broken—Clean 201
       Broken—Dirty 202
       Sound—Clean 203
       Sound—Dirty 204
    d. Any Odors Noticed Yes
       No
    e. Number of Windowless Rooms 21

12. Water Source
    City 221
    Well 222
    Spring 223
    Cistern 224
    Other 225

13. Piped to
    House ....
    Yard Hydrant ....
    Street Hydrant ....

14. Well Condition
    Good 231
    Fair 232
    Bad 233
    a. Protected by Curb Yes
       No

15. If no water on premises (state how obtained in comments section)

16. Toilets
    Water Closet Inside.................... 241
    Water Closet Outside.................... 242
    a. Condition
       Good 251
       Fair 252
       Bad 253
    b. Privy Vault Construction
       Pit 261
       Can 262
       Concrete Tank 263
    c. Privy Vault Condition
       Full 271
       Half 272
       Overflow 273
       When Cleaned ....
       Distance from House....................
       Double 281
       Single 282
       Shared by how many families

17. Lots
    Slope Steep 291
    Slope Even 292

18. Drainage
    Good 301
    Fair 302
    Bad 303

19. Walks
    Good 311
    Poor 312
    None 313

20. Flowers or Shrubbery
    Well Kept 321
    Poor 322
    None 323

21. Garden
    Yes 331
    No 332

22. Street Frontage in Yards
    Depth of Front Yard....................
    Width of Side Yard....................
    Depth of Back Yard....................

23. How Is Garbage Kept
    Cans 341
    Boxes 342
    No receptacle 343

24. Stories excluding basement.................... 35

25. Is there a basement
    Yes 361
    No 362

26. Is 1st floor used for other than residence
    Yes 371
    No 372

27. Construction
    Painted Frame 381
    Unpainted Frame 382
    Brick 383
    Other 384

28. Foundation
    Post 391
    Brick 392
    Stone 393
    Other 394
    None 395

29. Screening
    None 401
    Complete Good Condition 402
    Complete Bad Condition 403
    Incomplete Good Condition 404
    Incomplete Bad Condition 405

30. Roof
    Leaking 411
    Sound 412

31. Walls
    Good 421
    Fair 422
    Bad 423

32. Steps
    Good 431
    Fair 432
    Bad 433

33. Value (Fill in only when specifically instructed)

34. Approximate Age of House in Years....................

Comments: _____
_____
_____